MARC CHAGALL:
HIS LIFE AND WORK

MARC CHAGALL:
HIS LIFE AND WORK

BY

ISAAC KLOOMOK

PHILOSOPHICAL LIBRARY · NEW YORK

Contents

Illustrations

Paternal Grandmother
of the Artist
Courtesy of the Artist
PLATE I

Maternal Grandfather
of the Artist
Courtesy of the Artist
PLATE II

Mother and Father
of the Artist
(On Their Wedding Day)
Courtesy of the Artist
PLATE III

The Artist and His Daughter, Ida. 1945
Courtesy of the Artist
PLATE IV

ACKNOWLEDGEMENT

IT gives me pleasure to acknowledge with gratitude my indebtedness to the artist for his generous assistance. He gave me unstintingly of his precious time and patience. Without his help this book could not have been achieved. His kindness and friendship have been a constant inspiration and encouragement.

Thanks are due to the New York City Ballet and to Mr. Eukelson of the Book League of the Jewish Fraternal Order for lending me some cuts.

MARC CHAGALL:
HIS LIFE AND WORK

Heritage

THE plastic arts, in the European sense, were engendered by the same spirit as the sciences. Their intellectual background was the same. The same awakened human hunger to know the world outside of themselves led both the scientist and the artist of the renaissance; both were interested in nature, in man's relation to nature, in man's orientation in it.

The scientist soon discovered he could not trust his senses in his study of nature. The artist never had and never wanted any other instruments than his senses—more precisely, for the plastic artist, his eye and tactil organs. (The painter, too, brings into his work qualities of nature that come to his consciousness not only through his eyes but also through the touch of his hands and other parts of his body, such qualities as mass, texture, space.)

In short, nature was the foundation on which the magnificent edifice of the great European arts was built.

All schools and individual artists, with their diversity of outlook and aim, had one ulterior motif in their work: some kind of representation of nature.

The Naturalist aimed at portraying nature objectively, as he found it in his experience, deformed and disjointed, or grand and harmonious.

The Idealist looked only for the perfect and exalted —improving nature by his art to its ultimate best.

The Realist picked what is exemplary and beneficent to the eyes of man.

The Romanticist went out in search of the exotic, the rare and strange, the picturesque, and grotesque— or nature in moments of passion, of storm and cataclysm.

But all went to nature for instruction and direction. And from this point of view one might say that all the art of Europe was naturalistic. The Impressionist, as is well known, looked for a more scientific, more truthful representation of nature—he studied closely the effect of sunlight on the appearance of things in the open air. Cézanne, who simplified and distorted natural objects, did so to obtain a more fundamental plastic of nature: discarding the transitory and accidental details, he searched for the basic and primary: behind the changing multitudinous appearances, the one enduring reality.

Even Dali tries to persuade himself and others that his surrealism is scientific art—that he paints reality transmuted by Freudian dreams.

And Chagall?

Chagall takes nature as a Jew.

THE JEWISH GENIUS AND NATURE

The Jewish genius has no respect for nature. And that is not because his people lived confined in walled ghettos and did not know the grandeur of nature and had no love for it. This tendency came by inheritance from far more distant times. The ancient Jewish poets, the prophets, the psalmists, the poet (or poets) of Job—had shown a close observation of nature and often made intimate references to it. They could, with love, call the native landscape, its trees, shrubs and herbs, its animals and birds, also its mountains and valleys, its seas and rivers and the creatures that lived therein. Even more, they had a sublime conception of the whole of nature as a unified universe in its plentitude. But they looked upon this universe as upon a house that has a lord and master, that is inhabited by its master. And it is its master's breath that animates and quickens the whole universe. He turns his face away, and the shining beauty of the world vanishes— He takes his breath away, and all is dead and withered. This great lord of the world, its creator and ruler—the great almighty Jehovah—He it was that captured the imagination of the Jewish poets and filled their hearts with rapture, and only to Him and of Him was their shout of joy, their songs of praise and jubilation. Jehovah was their guide, their inspirer and their glory. Jehovah's personality captivated them with its majesty, and all of nature was little and trivial compared to him.

"Hallelujah. Praise ye the Lord from heavens;
Praise Him in the heights.

Praise ye Him, all His angels;
Praise ye Him, all His hosts.
Praise ye Him, sun and moon;
Praise Him, ye all stars of light.
Praise Him, ye heavens of heavens;
And ye waters that are above the heavens.
Let them praise the name of the Lord;
For He commanded, and they were created.
He hath also established them for ever and ever;
Praise the Lord from the earth;
Yea dragons and all deeps;
Fire and hail, snow and vapour,
Stormy winds, fulfilling his word;
Mountains and the hills,
Fruit trees and all cedars;
Beasts and all cattle,
Creeping things and flying fowl;
Kings of the earth and all peoples,
Princes and all judges of the earth;
Both young men and maidens,
Old men and children;
Let them praise the name of the Lord,
For His name alone is excellent;
His glory is above the earth and heaven."

(Psalm CXLVIII)

This intensive emotion and joy in God could not find expression except in psalm, in song. Plastic art is not for such experiences, not for such ecstasy—therefore, from the very beginning the Jewish genius picked the word as a means of expression, the word that he could make aglow with his breath, and did not create a plastic art.

Jews say in one of their morning prayers:

"Blessed art Thou, O Lord, God and King, great in praise, God of thanksgiving, Lord of wonders, *who makest choice of song and psalm."*

"Bless the Lord, O my soul. O Lord my God, thou art very great; thou art clothed with honour and majesty;

Who coverest thyself with light as with a garment; who stretchest out the heavens like a curtain;

Who layeth the beams of his chambers in the waters; who maketh the clouds his chariot; who walketh upon the wings of the wind—"

(Psalm CIV)

All very clear images—that cannot be put in paint on canvas: Nature created to serve God, named by the poet only as argument to prove Jehovah's greatness.

The poet of the psalms accepts his own thoughts and emotions as truths of greater significance than the facts of the external world presented to him by his eyes. All nature must obey him and disregard its eternal laws if it so pleases the poet for the honor of his God. He tells us:

"When Israel came forth from Egypt,
The house of Jacob from a people of
    strange language;
Judah became His sanctuary,
Israel His dominion.
The sea saw it and fled;
The Jordan turned backward.
The mountains skipped like rams,
The hills like young sheep—"

(Psalm CXIV)

This is the way Chagall paints.

The greatest of the Jewish poets, Isaiah, disapproves of the established laws of nature, and he plans to change them because in his own heart he judges them to be unjust. And because he has a vision of a more righteous order of the world, he is ready to abolish what God himself had ordained.

Isaiah says: (X–XI)

"And it shall come to pass in that day . . . . . .
. . . .
The wolf also shall dwell with the lamb, and the leopard shall lie down with the kid; and the calf and the young lion and the fatling together; and a little child shall lead them.

And the cow and the bear shall feed; their young ones shall lie down together; and the lion shall eat straw like the ox.

And the suckling child shall play on the hole of the asp, and the weaned child shall put his hand on the cockatrice' den—"

On the lips of the poet it may appear as rhetoric—but these are the words also of the prophet: he cannot leave a place for murder and plunder in his equitable world: "They shall not hurt nor destroy in all my holy mountain—."

In Genesis (XXVIII) we are told that when Jacob

The Artist and His Wife, Bella. Paris, 1935
(With *Betrothal*. Oil. 1927)

Courtesy of the Artist

PLATE V

"went out from Beersheba, and went towards Haran, he lighted upon a certain place, and tarried there all night, because the sun was set; and he took of the stones of that place, and put them for his pillows, and lay down in that place to sleep.

"And he dreamed, and behold a ladder set up on the earth, and the top of it reached to heaven: and behold the angels of God ascending and descending on it. (See Chagall's etching.)

"And behold the Lord stood above it, and said, I am the Lord God of Abraham thy father, and the God of Isaac: the land where upon thou liest to thee will I give it and to thy seed."

The Talmud, as is well known, amplified this by saying that God folded all of Palestine like a book and put it under Jacob. And therefore God promised to Jacob all of Palestine, and not only the ground where upon he was stretched . . .

The Talmudist in exile in Babylonia, for whom his lost fatherland was now a painful yearning, a hallowed patriotic emotion in his heart, an inspired burning principle in his brain—he who saw now the holy land as a divine history, he could unhesitatingly form an image of the whole of Palestine folded as a book and put under Jacob's side.

Thus, to the Jewish genius the world transfigured by his vision into which he transfused his own spirit, is of greater importance than the world of his sensuous experience.

And this attitude is not so violently opposed to the concepts of science as it is to the very foundation of European plastic art.

And that, it seems to me, is the reason why the Jewish people did not develop an authentic Jewish plastic art. Jewish artists, yes. Jewish art, no—not until late modern times.

Rabbi Menahem Mendel of Worki said, "three things behoove a Jew: to kneel and yet to stand; cry and yet keep silence; dance, yet be motionless."

The naturalistic arts are extensive—arts of space.

The Jewish spirit is intensive—incandescent within. Jewish ardor, the Jewish ecstasy . . .

INNER LIGHT

Even their bitterest enemies in their evil slanders could not say against the Jews that they were a blind people. On the contrary—the whole world knows that they saw clearer, deeper and further, with greater purity and sublimity of vision, than all the other peoples of the earth.

But they did not see with their eyes—only with the inner light that they possessed. As an exiled people they did not live by the sight of their eyes.

And how would their eyes avail them when they were not permitted to see the sun shine? They always lived in their own shadow, in fear and in threat. They had to accept the world like a chaste Jewish bride, covered with a thick veil, and as a shy talmudic student they looked upon her with downcast eyes.

Behind the ghetto walls there was very little sunlight. In the prison of the ghetto they had lost their living sense of space. They confined themselves from childhood on in small, dingy, airless schools, in closed study-rooms, in overcrowded stuffy prayer-houses—and from there came forth their seers and leaders; and they led them with a light that needs no eyes.

When the fervent Jewish mothers stood with covered eyes before their lit Sabbath candles, they prayed to their creator that He might give them sons whose eyes would shine in the Torah—and the good father in heaven often gave heed to their supplication and granted them their wishes.

The Jewish idyll was the assiduous youthful scholar who sat over the holy books day and night. The romantic idyll of a Jewish daughter was the pale maiden with lowered eyelids, secretly in love with the poor talmudic student who came to her house to eat his charitable meals one day a week. She would wake at night to hear, with yearning, the sweet plaintive voice of her beloved as he intoned the old traditional chant of the Talmud, bent over his volume with a candle in his hand in the midnight house of study.

How much light, how much color have their children seen, imprisoned in their wretched schools from early morning till late at night? How much of sun, of sky?

The Jewish workers were surely overladen with work from daybreak to midnight. When could they look upon the shining world?

When did the Jews as a people look at the sky? Only to see if the time had come to light the Sabbath candles, or to say the prayers at the departure of the Sabbath day—or, after keeping a long hard fast, to watch for the first star to appear in the sky.

If we were to look for a symbol of light in the Jewish life in exile, we would have to pick the candle, not the sun. Mother and grandmother light their Sabbath candles; father and grandfather perform the ritual of separating the holy day from the oncoming weekdays, with the wax candle; the ceremony of searching for crumbs of leavened bread was carried out with the help of a candle; to celebrate the victory of the Maccabees, they light candles for eight nights; they light candles at the death-bed for the departing soul; they put up memorial candles at the anniversary of the death of their beloved ones; they light wedding candles, and candles for the Day of Atonement, and candles for the Passover table—all lights with great radiance; but the outside world they do not illuminate.

The whole Jewish community comes out publicly to bless the new moon—but they have no ritual for the sun.

And because they did not see the shining light of the world, they so devotedly treasured and venerated their inner light. Speaking of a wise man they say he has "a luminous mind." When praising a great Rabbi, they say, he is "a luminary of the exile"—a light that spreads radiance in the dark night of the exile. A great light, but one that does not illuminate God's beautiful world.

ESCAPE FROM REALITY

The Jewish child with an untrammeled imagination, who lived in a poor home, in a wretched street, where the visible world was miserable and colorless, without joy and without beauty—did not have far to go to escape his unacceptable surroundings. Not far away from his bed and his table lay the path into an infinitely rich and bountiful super-terrestrial world— a free world, with no boundaries and no barriers, a world into which he could and did transport himself any hour; a celestial world into which he was carried away by the breath of his whole community in the hours of great festivity. The Jewish child began in infancy to learn the path of escape from the unrewarding world of reality.

When the Jewish child entered his Hebrew school, he entered a world of the imagination. In his daily lessons of the Bible he had to transport himself into a vanished past that was glorious with its great heroes, tragic with its martyrs, and sublime with its prophets and poets.

The story of the past was no mere history, no tale of days gone by. The Biblical story was contemporary with every generation of Jewish children; they had to live with the past more than with the occurrences of their own time. It was also their promised future: what was, would come again. This sacred history pervaded and superseded their everyday life. All the spiritual and creative energies of the Jewish people, all their national strength was consecrated to the task of making the divine history of the distant past the bread and sustenance of the children of the whole people. In danger of its national existence, the hope for the future depended upon the people believing in the promise of the prophets, upon the young generations clinging to the heritage of the past. From this heritage flowed national pride, strength and courage. And beginning with infancy every Jew was made to nourish from the sacred sources of the holy book, to drink its ever-living waters. The holy land, the destruction of the temple, the diaspora, the Messiah— the whole divine legend was as close to the Jewish child as the face of its mother and grandmother from whom the child first learned the destiny of its people, in their cradle songs and nursery tales. Together with its mother's milk the child received the knowledge of her people's sorrow and hope, grandeur and pathos.

Thus the Jewish child is taught to live by his imagination, to see what is not and to believe in an existence that has no foundation in reality.

The religious life of the Jew in the old communities of the not distant days—it is worth repeating—was full of symbolical objects which, seen in their bodily appearance, were insignificant and even trivial, but were transubstantiated and received a super-mundane beauty when used in holy service—all the objects used in the home and in the synagogue in the Sabbath and holiday celebrations and rituals were of that nature.

For the imaginative Jewish child who follows his father to the synagogue there to welcome the beautiful bride, the Queen Sabbath, and to greet the Angels of Peace that are waiting for him on his return home; who enters the Suko (tabernacle) to meet the highly honored guests that have been invited to visit, no less than the forefathers, Abraham, Isaac and Jacob, also Joseph the Virtuous, Moses, Aaron and King David— for the imaginative child these legends are a part of his living world as much as his relatives that he meets, only more exalted. And what a training in seeing the invisible; and what an exciting company for the young image-maker! And there is the Prophet Elija, for whom a chair is set, a seat of honor, at every circumcision ritual; and who comes to drink his cup of wine placed separately for him a.. .. ..er Table, the most beautiful wine-cup in the family's possession—a highly honored guest, one opens wide the door for him when his presence is invoked, and all rise from their seats to greet him. But he also comes uninvited, if one is deserving of his favor, at any time of great need to bring succor and salvation—though one may not recognize him, for he comes in all kinds of disguises, his most favorite that of a peasant in a horse-cart, or a wood cutter, girdled with a rope, an ax under it, and a sack on his shoulder, in which he brings his gifts when material aid is wanted.

And, of course, there are other celestial beings, devils no less than angels—on earth, devils more than angels—and ghosts too. The cemetery is there as a part of the city; the dead not really dead, though buried; they have two abodes now: their graves in the cemetery where you go to supplicate them for help, especially for the sick; and in heaven—first in Hell, of course, and then in Paradise . . .

For the Jewish child who grew up in the atmosphere of the small town, there were no frontiers to cross and no sentinels to stop him when he wanted to make an excursion into the heavenly domains—and he needed no chariot of fire to carry him there; the Jewish heaven was bent over the desks in the school room where the children were memorizing their lessons of the Bible—it was so close, almost resting on the roofs of the lowly Jewish houses (as you can see in Chagall's paintings). And when Chagall's grandfather got up on the roof and sat down on the chimney to eat his dish of stewed carrots dessert (see Chagall's sketch of it) and enjoy the fresh breezes, why with one bound he could leap into paradise and pick up the leavings on the table of the saints (as he and other Chassidim do at the table of his holy Rabbi) that sit around with their crowns on their heads and take delight in the splendor of God's glory.

It was difficult for the Jewish artist who grew up in the old Jewish communities to forget the super-real world which he left behind and find profit in painting the natural and factual world. The authentic Jewish poet and artist is not a realist in his art.

So it was long ago and so it is today.

When Rabbi Nachman of Bratzlav said: "Each tongue of grass has its own tune; it is beautiful to hear the field of grass sing"—he was a poet. But when he added: "When you pray in the open field, the grass and the flowers enter into your prayers and give them

power to ascend to heaven"—you hear a Jewish poet and mystic speak.

When Peretz wanted to describe the fields in early spring, he said with the Talmud, "you can sense how behind each blade of grass there stands an angel and urges it on: grow! grow!" *

To see behind each blade an angel nursing it, you need eyes with Jewish light in them.

And here you have Peretz's "Between Two Mountains," "The Golden Chain" and "In the Old Market Place."

And now you have Marc Chagall.

"PROMENADE"

In 1917 Chagall painted his "Promenade."

The artist relates that in this canvas he wanted to tell that he and his beloved Bella were in heaven with happiness. He painted himself and his wife walking in the fields outside Witebsk. They hold hands—but he walks on the ground and she follows him in the sky. No, he, too, walks not on the ground but in the air; they are both floating between earth and sky; she in a horizontal position high above over the roof tops. He receives the touch of her hand in mystic rapture.

The like of it could have come only from the brush of a Jewish artist.

And while painting a picture of himself and his wife, Chagall also painted in it a Jewish idyll—an idyll that lived for centuries in the air of the houses of Talmudic study in the ghettos, in its unwritten folk-lore: it is the idyll of the romantic Talmudic student, the cabalist, who is in love with the pale-faced daughter of the rich house where he comes to eat his charitable meals one day each week. When he goes for a walk in the fields, he takes his heavenly sweetheart with him. She hovers over him—she is no less real to his vision even if she is only the bride of his dreams. She is with him on his walk, even if it is only the creation of his mystic sense—how otherwise could she go with him for a walk and a picnic? He feels the touch of her hand through his mystic power, and his eyes beam with an unearthly radiance.

How substantial are the little houses in the background and the whole city left behind compared with the intensity of his love? Of what avail the laws of nature against this prince of visionaries? Watch how

---

* Rabbi Simon said: There is no grass without its guardian angel in the sky, which drives it saying: Grow.

he strides over the waves of air with his winged steps, with no gravitation pulling at his heels. How proud he is. He has conquered the impossible with his occult cabbalistic powers.

In the process of creating this painting, there happened to Chagall what happens to him many times in moments of intuitive creation—what happens to all great artists. He begins his work with a personal experience, an emotional impulse, an impression of something seen, an incident of the moment, or something remembered. He begins his composition by arbitrarily putting on a few lines, a few dubs of color, to fix his structural idea—but soon the man steps back, the artist takes over. The artist is now in control. He does not think any more of the original impulse, of the first cause. He becomes preoccupied with the possibilities that lie, invisible as yet, in his undeveloped subject matter. He busies himself now not with the cause but with the effect of his picture, with the work to be. As he proceeds in developing his composition, as he watches its becoming, as he searches for the plastic affinities, picking up the nascent suggestive directions—in the moments of concentrated effort, as his mind hovers and broods over the intimations of the masterwork to be, his deepest sources open to his inventive powers and supply his imagination with their accumulated riches, which he now feeds to his new creation. Thus enriched, the finished piece of work far transcends the original subject matter; is of greater vitality and of more general significance.

In Chagall these sources that nourish his genius are his childhood memories of Jewish life and his Jewish inheritance.

In the above-mentioned painting Chagall created a work of Jewish art—Jewish not only for its content but also for its form in which the spirit of the subject expresses itself so convincingly; a form imaginatively and truthfully evolved from the subject matter. This canvas could be designed only by a Jewish artist, by no other. Again and again we will find this creative process in Chagall's masterpieces; the artist becomes a folk-artist, and his work achieves a symbolic significance rich with the spirit and ideals of his people.

Chagall's pictures have a Jewish rationale behind them; and what looks strange and incomprehensible to an outsider looks understandable and acceptable to Jews who have a familiarity with Jewish literature and folklore. It is this rationale that makes his most bizarre subjects acceptable to men and women of the Jewish masses, even when Chagall's art values are above their understanding.

In his intuition and his emotions Chagall is Jewish and is therefore no realist. For Chagall as for Peretz, as for the poets of the Psalms, and as for the other great creative personalities of Jewish history, the truth of his own conception is of greater importance than the superficial truth of nature.

The Rabbi of Kotzk said: "Everything in the world can be imitated except truth, for truth imitated is no more truth."

"SOLITUDE"

Chagall sees the world with Jewish eyes—and Jewish eyes are sad and often filled with pity.

In 1933 Chagall painted a picture called "Solitude." A Jew sits in a meadow, his head covered with a white mantle, a Torah clasped tenderly to his breast. Near him on the ground a cow rests on her knees, under her chin a violin and bow. Above, in the sky, there is a small figure with wings—an angel. In the background, are visible the cupolas of a church and the distant small houses of a village.

The "realist" approaching this canvas can hardly be pleased. The animal looks like a cow, but not really; it has a human eye. Then, he is not pleased with the Jew; how come a Jew with a Torah in the midst of a field, keeping company with an animal?

The "realist" is displeased.

But look at the heart of the painting, get its true meaning and you will agree that had the artist painted everything in realistic copy, it would have been bad art.

Look at the face of the Jew and see how much kindness, tenderness, and gentleness it expresses, all permeated with a comfortless sorrow. Alone and forlorn. He did not find one human friend. The Jew is friendless in the world. Only God's dumb creature, a cow in the field, accepts him without malice.

Again, here you can see how the artist's Jewish feeling directs the plastic design and the result is a Jewish work of art.

Chagall's Jewish spirit, his warm-heartedness, reaches out with loving care to all things, also to the still and dumb objects, that through their coming in touch with human beings, in giving them service, have in themselves achieved a human quality, human significance and esteem. They all find place in Chagall's painting—the lamp, the clock, the pot, the samovar, the candlestick, the candle, the menorah, the violin, the flute, the book, the sacramental cup of wine, and other objects associated with Jewish life and ceremony, in the home and in the synagogue, as the artist remembers them from his childhood days—they all come into his pictures—to fill up empty space, of course, but always to help out the humans of the picture.

A greater love does Chagall show to living things, to animals, birds, fowls—that are busy in carrying out some important task for their masters, participating in their joys and sorrows.

This human kind-heartedness, and the sympathy that suffering always awakens in the Jew—that is the oil that softens Chagall's pigments, that transfuses his colors with a warmth, a tenderness and a refinement.

All add up to a plastic expression which is Jewish in essence.

Chagall who is against determining Jewish art, had said:

"And yet it seems to me, had I not been a Jew (with the meaning that I attach to this word) I would have never been a painter, or entirely a different one."

Home and Childhood

CHAGALL relates that on the day he was born a fire broke out in the neighborhood, and mother and baby were removed to the other side of the town—against the possibility of the fire spreading rapidly through the small wooden houses huddled together in the poor Jewish quarters.

This happened in Witebsk on July 7, 1889.*

The baby was still-born—but Witebsk ** and its little houses became a beautiful legend known the wide world over, told so eloquently again and again by the faithful citizen that gave so much trouble at his birth.

He stubbornly refused to open his eyes and had to be "slapped" before he accepted the painful duty of living—but only that one time.

I believe that in the commotion and confusion of the fire the mother did not see that an angel came, the guardian angel of the arts, and, solicitous for the future great artist, providently tied the severed umbilical cord of the baby back to mother's body, to the squares and streets of Witebsk, to the Witebsk sky, sun, and moon. Chagall to this day is still getting nourishment from his mother, from her blood and milk, from her people, and from the soil, air, sky, and sun of Witebsk.

And as distant from Witebsk as he may have traveled, to Paris, Berlin, Moscow, Tel Aviv, New York—Witebsk was never left behind. On the contrary, all his peregrinations in foreign climes were a homecoming to Witebsk.

After seeing the world, he first could say:

"More than once I have been thinking to myself that maybe Witebsk is no worse than Florence and Paris."

And again:

"In Witebsk all the little fences, the little cows and sheep, all the Jews, looked to me just as original, as ingenuous, and as eternal as the buildings in Giotto's frescos."

This eternity, we must remember, is a spiritual one, in measure of quality, of worth, not in measure of physical strength and endurance.

If in his canvases he gave them immortality, it is because he had for them this feeling and because he saw them in the aspect of their "eternal substance."

Placed back in their Witebsk landscape, on their native soil of reality, you will see his houses and their fences—small, poor, frail, as swallow nests on naked trees, that any strong wind could shake down. Fragile small huts that lean one against the other for support and comradeship—and over them a royal spread of sky, that bends low over their roofs, a friendly sky, where Chagall's people are at home, take a walk, or stretch out, as in their own yard.

And all Chagall's heroes, his cows and sheep and Jews, look frightened, as if living under the constant threat of a sinister doom. They do not feel secure on their earth—and that may be the reason why Chagall puts them up in the air time and again. When he paints Jews in groups, they are always on the run, running to get together, running away to escape. There is an atmosphere of panic and fate.

Even in his pictures of Jewish weddings, a favorite subject of his, you do not see the joy of healthy free people. You feel that Chagall pities them.

Did Chagall have a premonition of the storm of destruction that was to strike down the Jewish towns and cities, the "Witebsk" Jews, their cows and sheep? Or was it the old fear of Jewish history in the blood of their great artist in wakeful watching over them?

When Chagall came home from Paris he could not stop wondering how diminutive his parents' house looked to him.

---

* Some writers give 1887 as the year of the artist's birth. This was the date registered in the Witebsk city records and appeared in Chagall's passports.

In old Russia there was no strict rule about when a father had to register the birth of his children—it was done at any time after the birth.

When the artist's father went to register the birth of his two boys, he added two years to the age of the first born, Moshke (Marc), making him four years older than his brother—to secure for him the right to be exempted from military service on the ground that his brother is still a minor. The family, of course, knew the real age of the artist and told him so.

It was not an uncommon practice.

** Witebsk, an old city of about 60,000 population, on the Russo-Polish border.

He relates:

"When I looked down from the 'loftiness' of my present stature upon the little house where I was born, shrinking as far as I could, I asked myself how indeed could I have been born there? How could one draw his breath there?"

No wonder that Chagall's mise en scène is always in the open air, in the yard, on the square, on the roof, or in the sky.

Moshke (the future Marc) was a quiet thoughtful child, a born dreamer.

He tells that his favorite occupation as a young child was to sit in the yard with a large slice of bread and butter in hand, sitting and munching, and looking.

Looking:—everything in sight was an attraction, his eyes moving from object to object, taking it all in, but only with the eyes. Before he could form a clear perception of what was before his eyes, he relished the mere pleasure of seeing.

When the inside of the yard became too familiar and the allure of the "beyond" began to excite him, too little as yet to look over the fence, he found a log to stand upon; later he got up on the top of the fence, and still later, he got to the roof of the house.

Everywhere, in all places, he was first of all interested in all his eyes could take hold of, could watch, for the pleasure of the eyes in seeing things, people, earth and sky. The same in the yard, in the street, in his Jewish school, in the city school, in the synagogue. The eyes more than the mind were always busy, always preoccupied. The mind often could not follow, could not understand what the eyes were seeing; thought was left behind while the two eyes were moving and foraging. There was always something to watch: in the synagogue in the midst of service—the Jews, their prayer shawls, the holy shrine with its marvelous decorations, the pulpit, the chandeliers, the hanging lamps—and through the window, the sky, the clouds, a tree, a flying bird, and people passing by, children at play, a driver and his horse and wagon, a peasant leading a cow—looking more than praying. In school, looking more than studying. Everywhere the same, looking without thought or purpose, for the sheer pleasure of seeing.

There was and still is an unsatisfied hunger in his eyes.

The artist tells me with a smile that he loved to go to the outhouse and spend many quarter-hours there—because it stood at the far end of the backyard and had an open casement through which he could put out his head and look at the beautiful green world of trees and truck gardens and fields beyond, open vistas spreading into the far distance. The street about their little house was completely built up, and only from the outhouse window could he see the open landscape.

"The outhouse window opened upon paradise for me"—the artist says with his hearty laugh.

It was a pity when someone else had need of the outhouse and came to drive the boy out from his "paradise."

And that was the reason why the young fellow loved to get on the roof—from there an enticing panorama could be watched without disturbance.

He became so adept in walking on the steep roofs and disported there so freely that when a fire broke out in the neighborhood and the neighbors organized themselves in groups to protect the roofs in the vicinity from the flying sparks, he, the young lad, became their chief.

That is the reason that, when he later put the people in his paintings on roofs, he knew how to dispose them there securely and comfortably.

"One fine day (and there are no other than fine days) a 'melamed' appeared before me, a figure out of my canvases, or as one that ran away from a circus. No one called him, he came himself, as the matchmaker or the old undertaker."

He showed the child an "Aleph" and fell asleep, and the student, too. He came every day, and after a time something was accomplished. One term, two—and finally the child could read a few words.

"You know, your son has a sharp mind—" he said one day to the mother.

And the child began to go to "cheder" for the whole day and come home at night with a lantern.

"At night, my stars were patiently waiting for me at the school door and took me home"—

The father, Reb Yecheskel (Ezekiel) was a worker in a herring store. The artist writes in his "Ma Vie":

"My grandfather, a religious instructor, could think of nothing better than to place my father, his eldest son, as a clerk in a herring wholesale store while he was still a child, and his youngest son in a barber's shop.

The Sabbath. Oil. 1909–10
Museum of Düsseldorf
Courtesy of the Artist

PLATE VI

The Slutsk Preacher. Oil. 1914
Collection of Karl Im Oberstag, Basle
Courtesy of the Artist

PLATE VII

"No, my father was not a clerk but a simple laborer for thirty-two years.

"He lifted enormous barrels and my heart shrivelled like a Turkish cracknel when I saw him hoist these loads and rummage in herring barrels with his frozen hands."

With all his hard work the father's wages were not enough for the upkeep of the family—a large one of eight daughters and two sons.

But the mother was a clever and energetic woman. Not only did she manage the whole family and her husband, but untiringly built up a store, got drivers to bring her loads of goods and opened a grocery—without having any money of her own, all on credit.

Her life was hard and not very happy. As a girl she was pretty. But giving her strength to bring her big family into the world, her care and worry to provide for them, her unremitted work in the house and in the grocery, brought her down. Some of her old charm remained, however, and on the Sabbath or on a holiday she would dress up a bit and try to revive her faded good looks for the sake of her husband and children.

But her husband, exhausted by a day's toil, would no sooner get through with his supper than he would fall asleep at the table.

And the children were as yet too young to understand their mother's inner needs. Only Moshke, the oldest son, would see and understand his mother's bitter days—and there was a close bond of sympathy between them.

The artist relates:

"Friday night after supper. Father is already asleep at the table, hardly had time to finish his blessings after the meal. Mother's eyes grow sad. She raps with her knuckles on the table a few times, as was her habit: 'Everybody is asleep already. What kind of children have I got? There is nobody to talk to, not even one word. You, my son, you talk to me!'"

But the son felt so young and so silly—and his mother looked to him like a queen. What could he talk to her about?

"She raps again on the table: 'Children let us sing together the Rabbi's tune. Help me!'"

The children would sing—but soon began napping and their Mother would cry.

"'Well now, mother, if you cry, I, too, will stop singing'—her son pleads with her, all melting in tears inside."

Pity—pity for the father that had to wake every morning, summer and winter at six o'clock in the morning and run to the synagogue to say Kaddish—he always had to say Kaddish for somebody dead—and then toil a whole long day at heavy barrels of herring, and fall asleep at the table; pity for the mother and her lonely, unrelieved life.

This feeling of pity, sympathy with the suffering of people, this, says the artist, was his strongest emotion—and still remains so. He could never forget that his father was a worker and toiled his whole life for his rich employer. He could never forget the hard and careworn life of his mother, her unsatisfied needs and yearning and her heroic struggle to keep up.

The artist has a later memory of his mother.

"Here she is coming to my room. I hear her knocking at my door. Are you there, my son? What are you doing? Was Bertha (Bella) here today? Do you want something to eat?

Look, mama, how do you like it?

She examines my painting with God knows what eyes. I am waiting for her judgment. At last she remarks thoughtfully: Well, my child, yes, I see, you have talent. But listen to me, son, wouldn't you rather be a clerk? I am sorry for you with your big shoulders. How did this thing ever come into our family?"

At another time the artist gives this description of his father:

"Did you ever see one of the accidental personages in the Florentine paintings, with a beard never trimmed, eyes brown and ashen at the same time, a face of burned ochre, wrinkled and creased? This is my father.

"Or, have you seen one of the figures of the Haggadah with his paschal and doltish aspect? (Forgive me, father.)

"I made a study of you, do you remember? Your portrait should have produced the effect of a candle that flames up and goes out at the same time. Its smell that of a sleep."

And this is how he reminds himself of his mother:

"I seem to see you, mama. You come towards

me slowly, so slowly that I have a desire to help you. You smile with my smile. Oh, that smile is mine. . . .

"I see the river receding, the bridge further away, and nearby the eternal fence, earth and a grave. Here is my soul. Look for me here, this is where I am, here are my paintings, my birth. Sorrow, sorrow.

"That is her picture. It is all the same. I am in it too. Who am I? (You will smile, you will wonder and laugh, passing stranger.) A well of sadness, untimely greyness, eyes—gates of tears, a soul that barely exists. What remains? . . .

"I want to say that somewhere in her was my talent hidden, that she gave me everything, except her wisdom."

You must also get acquainted with a few of his relatives.

There is his grandfather on his mother's side, a butcher in Lyozno, a village near Witebsk:

"My grandfather spent half of his life lying on the stove, a quarter of his life in the house of prayer and the rest in the butcher store."

About this grandfather the artist relates:

"One of the days of the Feast of the Tabernacle, on Simchath Torah, they were looking for my grandfather—but he was nowhere to be found.

"In the end they discovered him. In the fine weather he got up on the roof, sat down on the chimney and was eating his dish of stewed carrot dessert, enjoying the fresh breezes at the same time.

"Not a bad picture."

Chagall made a drawing of it.

"My mother told me about my relatives in Lyozno. One of them could think of nothing better than to walk in the street of the village clad only in his long undershirt. What is so terrible about it? The memory of this sans-culotte will always fill my heart with sunny joy. As if on the streets of Lyozno the paintings of Masaccio, of Piero della Francesca had been re-born. I felt close to him.

"I forgot about you, Uncle Noah. With you we used to go to the village for cows. How happy I was when you consented to take me with you in your jolting cart—but no matter, one could go in it.

"On the way back I decided to show my power and skill by dragging a cow along by its tail after the wagon, admonishing her not to keep back."

Chagall has painted such a picture: he sits at the hind end of the wagon dragging a cow by the tail. You can't tell which way the wagon is moving: after the horse, forward; or after the cow, backward.

He also has painted several pictures of his Uncle Noah and his horse and wagon with his cows and calves.

Uncle Noah was a Chassid and possessed a violin. After a hard day's work he would try to play the tunes he had learned at the Rabbi's. Uncle Noah and grandfather, the butcher, had a romantic influence on the boy.

The slaughtered cows and sheep and their dried hides stirred the imagination of the impressionable lad, waking pity in his heart and making him thoughtful.

His relatives exerted an influence on the sensitive future artist with their very lives, with their queer and quaint personalities.

There remained with the artist all his life a love for the simple folk, for the lowly and their ways of life.

In addition to the ones mentioned, he had "another half-a-dozen and some more"—as he himself puts it—uncles and aunts who enriched the memory of the artist with their folkways and folklore, that he later used in his paintings.

"If my art did not play any part in their lives—they and their stories influenced me greatly. And I do not mind if people discover with pleasure and joy the riddles of my canvases in the innocent adventures of my relatives"—

the artist confesses.

Many times in conversations the artist said to me that he tries to bring to his art the simplicity and truthfulness with which his father and mother lived their lives.

Talking with the artist about his contemporaries in French art, the great artists Matisse, Picasso, Rouault, I suggested that he, Chagall, differs from them in his art by his Jewish spirit and his Jewish heritage.

"As my father differed from their fathers"—Chagall assented.

Up to his sixteenth year Moshke (Marc) was still going in the Hebrew schools. The hard working father had made sacrifices to pay for his son's studies—"that he may know what a Jew must." Well, by then Moshke could read by himself the weekly portion of the Sacred Law with Rashi's commentary, and he could also write a handsome letter—and that is about all his father could do to help him. What else? He will never be a rabbi!

And the lad agreed. What did he gain by going to cheder? And he hated to take away even a small part of his father's earnings, gained so painfully—the less he accepted the happier he would be.

And though he had as yet no notion of becoming an artist, he had already tasted the intoxication of using a pencil to draw. The truth must be told that he had no more heart in his studies.

Now, when the artist recalls those days, he confesses, somewhat abashedly, that all the subjects of his studies really did not engage him much. Neither the stories of the Bible nor the poetry of the prophets made a deep impression on him—not then. Now, coming back, well, of course!

We can assure the artist that he is not the only one at the age of sixteen or seventeen who could not fully grasp the sublimity of the literature that he was made to study. We may ask the artist, how much at the age of sixteen could he have apprehended what is in the art of Rembrandt, of Tinteretto, of El Greco? It is above the understanding of a youth—and so is the literature of the holy books, as it is forced upon the youth by the old rabbis.

The question arises, would the Europeanized Jewish intellectual have come back later to the same old sources with so much hunger and avidity if they had not tasted of them in their younger days? Something remains from the chedar days that pulls them back with a passion to the old tomes. Unknowingly, a love was planted in their young hearts for the sacred pages, a love that could not be uprooted in the later years of questioning, doubting, and rebelling that made their hearts more lonely and increased their hunger for the discarded old volumes; a hunger which could not be satisfied at any other source.

Perhaps the rabbis knew this and for that reason kept the Jewish child in their old schools.

Chagall, too, came back—came back to partake of the precious heritage of Israel and to enrich his spirit and his art with the sacred lore of the "book" he once held lightly, as his superlative recreation of biblical subjects show.

But about that later.

The mother of the artist was not entirely pleased with her son getting a Jewish education only—and she put him in a government school to acquire secular knowledge.

For a Jewish child it was very hard in those days to break through the door of the government schools, and few Jewish boys found their way there.

But the wise mother knew that with a gift of fifty rubles she would find a "kindhearted" professor who would quietly open the doors for her son. Soon she discovered that "softhearted" man, and her son was accepted in the third form. Why in the third?—because the "kind" professor was the head of that grade.

But he was in—

For the young Movsha * (no longer Moshke) it was no great joy to go to that school—and no great profit either. His "two's" (out of possible "five") he easily obtained—though he learned his lessons well. It is true that sitting up nights over his books, he more often than not lost himself in dreams; or his imagination carried him off to his friends in the streets, on the river, or bridge—forgetting his book, until mother, waking up suddenly, would berate him for burning the lamp so late for nothing. But he did know his lessons. Only it always so happened that when he was called to the platform to recite his lesson in front of the class, his tongue somehow twisted, and he could not show his learning . . .

Besides, there was an uncovered window and through it the allure of pretty young faces of girls, students in the next-door school. And the inspector always happened to appear, as if out of the ground, just when the lad was throwing a kiss through the air to a pretty face showing at the window—so his "twos" were growing fast. Well, so what? He was satisfied with them. Oh, no, not in the geometry class—there he was a wizard and artistic figures ran out from under his fingers as if by magic.

But his throne was in the drawing-class room. Here he was king and his sovereignty was generally acknowledged, everybody looked up to him and took him as an example. Here was the center of the world for him; here all abuses and all discriminations were forgotten. Here he was happy.

_____
* Russianized. Later, in Paris, the artist changed it to Marc.

Funeral. Oil. 1909. Collection of L. Bernheim, Paris

Courtesy of the Artist

PLATE VIII

Wedding. Paris 1910. Oil

Courtesy of the Artist

PLATE IX

YOUNG AMBITION

If you sometimes find Chagall in a good mood, after a fine dinner and a glass of wine, in congenial company, ask him to give you a choice piece of synagogal music, a passage of the services of the Days of Awe; for instance, that soul stirring piece beginning with, "As a shepherd examines his flock"—and the artist will sing it for you exactly as he received it from the Witebsk cantor, with all the trills and quavers, nothing lacking. It is all still fresh in his memory as if it were only yesterday that he stood in the crowded synagogue, at the side of the cantor, as one of his helpers. You must know that at one time Marc was almost a professional singer and received for his professional services the respectable sum of two and one-half rubles, for helping the cantor in the Days of Awe only. It is true that the cantor did not need him any other time—but just the same, it was a fortune of money—and what did he do for it?—he just sang. And remember the honor that went with it. Just imagine yourself standing in the crowded synagogue, filled with a holiday spirit; you open your mouth and the holy words flow out sweetly, tenderly, carried aloft and spreading out over the heads of the whole congregation by your ringing soprano—and you know with trepidation that everyone is listening—you yourself listen too —with appreciative delight to the sweetness of your voice as it swells and rises out of your "golden" throat. Oh, what joy, what rapture! . . .

The world-famous artist recalls that joyful time with pleasure—though, as he remembers, his enjoyment was not unmixed with the gall of envy—at his side there was another little fellow who not only had a beautiful voice, but could also read music and was a fine singer, admired by everybody.

However, this did not prevent the young Moshke from appreciating his own "instrument," and he dreamed of going to a conservatory of music to become a world-famous cantor . . .

But he was not too sure whether that was the best that he could choose for his life's career. When he and his sister went dancing together, everybody gathered around them to applaud. The neighbors invited the two of them to their homes to see their beautiful dancing. And a handsome lad he was with his elegant figure and curly hair—a handsome lad, why, he could become a famous dancer . . .

But then again, he was taking violin lessons from a neighbor. His teacher, who was a clerk in a hardware store, would always beat time, one-two-three-that's it! —excellent, my boy! excellent! Well, then, he might become a famous violinist and give concerts in all the big cities of the world . . . Excellent!

And all the time, day and night, he made poems, true poems with good rhymes, that people said were fine, *very* fine. So, he might become a famous poet . . .

But then . . . When he was in the fifth grade in public school, there was a big fellow sitting in the front row of the drawing class, a bully who always provoked him.

One day this bully showed a drawing he had made on silk paper, a copy of a picture in the magazine "Nivo"—"A Smoker."

For him, right there, an abyss opened suddenly, a great misfortune befell him. What?—this accomplishment was not his own but that block-head's? A rage flamed in his heart, a leopard woke in him—wait, he will show him!

And immediately he ran to the public library, grabbed the thick volume of "Nivo" and sat down to copy a portrait of the composer Rubinstein, then some Greek statue and other illustrations—maybe not altogether faithfully copied, but much improvised . . .

Up to that day he had known nothing of the world of art, of pictures. All that he had ever seen were a few faded family photographs. It was a holiday for him when he discovered in his mother's grocery a wrapper with a picture on a piece of chocolate or on a can of cocoa. This was a rare occasion, a precious find.

And now the "Nivo" opened a new world to him, thanks to that rapscallion.

The copies and the improvisations that he made he treasured very dearly; the best he pasted on the wall of his corner of the room at home.

THE GREAT DISCOVERY

The artist relates:

"I knew all the street slang and other expressions less popular—but one word I did not know, a fantastic, a literary word that came from an entirely different world; the word "artist," that I might have heard, probably, but which did not 'stick,' a word that was not in use in my environment. It was so far away from us.

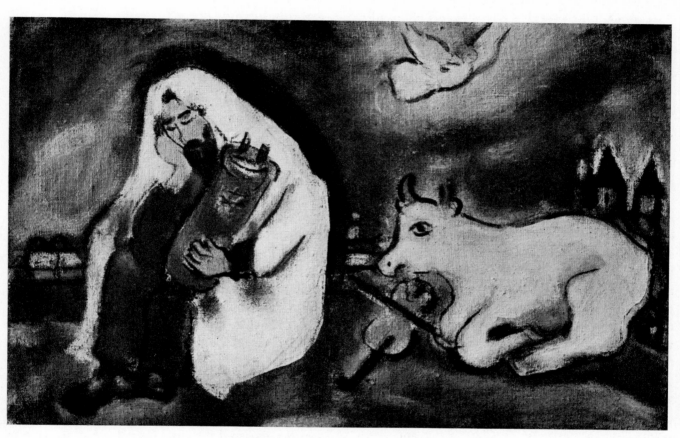

Solitude. Study for Oil Painting. 1933

Courtesy of the Artist

PLATE X

"For myself I would have never been so bold as to let that word slip off my tongue. But one of my school friends came to visit me and, looking over my drawings on the wall, he turned to me with admiration exclaiming: 'So you are a real artist!'

"'What are you saying? Who is an artist? What is an artist?— — —'

"My friend left without my getting much out of him.

"I soon reminded myself that somewhere in a street of our city I had seen a big sign, such as on stores, with the legend: a school for drawing and painting, run by the artist Pen.

"I thought to myself, here now my destiny is decreed. There was nothing else for me to do now except to get into that school and become an artist.

"My mother's illusions that she was going to make a clerk out of me, or a bookkeeper, or better still, a photographer, forever destroyed."

Moshke finally persuaded his kind mother to take him and his work to the art teacher Pen. It was no easy job to move his mother to such a step, but slowly she gave in—and as she was the sovereign of the family, her son gained his objective. His father angrily threw on the floor the five rubles monthly tuition fee—but the son picked it up in humility and carried it hopefully to pay for his entrance into Pen's academy, the only art school in Witebsk. Marc was then seventeen years old.

It took him not more than three months to find out that Pen couldn't give him anything, and he left his school.

The ambition of the family now revived and new plans were discussed how to make Moshke a successful businessman in Witebsk—an ambition latent in the heart of his father, who could not himself attain to it. But the youthful artist had already been planning to get to an art school in Petersburg—planning it with one of his friends from the Pen school, so far secretly because he saw no way of carrying it out.

It was an accepted rule for the parents in the small Jewish cities, when a son showed artistic abilities, to make him a photographer: photography is "artistic" and it provides a livelihood.

And so Moshke was apprenticed to a photographer.

But Moshke immediately disliked the tedious work of sitting for hours retouching, and he began to beg his mother to send him to Petersburg.

He finally achieved his heart's desire. With the huge treasury of twenty-seven rubles, a veritable fortune scraped together from their poor pockets, the mother sent her son on the way to the Tzarist capital, St. Petersburg, to begin a new life.

ART SCHOOLS

And now began for the young Chagall the trials and tribulations of the poor artist, a Jew in the bargain, without the right of residence in the imperial capital.

The ambition of the young man was to get into a first-rate school at once—which would also give him, as an enrolled student, the permit to stay in the capital.

But he had to pass an academic examination for which he was not prepared; small wonder that he failed.

Time to prepare himself he had none. And so he bent his proud heart and applied now to a third rate school, which was known as "The School of the Society for the Protection of Art." Here he not only passed the entrance examination, but did so well that he was granted a year's free tuition and also a stipend of ten rubles monthly.

After that he managed to get some help for short periods from one or another kind person. He lived with poor workers. He took a job as a servant in the house of a lawyer—and got along somehow.

Much worse was it for him to get along with the police inspector, who gave him no peace because he had not procured the right permit to live in the city. The enrollment in "The School of the Society for the Protection of Art" did not carry the privilege of the right of residence. One had to get it in another way— but meanwhile it was a game of avoiding the clutches of the police.

After he tasted a term of imprisonment, Chagall decided to learn some kind of a recognized skilled trade that entitles the practitioner the right of residence in Petersburg. He picked the trade of sign-making and quickly began to work at it, keeping up meanwhile his studies in the art school.

After two years of attending "The School of the Society for the Protection of Art," he discovered that he was only wasting his valuable time there and quit.

In the year 1908 an exhibition of the works of the "new" French and Russian painters was held collectively in Petersburg.

It proved that the Russians were far behind. The modern art of Paris captured the imagination of the young.

In those days the fame of the artist Leon Bakst began to spread through Petersburg. He was making the brilliant decorations and costumes for the Russian Ballet Theater.

Bakst belonged to the society of the progressive artists grouped around the magazine "Mir Iskustvo" (The World of Art), that led the fight against the academicians under the banner of "Art for Art's Sake." In this periodical appeared articles dealing with the latest directions in the art of Paris.

When Chagall heard that Bakst was also a director of a school where the spirit of the new art was dominant, he at once knocked, somewhat fearfully, at Bakst's door with a number of his paintings under his arm.

Bakst accepted him.

Three months with Bakst was enough for him. By then he knew that nobody could teach him, anyway.

He left Petersburg and returned home to Witebsk. The young artist had a word of praise to say for the schools of Petersburg: they did not injure him.

On the Way to Himself

AFTER his experiences in Petersburg, the young artist felt that he could now work on his own.

At all events, others could not teach him. He had to find his way himself.

What his way would be, his first pictures painted after his return to Witebsk give a clear indication. A few of these early paintings were fortunately retrieved, and it is very interesting to examine them.

It is all very surprising and provoking; nothing that you would have ever expected. Here is a small-town young man come back from Petersburg, an imperial capital, a great metropolis, a world center. One would have expected that the young artist brought back many sketches of the big rich city, which he would now develop into big canvases. He had surely seen the grand palaces, brilliant squares, boulevards, old churches, beautiful women, actresses, diplomats, generals, elegant equipages, peasants with their horses and wagons, workers, soldiers, sailors, beggars—and what not, people and things to win the eye and fancy of a young artist; a big rich world to pick from.

And what do you think he did?

"BURNING CANDLES IN A DARK STREET"

Here is one of his first canvases. It is called, "Burning Candles in a Dark Street." A Witebsk alley with little houses, the oncoming of evening. At one side of the street a dead man is lying on the ground, covered with a black cloth, his dead face and naked feet exposed; burning candles in candlesticks stand around the body. Towards the other side of the street is a screaming woman with her hands raised above her head. A street cleaner, unperturbed, is sweeping the street at the head of the corpse. Unperturbed is also the fiddler who is sitting on the roof of a low neighboring house, fiddling. But a man was so frightened that he had crashed into his door, the upper part of his body disappearing in the house, leaving the hind part and legs in the street. His violent action caused a flower pot to come tumbling out of a window.

Where is Petersburg?

A disconcerting picture—but looking at it now, retrospectively, one may discern in it, in embryo, as it were, the features of a Chagallian work of art.

Why does the dead man lie in the street?—because Chagall wanted him there.

Why does the street cleaner sweep the street unconcernedly?—because the artist made him do it.

Why does the fiddler sit on the roof, fiddling?—because the artist put him to it . . .

The logic of the scene lies in Chagall's fancy. He wanted to create a new reality.

Preposterous, you will say; madness.

There is logic in its irrationality.

Some critics, in discussing this picture, seem to assume that Chagall recorded disparate acts as they tumbled out of his memory; with no kinship of one figure with the other, except that all are in some way associated with Witebsk.

But to assume that the artist had no central idea and no purposeful plan in introducing and distributing the characters in his mise en scène is to fail not only to understand this picture, but also to miss one of the fundamentals of Chagall's art, which manifests itself from the earliest moment of his creative labors.

Chagall conceives a picture as a living thing that has a "soul."

And it is for this "soul" that he was later to take up a fight with the Cubists and with himself. We will witness it in its due time.

But the "soul" must be a new reality—not a transmigration from the old world, from nature. It must be created by the artist.

Stop to examine the picture, and you will see that there exists an inner psychological unity among the different actors of the little play. And this unity is first established when the artist puts the corpse and burning candles in the street. Take out the dead man and the candles burning for the departing soul, and there is no central idea to hold together the little drama. You would then have separate and unrelated actions: a fiddler is fiddling, a street cleaner is sweeping, a woman is screaming—no binding motif and therefore no unity. The dead man ties them all to himself psychologically and through him all the living people and their actions come into a dramatic conflict. Unity is here created through antagonism. The indifferent, unceremonious street cleaner, by his very profligate action, by his preoccupation with his trivial trade in face of the solemnity and awesomeness of death, desecrates the corpse and the burning candles. His very contrariety makes him a necessary character in the mise en scène.

And the comical figure of the fiddler, sitting on the roof and playing, with his back turned to the dead man, despoils the dead man of the dignity and mystery with which death invested him, and which the burning candles consecrate.

The corpse reproaches them for their levity—and they scoff at him by their disrespectful attitude—and thus their relationship is established and the unity of the legend of the picture maintained.

Though the scene is laid in the open street, the artist closes the exit of the alley by the figure of the street sweeper—and with that, the public domain changes into a sort of a private yard, encompassing the group of actors with a unity also of space.

The corpse being the protagonist, the mood of the picture is in sympathy with him—and the mood, as always in Chagall's canvases, is carried by the colors. It is early evening and the street is dark. The green, yellow and red colors have a low smouldering glow. The candles flame mystically. The green sky is sinister. . . .

Is the picture Witebsk? No. No dead are put out in the street in Witebsk. No fiddlers sit on the roofs. It is all in Chagall's fancy—which transfigures reality.

It is an old Jewish traditional custom to remove the corpse, soon after death is ascertained, from its bed—be it a rich man's or a poor man's bed—and put it on the ground on a few straws. Burning candles are placed around the body. The corpse is raised from the ground for the ritual of washing and purification and putting on the grave clothes; then it is put in a place of honor until the funeral.

But Chagall puts the corpse on the ground in the street, for his plot—as we have seen.

He does not hesitate to change the order of the world. He has no respect for reality. He makes his new reality as it is dictated by his fancy and the needs of his art.

But always—may it be in a strange way, his own way, sometimes with a whimsical, or sardonic, or poignant humor; sometimes with a lyrical tenderness, or with pity and compassion—his art expresses essences of his Jewish human soul.

"Art is first of all a state of the soul"—he maintains.

The "Burning Candles in a Dark Street" is not Witebsk. And yet a denizen of Witebsk—and Witebsk is, of course, a symbol of all Jewish towns of the not very distant past—will at once recognize in it a certain Witebsk atmosphere and aroma, a Witebsk rite, a style of living—the style of living of the artist's grandfather who climbed up to the roof and sat down on the chimney to eat there his dish of stewed carrot dessert. Or, the style of his precious relative who left his breeches home and went out for a walk in the bright sunshine in his long undershirt—as if he were one of Chagall's angels.

"A WEDDING"

Altogether in the style of Witebsk is another canvas of Chagall's of those early days, "A Wedding."

Here we have an almost realistic representation.

This canvas is interesting because it shows Chagall's vein of folklore and good natured humor. His laughter at the simple Jewish folks and folkways does not hide his love of them.

Notice that the one musician who leads the wedding procession through the village street is in an old soldier's uniform, is probably blind in one eye—the only man in the village that can fiddle. He is one of the "Nicholas Soldiers"—a Jewish soldier of the time of Tzar Nicholas the First—he was kidnaped as a young lad, put into military service and served for forty years, returning to his native village a stranger who can hardly speak his people's language and can say only a few simple prayers, mixing his Hebrew and Russian words in his own melange. He still puts on his soldier's uniform on holidays and on other festive occasions, or, as in Chagall's picture, to proudly lead a wedding procession.

These soldiers were a rarity even in Chagall's early life—but a priceless find for a picture like this.

See the Jewish water carrier who meets bride and bridegroom with full buckets of water as an omen of good luck (expecting a few coppers would be dropped in the buckets by the passing wedding guests). See his comical square figure and his legs parted wide, for a secret reason that he cannot hide. But look at his rabbinic beard, how well kept; and how proudly he displays his long striped four-cornered ritual garment with the full fringes.

See the Jewish children, small street urchins, but already little Jews, droll and enchanting.

The artist dressed up all the figures in this picture in their blessed Jewish provincialism from head to foot; all heavy and hairy, all with the small-town air and smell—yet each one separately touched up with an individual humorous mark, but still typical of the simple folk life; all showing the knowing and loving eye of Chagall the folklorist.

A Jewish spectator who retains nostalgic memories of the old "home-made" folks will relish this canvas of Chagall like grandmother's old-fashioned fruit cake chock full of delectable bits. You can stop at every figure and find something to regale your eye.

This is the first of many wedding pictures—and from here one can well measure the artist's progress.

"PORTRAIT OF MY FIANCÉE"

Another picture of that year (1909) has particular interest for us—his "Portrait of My Fiancée in Black Gloves."

Here is a surprise again. The young artist of twenty, the future poet of love, never tiring to sing of the young lovers, here paints his own sweetheart, a young and tender girl, graceful and lovely, full of spirit and sparkle, full of fun and the joy of living—the young and soulful Bashke (Bella), fresh, imaginative and playful (as we know her from her autobiographical tales written later in life)—here her fond lover paints her stiff and frigid and painfully serious, as if she were the tragic muse. Not a drop of young warm blood, not in the girl nor in her lover—as if he had no joy in her, being insensible to her.

And it is a well-painted picture. It has the beauty of a Greek vase. But why is the artist so "professional" here, why so distant, cold and classical?

The artist tells me that his love for the very young girl was unusually pure and ideal. Though he fell in love with her at first sight—nay, even before he saw her, by just hearing her voice for the first time, he could honestly and from an innocent heart call her—as King Solomon called his Shulamite—his sister-bride. If he had a young man's ways with other girls, for his fiancée he had only a spiritual love, his male instincts completely disguised or sublimated. He knew only of pure, idyllic and chaste relations with her.

This pure and coy first love Chagall painted again and again, but in later years.

Here we want to note that the idyllic songs of love, that Chagall so beautifully painted later, were no mere conceits, inventions of his imagination—but he knew them well in his own heart. Let this canvas, "My Fiancée in Black Gloves," not witness against him.

Here, in this picture, as he always does, he changed his own personal experience into a strange art motif.

We will have occasion to study again and again the artist's way with his material—here we can see it very clearly for the first time.

"A FUNERAL"

Another canvas of the same period is "A Funeral." Again very interesting, but from a different point of view.

A wintry, snow-covered street, evening. In the background small houses are grouped on one side of the street only. A small church with a broken cupola, the upper half, with the cross on it, falling down, stands out among the group of buildings. Birds are flying over it. Standing on a ladder, a man is lighting the street lamp.

In the foreground is the funeral procession. Six figures in all, including the little horse. The seventh, the corpse, lies in the black wagon, only his dead white face showing. A dog follows the procession in deep snow.

The composition is primitive in style. The perspective is primitive. The buildings are in the upper part of the canvas, the funeral procession in the lower part. Both, the row of houses and the procession, go parallel to each other and to the surface plane of the canvas. All the figures are flat, almost two dimensional. It looks as if the whole procession were made of cardboard and pasted on.

This is, in fact, the method of flat painting accepted by the Cubists; they objected against making the canvas "hollow" by depth-perspective. They were against creating the illusion of deep space, thereby denying the nature of the plane of the canvas.

Critics have pointed out that when Chagall was in Paris he accepted the opposition of the Cubists to a "hollow" canvas. It is therefore very interesting to see that here, in 1909, Chagall painted a "cubistic" picture, before he set foot in Paris—which happened at the end of 1910.

I do not mean to deny that Chagall came under the influence of the Paris Cubists. But it is very possible that Chagall found his inspiration for the flat design of his "Funeral" in other, far from cubistic, pictures.

For me, for instance, the whole "Funeral" with its figures savors of the Passover Haggadah. Do you remember how the "Four Sons" are ranged over the page of the popular Haggadah? Chagall's figures, each with its fixed pose, have the naive charm of those famous four heroes.

One thing is certain, the canvas as it was conceived and painted cannot be associated in any way with Paris. The picture has the mystery of a primitive ritual. It has the flavor of one of the tales of Genesis—as the story of Lamech and his two wives, naked and stark in its simplicity.

One more canvas must be mentioned—"Birth." Here is a realistic picture of a Witebsk woman in child bed—except that here, too, the woman in her bed is placed in the open street, as happened to his mother because of a fire in the neighborhood. The artist relates that his mother advised him to tie the woman's abdomen with a kerchief to make her feel more comfortable—and he painted it as his mother suggested.

Here is novelty and originality enough for the artist —bizarre and strange, nothing need be added.

The subjects that Chagall chose to paint at this first period are characteristic in many ways. He took the "great" moments in the life of his Witebsk relatives. He painted a birth, a wedding, a funeral and again death ("Burning Candles in a Dark Street"). His interest in the people, which remains the passion of his artistic life, is here clearly manifested. Also clearly manifested is the lyrical poet, who takes the outside world as if it were a part of his ego and responds to it emotionally—no, not to the whole world, but to that segment of it that he can make his own.

It is worthwhile to stop here a moment to note how unjust are those critics who have claimed that Chagall continued to paint his Witebsk subjects even in Paris for the reason that he found it to be the fashion among the artists of Paris to pick strange, quaint and exotic subjects for their pictures.

Now, we have just seen that Chagall had come from Petersburg where he spent three years—why did he not paint Petersburg?

Because Petersburg did not take in the Chagallian

soil: he saw, heard, smelled Petersburg, but felt Witebsk. What he does not feel, he does not paint.

We have seen that Chagall was already "mad" when he painted his first pictures in Witebsk—that in this respect, in respect to the temper of his work, he was as "madly" modern in Witebsk as the Parisians, whom he joined later. We must also remind ourselves that Chagall must take his share of the guilt, as much as anybody, for the spread of this "madness of modernism" over the whole world.

For the rest, we can note that his canvases of this period show that the artist was still young . . . young in his emotional experience and young in his art. His paints served his needs—but he had no need yet to sing out his pictorial ideas in scintillating, fresh and ravishing chords of color and melt his tones in tender beauty. His poetic lyricism was still constrained and severe, both in feeling and expression. His architectonic, which depends on the artist's living sense of space, was also not fully developed—though his "Funeral" shows how well the artist could make a design of space. He also shows in his "Portrait of My Fiancée" how well he could put a figure into the pictorial space and make it feel as if born there.

After trying out his powers and accomplishments so far, the young artist knew now that he must go on—and to go on he needed Paris. He had learned while in Petersburg that Paris is the center of the world for the young artist.

But for a while he had to be satisfied with Petersburg. He had no means for Paris.

"I am leaving you Witebsk, goodbye to you and to your herring"—and he went back to Petersburg, which was nearer to Paris in many ways.

In Petersburg he was introduced to the famous Jewish advocate, Winaver, then member of the Duma and leader of the "Constitutional Democrats."

Winaver befriended the young artist, bought two canvases from him, the first ones that the artist ever sold, and encouraged him to go on.

Chagall said later:

"My father brought me into the world, and Winaver made me an artist. Without him I would probably have remained a photographer in Witebsk, without any knowledge of Paris."

At the end of 1910 Winaver gave Chagall a monthly allowance, enough to keep soul and body together and paint—and Chagall left for Paris.

Paris

NOW he was in Paris.

But the shock of the strange and foreign city was so powerfully anti-Witebsk that he had a strong impulse to run back home. If it were not so distant, he would have gone back at once, the same week, the same month—he confesses.

It was not the distance, of course. He knew very well what prospects Witebsk offered—and he stayed in Paris, finding comfort in the Louvre, in the masterpieces of Veronese, Manet, Delacroix, Cézanne.

The very next day after his arrival he went to see the exhibition at the Salon des Independents and then to the other galleries.

But he loved the Louvre best; there he felt at home.

"No academy could have given me all the things that I have discovered gnawing at the canvases in the Paris exhibitions, through the windows of the galleries, and in the museums."

Later, in retrospect, he could say: "I penetrated to the heart of French painting of 1910. I hooked myself there."

For a short time he lived in a studio in the Impasse du Maine, but soon moved into a cheaper place, more suitable to his meager pocket. It was a "cell" in the "Bee Hive" (La Ruche), as it was known—a two-story building constructed by a certain sculptor, Boucher, out of the lumber salvaged from the demolished Paris exposition. It was divided into small studios, twelve on a floor, the ground floor for sculptors, the upper for painters.

It was an international "bee hive," a bohemia, where artists of different countries, all young and poor and struggling, lived as neighbors; in later years some of them were to become famous the world over. Modigliani had a studio next door to Chagall; Léger and Soutine on the same floor.

Chagall relates how he lived then:

"When in the Russian studios an insulted girl-model was sobbing, when in the Italian studios songs were heard accompanied by a guitar, when the Jews were carrying on their heated discussions—in my studio I remained alone with my kerosene lamp.

"The studio is littered with pictures and pieces of canvas, or more specifically, my table-cloths, bed-sheets, and night-shirts torn into pieces.

"Two, three hours before sunrise. The sky is blue. It begins to dawn. Somewhere, not far away, they begin to slash the throats of the cattle (the "Bee Hive" was located in the vicinity of the slaughterhouses); the cows bellow, and I paint them.

"So I am up all night. Here now a whole week passed by and my studio is not swept. Picture frames, egg shells, empty two-sous cans of bouillon are scattered everywhere.

"The lamp burns and I with it.

"It burns until its flame hardens in the blue of the morning.

"It is only then that I climb up upon my bunk. I should have gone down into the street to buy, on credit, a few hot rolls, but I go to sleep. Later the woman house-keeper will come. I am not sure whether with the intention to clean up the studio (Must you? At least do not touch my table!) or with the wish to climb up to join me.

"On the boards of my table lie together reproductions of Cézanne, of El Greco, the remains of a herring which I have cut in two, the head for today and the tail for tomorrow, and thank Heaven, there are still a few pieces of crust.

"But perhaps Cendrars will come to take me to lunch with him.

"Before you come into my studio, you must always wait. This is necessary to give me time to put on my clothes, to adjust myself, because I work naked. Generally, I am uncomfortable in any kind of clothes; I do not care for clothes, and dress without taste.

"Nobody buys my pictures and I don't think it is at all possible—"

Still Life. Oil. 1910. Paris
In the Collection of Paul Eluard, Paris

Courtesy of the Artist

PLATE XI

The first friends that Chagall made in Paris were the poets Blaise Cendrars, Rubiner and Canudo. Later were added Max Jacob, André Salmon, and the painter Delauney.

Every Friday there was a gathering at Canudo's where all the latest tendencies of Parisian art were hotly discussed. Among the participants were Gleizes, Léger, La Fresnaye, Segonzac, Lhote, and others. There the young Witebsk artist became acquainted with the ideologies of the different groups. The rising new cult that captured the imagination of the young people was cubism.

After listening to all the arguments, getting acquainted with all the enchanting theories, Chagall went back to his studio to paint—Witebsk.

Witebsk, but painted with a new power, with a new consciousness.

"In Paris, it seems to me, I have found everything, but above all, the art of craftsmanship.

"I owe all that I have achieved to Paris, to France, whose nature, men, the very air were the true school of my life and my art."

Everything?

What did he bring with him to Paris?

Not so very little as it might appear from the confession of his love and gratitude to France.

The greatest possession of an artist is what nature gives him as a gift—and that he already has in his cradle.

One can learn to draw—but the true colorist, like the poet, cannot be made, he must be born.

According to John Ruskin, to be a great colorist one must be born with the genius for it; but that is not enough, one must give all one's life to achieve it.

Nature greatly qualified Chagall for his métier by giving him a rare poetic sense of color and the power to express himself with pencil and brush as freely and as naturally as with his mother tongue.

In addition to these endowments, Chagall took along with him to Paris his Witebsk—which means Jewish life that was rooted in Witebsk soil for many generations; established patterns of Jewish life, images of men and women, carved out of time and eternity, as complete as a work of art, replete with inner harmony, covered with a poetic patina of folklore, rich in ritual, seductive in their somber beauty—waiting for the artist with an understanding heart to view them in their fullness and entirety and see them "as original,

as ingenuous, and as eternal as the buildings in Giotto's frescos." (And with this emotion he painted the Witebsk fences and little houses, cows and calves, Jews and angels.)

In addition, we must remember that in his heart he carried a blood saturated with Jewish culture, a heritage of four thousand years of ingenious creativeness. And this heritage does not lie quietly in the blood, does not let itself be forgotten, but cries out from the very depth of being in the gifted and chosen children of the Jewish people.

Another Jewish artist, Ernst Block, speaking of himself and his music said:

"It is not my desire to attempt a reconstitution of Jewish music. . . . It is the Jewish soul that interests me, the complex, glowing, agitated soul that I feel vibrating through the Bible . . . In my work, termed Jewish, . . . I have not approached the problem from without—by employing melodies more or less authentic (frequently borrowed from or under the influence of other nations), or oriental formulas, rhythms, or intervals, more or less sacred. No! I have but listened to an inner voice, deep, secret, insistent, ardent, an instinct much more than cold and dry reason, a voice which seemed to come from far beyond myself, far beyond my parents . . . a voice which surges up in me on reading certain passages in the Bible, Job, Ecclesiastes, the Psalms, the Prophets . . . This entire Jewish heritage moved me deeply, it was reborn in my music." *

The German-Jewish poet, Richard Beer-Hoffman, expressed it succinctly in the last stanza of his "Schlaf-ied für Mirjam":

"Schläfst du, Mirjam?—Mirjam, mein Kind, Ufer nur sind wir, und tief in uns rinnt Blut von Gewesenem,—zu Kommendem rollts, Blut unserer Väter voll Unruh und Stolz. In uns sind Alle. Wer fühlt sich allein? Du bist ihr Leben,— ihr Leben ist dein,— Mirjam, mein Leben,— Mein Kind, schlaf ein." (Are you asleep, Mirjam? Mirjam, my child, we are but river-banks, and deep in us flows blood of the past,—to the future it streams, blood of our fathers full of unrest and pride. All are in us—who feels himself alone? You are their life, their life is yours.—Mirjam, my life,—my child, sleep.)

* Quoted by Kurt List in *Commentary*, Feb., 1949.

For the Jews in Witebsk, for Chagall's relatives, culture was a cult. They knew of no division in culture between the secular and the sacred—the book was still a holy book which must be touched reverentially and when inadvertently dropped, must be picked up and kissed in atonement. The poets and writers of Israel were in the category, if not in the office, of priests. This tradition, coming down from ancient times, had not lost its power up to the days of Chagall's childhood. The secular Jewish poets of the not far distant past still used the "holy tongue" for their poetry; and part of their poetry was devotional in character, whether their subject was the love and yearning for Zion or their anguished cry over the tragedy of their people. Some of their poems were hymns and were accepted into the services of the synagogue. The Jewish artists and poets of today who grew up in the atmosphere of the small town, as Chagall, still carry deep in their hearts the conviction, which they will not admit, that they have been "called," that they are "dedicated."

Speaking later of that early period in Paris, Chagall said:

"It did not seem to me that pictures were destined solely for decorative or domestic purposes. I said to myself: Art is in some way a mission—and don't be afraid of this old word."

Chagall told us that among his people the word "artist" was unknown, that he had never heard it in his neighborhood.

Why then was he so strangely agitated when it was first applied to him by a school friend?

The "artist's blood" in him, no doubt, responded immediately to the call of this word. He sensed the meaning of the word intuitively, as soon as it touched his ear, and knew it designated the creative forces that were beginning to stir in him.

But though it is true that the word "artist" was not in use, and perhaps the concept of art was foreign to his neighborhood, his people were not altogether without the knowledge of art in terms of beauty, not only as applied to nature, but also as applied to things made by the hand of man, the beautiful object.

No Jew is so poor and so lowly that he has no desire to mark his Sabbath and festival with some distinguishing object of adornment, to show his love for his God by worshiping him with beautiful things. At home, in communal festivity, in the synagogue, all objects used in the services of God were decorated and adorned.

Beauty was associated with sacred things, expressing piety, and thus spiritualized.

This was the traditional background of Chagall's tender, impressionable, and absorptive years.

He grew up with a norm by which to measure, a guiding principle in approach, an intransigent outlook on life and nature, which came into conflict in Paris with the new art that he saw—an art that left no living breath in the picture, no vestige of a "soul," no warmth of spirit—an art that was sufficient to itself with a dead geometric structure—cubism.

His canvases of those days show his struggle not to submit to the materialistic spirit of the Cubists.

"Art, it seems to me, is first of all a state of the soul"—he protested.

And yet, captivated by the craftsmanship that he was seeing everywhere, he paid the tribute that was demanded of him, and learned.

We must pause here to see if we can fully understand what Paris did give to the Witebsk artist.

For the reader not freely conversant with modern art, we have to digress to make a few points clear.

The Talmud found a good reason why, when Jehovah created the world, He created man last. If man were created first, he would have interfered with God's plans and then claimed partnership in the Lord's rule and co-ownership of the world.

Prescient Jehovah knew of man's propensity to find fault with the works of others—that man, seeing before him an abysm full of chaotic elements, would not contain himself and would attempt to make a world of his own—so deeply human it is to want to change, to fashion, and to build.

But, providentially, Jehovah did not wholly deny man the joy of creating. In giving man understanding and imagination, He made it possible for man to satisfy his creative urge by reshaping and rebuilding the *images* of the world, in art, according to man's own design.

When Jehovah called a halt to anarchy, disciplined chaos, and bid the elements "stay put" in planned order, He opened up for mankind the richest source of esthetic pleasure.

It is a primigenious trait in man, inherited from God himself, to take delight in this prime act of creation. The modern artist calls it "organization"; in modern art it is even more important than color.

But to tame chaos is not sufficient; to chain the recalcitrant elements is only the beginning: you must lead them to follow a plan. With this begins everything man makes. And still art is not achieved. Art must have organization according to a *planned design* —this is the fundamental outset of music, of poetry, of the plastic arts.

But that is an old story—what is modern about it?

This is what is modern.

When the poet and musician come to their store of materials for words and sounds, they find them heaped freely, uncombined, like sand and bricks to the hand of the builder. They can begin with their elemental units, words and notes, and build them up in patterned phrases to please their own fancy.

The painter has no such free units. His elements of expression are: line, light and shade, color, and space. But they are not free; they are bound up by nature in patterns and forms, and the painter cannot disengage them—he must accept and follow the model nature prepared for him.

The poet too, is not as fully free as the musician— the words that the poet selects for his use have already a meaning, which he must abide by; and the words have sounds and accents, weight and color, which he cannot alter freely. Fully free is only the musician because his units are abstract sounds—sounds that come not from nature but from musical instruments, with no established patterns for their use. The musician is at liberty to organize them in patterns of his own invention.

And that is why music is the ideal art.

When the painter wants to paint a man with a blue face and green hair, he is up against nature, that denounces him publicly. If he wants to paint a Jew walking in the sky, he must abrogate the law of gravitation—and become an outlaw in your eyes.

The modern painter takes for himself the prerogative of the musician. He refuses to let nature dictate to him her forms, shapes, and colors. He aims at free creation on his own terms with nature. The modern artist will distort, bend, and break the natural image as much as he finds it necessary for his purpose. He will violate the model in an act of a new creation; and if nature demurs, he banishes her out of his studio and works fancy free.

Evidently, the realist and academician will not commit such folly. But the modernist creates a whole new category of art values, a new order of pictorial expression. And if he is a great artist, you will derive an esthetic delight from his revolutionary organizations.

And now, what bearing does it all have upon our discussion of Chagall?

Chagall came from Witebsk with Jews who want to eat their dessert sitting on the chimney; who want to walk over the roofs; who want to promenade in the sky—and whatever else they might take it into their heads to do. And goats and cows, asses and angels that have no discipline, that come and go in places where they are not expected. What could Chagall do with them?

Paris said: let them!—let them do as they please. If your Jew wants to walk in air, let him—you get to work, use your craftsmanship in his behalf; organize your canvas as if it were a world by itself, with its own laws, where such traveling is possible. Only look to it that your Jew fall not out of your canvas. Tie him up plastically with your landscape, with the houses and fences, with the sky and earth; hold him in design, in space, in color—make him hold the composition together; make him feel that he is needed there, that he belongs where he is, as he is . . .

And this, as we had seen in Witebsk, Chagall liked to do even before Paris. Now in Paris he learned to do it masterly.

This is one thing.

And then again—

The artist of the Paris school uses color as the potter clay, to give body to his idea. Everything is done with color. Color is the primordial plasma that gives birth to all things. The modern artist does not draw his figure first with line, or light and shade and then tint it—he creates it in color.

This is not altogether new in French painting. However, with the Impressionists, with Manet, Monet, Pissarro, Sisley, Cézanne, Renoir, Van Gogh, Gauguin, and later Matisse, the picture obtained a richness, an intensity of color, a luminosity, freshness, purity, and sparkle as never before.

Here Chagall's sense of color was stimulated and invigorated, and he immediately began to display his ingenious inventiveness and prodigious creative powers that made him one of the greatest colorists in the world. But so far his vein of lyric beauty lay still unopened in his palette—he had no need of it as yet. His canvases showed an abundant richness of color—but his riches had a glow that was frigid and a glory that was cold. His brilliance was not as yet suffused with feeling. But at the very inception of his mastery you can see in his canvases a painter who makes color the vehicle of his moods. Color will be the medium that he will use to communicate "the state of the soul."

Meanwhile he was fully appreciative of the craftsmanship that he witnessed everywhere in France. What he admired most was the neat taste for measure, the exacting sense for form that he saw—in the worker in his blue apron in the market place as well as in the most zealous disciple of cubism, and a painting that was most painterly even in the second rate artist.

About two-score years later he said:

"In Paris I visited neither academies nor professors. I found my lessons in the city itself at each step, in everything. I found them among the small traders in the weekly open-air markets, among the waiters in cafés, the concierges, peasants, and workers. Around them hovered that astonishing freedom-light (*lumier-liberté*) which I had seen nowhere else. And this light, reborn in art, passed easily onto the canvases of the great French masters.

"I couldn't help thinking: only this *"lumier-liberté"* (more luminous than all sources of artificial light) can give birth to such sparkling canvases, where technical revolutions are just as natural as the language, the gestures, the work of the passer-by in the street."

Wrestling with Cubism

CUBISM brought a revolutionary innovation in art. Up to the advent of cubism the French painters respected the natural form of man and thing. The changes that they permitted themselves to make in the image of their model were well within the limits of the basic plan of nature.

Far as Cézanne ventured in his search for primary forms, eliminating the details of individual variation, reducing all structures to a combination of a few geometric forms—simplifying and distorting as much as he dared, he still maintained in his figures the order of their basic natural architecture. Moreover, by his simplification the ground plan of nature was exposed and supported.

Picasso and Braque, and their followers, dissented completely from this pietism in the respect for nature. They split up and broke up each animate and inanimate object into a multitude of component geometric segments and reassembled the segments into a new organization in accordance with their own design. They placed the value of the new image thus obtained on the quality of its construction only, on the esthetics of the clever organization.

The cubistic picture is a fine mechanical, even if an artistic, contrivance without life and without any relation to life. Its significance lies purely in its craftsmanship.

Chagall could not accept this dispassionate intellectualism of the Cubists.

He knew that his new friend, the poet Guillaume Apollinaire, was closely associated with the Cubists and supported them ideologically—he was the first to formulate their credo. And for some time Chagall was reluctant to show his pictures to Apollinaire.

Once, while walking with the poet, Chagall confided to him his objections to cubism.

"I know that you are the inspirer of cubism. But I demand other things of art."

He brought Apollinaire to his studio.

"Personally, I do not believe that the inclination towards science is beneficial to art.

"Impressionism, cubism are alien to me.

"Art, it seems to me, is first of all a state of the soul.

"The soul of everyone, of every two-footed in all the corners of the earth, is sacred to me.

"Only that honest heart is free that has its own logic, its own understanding.

"That soul is the purest that by itself has reached to that position.

"Not of the old realism am I talking now, neither of symbolism—romanticism, that brought very little.

"Still less do I have in mind mythology, or any other fancy. Well, yes, Heavens, but what do I want?

"One may say that all these schools are only formal baggage.

"The most primitive art already knew of the technical perfection to which all our modern generations are striving, meanwhile indulging in all kinds of tricks, and even falling into stylization.

"I compare this formal baggage to the Pope in Rome, dressed up in all his pomp, besides a naked Christ; or a decorated church to a prayer in the field." *

Apollinaire listened to him, sat down, looked at his pictures, blushed, puffed, smiled, and muttered: "Supernatural!"

Next day the artist received a letter from Apollinaire with a poem, "Rotsoge—to the painter Chagall."

Thus we see Chagall protesting against cubism—and still falling under its influence. He submits and revolts, capitulates for a time—until he liberates himself completely; and in liberating himself, he introduces a new influence in French art and in the art of the whole world.

While wrestling with cubism, he created works

---

*   " 'Tis mad idolatry
To make the service greater than the God."
Shakespeare

Lovers. Oil. 1911. Paris
In the Collection of Tennenbaum, Rye, N. Y.

Courtesy of the Artist

PLATE XII

that battled in essence against his Witebsk soul, against his Jewish feeling. But they were also unacceptable to the orthodox Cubists—though the sin of cubism engendered them.

A true-hearted Cubist Chagall could never become and never did.

At this period Chagall began a revision of his Witebsk ideological approach to art. Stimulated by the Cubists' revolutionary daring, he began to think that the Cubists did not go far enough in their subversion of nature; their efforts were directed only against the appearance, against the external layer, the body of nature.

> "I had the feeling that we were all fumbling on the surface of matter; that we were afraid to rip open, to overturn, to smash and trample under foot the top layer to which we were accustomed; that we did not dare leap into chaos."

But what did he want?

The Cubists, as we have seen, busying themselves with the structure, founded the value of their picture on its masterful organization. Essentially they were interested in the "how" only. Therefore they permitted the life-content to fall out and vanish from their picture. In this way they divorced themselves completely from nature, using the model only as a starting point from which to depart more and more as the work progressed to completion. In their finished pictures not only was there no human soul, there was no breath of the living left. The cubist artist endeavored to appeal with his clever organization to the esthetic sense of the spectator and to no other sense—no, not even to all his esthetic sensibilities, but only to one part of him. The "pure" Cubist set out to create a piece of art that would contact only the constructive faculty of the mind, avoiding all and everything that would arouse emotion—a work of art so austere, so ascetic that it feared rich colors; rich colors being too sensual, they might stir up emotion and befog the clear light of the mind that must admire coldly and "scientifically" the accomplishment of the artist in organizing the structure of the picture. No other human response to the picture was wanted.

Chagall, as we have seen, could not accept this limitation. Art for him was first of all a state of the soul.

But what prevented Chagall from painting the states of his Witebsk soul?

Chagall was now no longer satisfied with his Witebsk soul. He wanted to do with the soul what the Cubists did with the body—to split it up, rip it up, smash it, trample it under foot, and build up a new soul of his own design. He was not pleased with a change in the envelope, in the body; he wanted a "cubistic" soul, a "cubistic" psyche. His aim now was to shatter and trample underfoot the logic of natural living and to make the spectator accept experiences (be it only in the picture) that are irrational, that one can perceive to be occurrences impossible in the world of reality.

But why not, please?

It took eons before man's brain washed itself (partially) clean of the primeval slime from which it had emerged—before the noble power of reason struck a light in the abysmal murkiness of animal consciousness and led man up the road to clear vision, and to a sensible understanding of the world outside and within himself. We needed the long laborious history of human culture to polish the mirror of the eye before the norms of logic, beauty and dignity came into focus and established themselves in the brain in patterns of rational concepts.*

For an artist to try to bring into being a human consciousness contrary to the historic logic of reality and to build a psyche upon anti-rational bases, means to plunge into chimerical fantasy and to go phantom hunting.

And Chagall attempted it. He set out to create a pictorial world of phantoms, an anti-rational world that had logic, but the logic of perversity; that had a soul, but the soul of contrariness, of corruption, of nihilism —and as a matter of course, pessimism.

If Chagall did not get lost in the marsh of glamorous vacuity and perfidious absurdity, as many of his followers did, it was because cubism saved him, the very cubism that led him to the brink of it.

Chagall's new mastery of organization in which cubism had trained him, and his awakened artistic awareness that a picture must be fully and harmoniously strong in form irrespective of content, gave him

---

* "When you slowly emerged of the den of Time
And gained percipience as you grew,
And fleshed you fair out of the shapeless slime."
Hardy

the necessary knowledge and guidance to make a work of art out of chaotic nonsense.

On the other hand, precisely because he was now working with chaotic material, he was entirely free with his formative powers to experiment and to prove his abundant skill and inventiveness in plastic construction.

That Chagall was predisposed to artistic "madness," we can witness when we bring to mind his "Burning Candles in a Dark Street."

Of course, that picture is still a Chagall primitive— but already quite crazy . . .

The symptoms are all there.

It is interesting to note here that this was long before the Dadaists and Surrealists came into the world. Now the Surrealists claim Chagall as one of their progenitors and bring as witness family traits. But Chagall did not give them their credo. What they inherited from him they picked out from his canvases of this period.

In War with Witebsk

IT IS characteristic of the rebel against the human soul that once he sets out, he can only follow the road of negation, sin, and destruction that leads to Satanism * and ends in pessimism. Suffice it to point to Byron, Baudelaire, and Picasso.

Picasso has no means by which to express a lofty and noble human emotion. To depict the gruesome grotesquery of Guernica he is well qualified—he developed his mastery on the road of negation.

Also in Chagall's period of rebellion—and its pernicious effect is felt even today—you will easily find evidence of a demoniacal aberration.

Later Chagall changed and turned with love towards the world and man—and only then did his vein of lyric song open in him, that distinguishes him among the great artists of all time.

We remember Chagall's fervent pleading for himself before Apollinaire:

"Only that heart is free that has its own logic, its own understanding.

"That soul is the purest that by itself had reached to that position."

Every young artist who is worth his paint brush is a rebel. At first he goes to school to the old masters—but soon he discovers that to be faithful to himself he must strike out a new road of his own. And little by little does he free himself from the bondage of tradition.

Much more difficult for the young artist is to go against the successful tendencies in vogue in the arts of his own time.

If you have an interest in the conflicts that develop in the heart and mind of the young artist as he is struggling for his independence, as he is carrying on his passionate endeavor to find a genuine and pure expression of his own artistic soul, to gain his own logic, his own understanding—if you have an eye for

it, you will enjoy examining Chagall's canvases of that first period in Paris.

"A WEDDING"

Here is one of his earliest, called "A Wedding" (1910).

It is still Witebsk, and yet not altogether. There are the small-town wedding guests like those of his "Wedding" of 1909. But now in Paris the artist does not show any family kinship with his people. In the earlier canvas you will find the good-natured humor and fun of a friend who is indulgent and enjoys the peccadillos of his kin. Now, in Paris, he draws them with biting satire and exposes them to derision and mockery. It is the beginning of his insurrection and change of heart.

The composition of the canvas is more ambitious and more involved. It shows that the artist is paying more attention to form and is working for a greater plastic unity. He is now grouping his figures with an eye to the design as a whole. The arrangement here is a step nearer cubism. In the earlier picture ("A Wedding," 1909. See page 17) the procession comes forth out of deep space. The canvas there is "hollowed out" with deep perspective. In the Paris picture the procession proceeds from right to left over the surface plane of the canvas. The small houses of the street are flattened out and follow the flat surface of the canvas.

The colors are no longer local and though richer and more playful, they are still cold and exterior, not uncompromisingly bound up with the mood of the picture.

There is something entirely new in the canvas: a patterned rhythmic movement; and the whole picture is decorative and pleasing to the eye.

"DEDICATED TO MY FIANCÉE"

In another canvas, "Dedicated to my Fiancée," painted in 1911, his rebellious spirit got the upper hand. The artist demanded a destruction not only of

---

* Mephistopheles:
  "Do but scorn Reason and Science
  Man's supreme strength
  Then I'll have you for sure."

To Russia, Asses and Others. Oil, 1911.
Musée d'Art Moderne, Paris

Courtesy of the Artist

PLATE XIII

the natural body but of the soul of the picture—and here you have a ripping up and trampling underfoot of his Witebsk soul; here is chaos.

It is a canvas hard to describe because it has no unified content and no clear sense, though it does have unity of design and its purpose is discernible. You have here large segments of a gigantic human figure that has the head of an ass but with horns . . . one tragic human eye, a very big open mouth without teeth, hollow but smiling. The head rests on one hand, the second hand holds on the lap a naked dissevered leg of a woman, another naked leg lies on one shoulder. Close to this shoulder is a cut-off head of a woman, dead but smiling, with closed eyes, all dressed up in an ornamented kerchief, its mouth turned to the mouth of the ass-man. A cut-off hand appears on the right side, and a big fat leg is leaving on the left. In the lower right corner stands a glass kerosene-lamp, its chimney down on the side.

The whole picture consists of fragments—which are not assembled in a cubistic formation. Everything in the picture is in disorder and in chaotic rhythm.

The colors are strong: gold, vermilion, and green.

Looking at this picture you begin to understand what Chagall had in mind when he scoffed at his colleagues for being afraid "to leap into chaos."

The artist tells an interesting anecdote about this canvas. When it was hung on the wall for exhibition in the "Salon des Independents," the censor came and ordered the picture removed; he called it "pornographic."

The artist and a friend had to assure the censor that no such thought ever entered the artist's mind—and only then did the censor permit the picture to stay in the show.

I presume that the incident that brought on the censor's suspicion was the title of the picture as it appeared in the catalogue, "The Ass and the Woman," with its hint of perversity. "Dedicated to my Fiancée" makes it respectable.

Another canvas of the same year is called "Half Past Three." This picture is completely in the power of cubism. The subject has no content of time, in spite of its name—it is timeless in its nonsense. There is so little "soul" in the picture that you cannot even accuse it of perversity, though the artist did try to introduce some evil. But cubism interfered. It is cubism, but, of course, a Chagallian cubism—and from this angle it is interesting.

"I AND THE VILLAGE"

A definite compromise between Witebsk and cubism is his now world-famous picture, painted in 1911, "I and the Village" (in the collection of the Museum of Modern Art, New York).

Here Chagall, in a very interesting original manner, employs a cubistic idea in the formal structure of the picture—but the whole picture is alive with the innocent guiles and charms of a Witebsk folkloristic idyll.

The big head of a young peasant meets with the head of a cow, eye to eye, and almost nose to nose. They recognize each other as countrymen and both enjoy the meeting.

The young man is all spruced up for the occasion—on his large head a small cap of pretty colors and with an ornamented vizor; on his neck, a string of colored wooden beads from which a cross is suspended. A ring with a red stone adorns a finger of his right hand, with which he offers the cow, as a gift from his heart, a bunch of some kind of a paradise plant.

Looking at the cow, the young man bethinks himself of his sweetheart sitting on a stool, milking a cow—and the artist obligingly paints his vision in miniature on the cheek of the cow.

Both heads, the peasant's and the cow's, are "idealized" by the use of geometric forms.

In primitive perspective, on the top of the canvas, and diminutive, as seen from the distance, is a village street with peasant huts, two upside down, and a tiny church with the face of the priest framed in it. A man with a scythe on his shoulder and his wife, she with her feet up in the air, are passing by.

The whole canvas is lighted up by a childish innocence. It is not a transcription of the artist's childhood memories, but a lyric poem improvised on a motive from childhood memories—a pastoral based on the sentiments of a naive heart. By no means a vision of a child—and there can be no doubt that it is not the creation of a naive imagination; on the contrary, you see here the knowing sophistication of the artist who stands smiling good-humoredly behind the canvas and is not against showing his warm interest in the sentiments expressed.

The colors of the canvas are "morally" tied up with the character of the subject. The face of the peasant lad is grass-green. There is fresh and naive sentiment in the red, green, blue, yellow and white, and their shades. The very texture of the colors indi-

The Pregnant Woman. Oil. 1913
Municipal Museum, Amsterdam

Courtesy of the Artist

PLATE XIV

cates the character—makes the character—of the picture. Such purity, freshness, transparency and lightness of color can only be associated with the purity, freshness and brightness of a sunny morning in spring on the village pasture—or with the innocent joy of a primitive poet.

And the colors go harmoniously with the soft round forms and lines of the main figures. Much of the sentiment of the picture can be attributed to the design of its structure which is based on circles and arcs.

The cubistic anatomy—the stylized geometric simplicity and precision of outline of the separate parts—helps in establishing the reality of the *illusion*, giving substantiality and solidity to the imagined fiction, without diminishing the certitude of the impression that you are looking at a new reality, an art reality, beyond nature.

Here you have Witebsk in cubistic terms.

"TO RUSSIA, ASSES AND OTHERS"

Another canvas of the same period (1911) is entirely in the power of a perverse spirit, a demon.

The picture is called, "To Russia, Asses and Others." The name was suggested to the artist by his friend of those days, the poet Cendrars. It is supposed to have been a satire on Czarist Russia—though the god of perversity only knows how this "political" quip could attach itself to this canvas.

But this is quite apart.

As a painting it is brilliant, one of the most original of Chagall's masterpieces. The composition is the triumph of the artist's organizational skill; the evidence of his architectural mastery over space. Chagall shows here that he can do anything and everything his fancy can suggest. His craftsmanship will carry him safely through all risky adventures. If you are not looking for a human, a Witebsk motif, this canvas will please you immensely.

Indeed, when you are in front of the canvas contemplating its sheer act of free creation, you forget your differences with the artist. Only in comparing this with other masterpieces of the artist do you come to feel that Paris had been pilfering bit by bit the Witebsk heart of the artist, and nothing of it was left for this canvas. And the result: a cruel, villainous, murderous work . . .

Here is its fable.

Somewhere over the roof-tops, near a dome of a small church with a cross on it, there stands a flat cow on the steep incline of a roof. She has only two legs. Her tail is up in the air, a bell on her neck, and her tongue is stuck out to the tub of feed that stands on the nearby roof. But she will never reach her food: the heartless artist decreed that she stand there forever and aye, stupidly wanting her food, with her tongue avidly out . . .

A maid, cut out of some magical sheet-metal, the separate parts riveted together with big-headed rivets that look like eyes, steps down from the sky with a milk pail, obviously to milk the cow. She is one step from the dome and from there one more step to the next roof where the cow stands—and already she had stretched out her hand with the pail towards the cow, but, alack, poor girl! Her hand moved forward and became twice its length—but the poor girl can't make another move: she had lost her head about a meter away behind her, up in the air!

In the meantime some green goblin, or elf, (or is it a small devil?) with two boyish legs, one hand, and a dog's head, got under the cow and sucks her dry without giving one drop of milk to the hungry three-legged calf that stands by enviously . . .

The canvas is brilliant in composition and color, as mentioned above. It is built up of planes. The design is asymmetric and the structure is unbalanced in mass—yet the picture as a whole has perfect stability. By the expedient use of brilliant color, the artist made the air of the empty pictorial spaces stand out vibrantly with the force of formed masses and take an active part in the structure of the picture. All empty spaces are so divided and so patterned that the canvas has the overall unity of spatial design. Thus the canvas is held together by the organization of its colors and its space.

And though the picture does not possess the logic of naturalism, nor of common sense, it has the logic of art—a plastic logic—born of the conditioning of the canvas by the free, if capricious, choice of the artist's fancy.

Again you have a new reality, an art reality, created by the artist.

The colors are accordingly related to the subject by their unnatural textures—unnatural for cow and maid, but "natural" for the fiction established in the picture.

The texture reminds you of the hard shine of glazed ceramics. Here and there a spot of color flickers up with the fire of a precious stone—a cold glimmering without the warmth of emotion.

Comparing this canvas with "I and the Village," you will find in both an unnatural, an entirely contrived, and, if it so pleases you, an "impossible" life content, completely beyond the boundaries of rational experience—taking it as it appears in the canvases—and that is what the artist aimed at.

But behind "I and the Village" you can discern a human attitude, a human emotion—and the colors sing it out. Behind the later canvas there is no trace of an emotion—not even of the artist's malice, though he treats his creatures barbarically—and the colors have nothing to sing; they only tell in cold beauty the praise of the artist's achievement.

We must admit, no mean achievement and no small triumph for the artist's skill.

But if you apply to the canvas the set-up requirement with which Chagall confronts a work of art, namely, that it must be an expression of the state of the artist's soul, you can judge in what a nefarious state Chagall's soul was in his attempted murder of Witebsk . . .

And yet here, in this canvas, he was still attached to his Witebsk.

"CALVARY"

One of the strangest and most powerfully effective of Chagall's canvases of that period, and perhaps of any other period, is his "Calvary" of 1912.

For many years this canvas was in a private collection in Germany and is little known. Fortunately it escaped Hitler's destructive hands, having been kept hidden in England by its owner, a German but not a Nazi.

(Chagall was on the honor list of the modern artists whom Hitler held responsible for the "Jewish degenerate art.")

After the war it was brought to the U. S. and the Museum of Modern Art of New York acquired it for its permanent collection.

Without looking at its date, one could easily place this canvas in its time by its style and spirit.

Chagall was still testing his human soul, still trying it with cubism, attempting to "trample it under foot." Or did he, on the contrary, want to prove to himself that one can use all the formal strength of the new art and still give expression to the deepest human experience? Was he fighting against the human soul, or for the human soul?

Who but Chagall would have picked a crucifixion as a subject for a cubistic picture?

On the occasion of its first showing in the Museum of Modern Art in 1949, Chagall made the following statement:

"The symbolic figure of Christ was always very near to me and I was determined to draw it out of my young heart. I wanted to show Christ as an innocent child. Now I see it otherwise.

"When I painted this picture in Paris, I was freeing myself psychologically from the conception of the icon painters and from Russian art generally."

On another occasion Chagall stated:

"I recognized the quality of some great creations of the icon tradition—for example, the work of Rublev. But this was essentially a religious, an orthodox art; and, as such, it remained strange to me. For me Christ was a great poet whose poetical teaching had been forgotten by the modern world."

In the "Calvary" Chagall painted the Christ as a child, but an overgrown child, precisely in the tradition of the icon painters who had always made the child Jesus with a large body to indicate his divine nature.

The child is painted with cubistic simplification. The forms are geometric, hard and heavy, as if a plaster figure was intended and not one of flesh.

Chagall uses space concreted into forms—here it is large spheres and segments cut out from the spheres, that go into the organization of the canvas; forms that have no logic of being, but have plastic function. The cross is only suggested by the crossing of painted spaces, without a material structure.

Chagall said that he used his own father and mother as models for the "eternal father and mother idea."

Father and mother are standing at the foot of the crucified—all dressed up, whimsically, in finery; a reminiscence of the rich robes with which the icon painters adorned their saints—here definitely of Chagall's own tailoring.

The father with his tall figure and carefully trimmed beard has dignity and pathos. The short mother (Chagall's mother was half the size of her husband), on the other hand, has little divinity about her, neither in her figure nor in her face—though with half of her face rubbed out and the other half with an enlarged eye, black and blind, she looks the most pathetic *Mater dolorosa* a painter ever created. (It gives you a feeling as if she cried long, and that was her undoing—of course, this again is against tradition.)

It is interesting to note that one of the mother's breasts is uncovered, which again makes you think of Jesus as still a child.

But the strangest of all Chagallian creatures is the little Judas. He is a villain if ever there was one, a treacherous, vile, scheming dwarf. The artist painted his Judas realistically, keenly analytical, with psychological insight, even as to the cap on his head and kerchief on his neck . . . If he were not so little, one would think him a gypsy horse-thief . . . To "kill" the realism of the figure Chagall made a dwarf of him with a full-sized head and face—reminding one of the small figures in Russian folk-art.

How did this figure get into the picture—and with a long ladder? (Chagall said he gave him a large ladder because he is so small . . . .)

The artist will forgive me, I hope, for finding my own reason why the "Judas" (except for plastic needs) came into the picture.

It is obvious that Chagall was not following any tradition here, nor any consistent or logical story. On the contrary, he was breaking up the logic and the historical sense of the picture. He "smashed" its old soul, building up his own, free and contrary. Judas is the personification of the spirit of perversity and Satanism—that is why of all the apostles Chagall thought of Judas. The ladder, of course, suggests the descent from the cross—and to make Judas think of it! That again is part of the contrariness of which this picture is full.

Chagall once said that he is an "unconscious-conscious" painter. Some things come into his pictures unconsciously—but usually they have an inner connection with the subject painted, even if he is only conscious of their plastic value, and he uses them for that purpose only.

There is also a tiny figure in a boat with an oar and sail, on a very colorful river which runs across the canvas.

A purely cubistic picture Chagall did not aim to make out of it—that is evident. And the picture is rich with an imaginative, even if a furtive, logic—with a good measure of contrariness and perversity, of course.

But the amazing thing is that the whole picture is

ultimately unified—a triumph for Chagall's organizing power. And what is more strange—he succeeded in giving a profound tragic spirit to the canvas. Calvary is there! A new one, his own.

It may sound paradoxical, but Chagall built with partly cubistic means a very impressive expressionistic picture, without as yet knowing of such a "kind" of art.

No wonder that the German Expressionists were so enthusiastic about Chagall when they first saw his pictures on exhibition in Berlin (in 1914).

In other pictures he was "surrealistic" before the Surrealists; here, in this canvas and in others, he invented "expressionism" for himself.

It should be noted here that in 1910 when he first came to Paris, Chagall painted "My Studio" which is stylistically a "Soutine" (before Soutine came to Paris, in 1911).

"PARIS THROUGH MY WINDOW"

In the next canvas that we will examine, his flight from Witebsk is accomplished. He broke all ties with Witebsk and he does not even have any memories of it.

It is a picture called "Paris Through My Window" (1913).

Through an open window you see the city landscape with the Eiffel Tower. An elevated train is travelling with its wheels up in the air. The locomotive, with its smokestack down, puffs on, a sign that it is pulling hard . . . Two well-dressed Parisians, a man and a woman, take a walk horizontally. Coming from opposite directions to one point, they will soon meet head on in a collision. A man is up in the air, hanging from a kite. In the house a fat cat with a human face sits on the window sill. Near the window, inside, a head of a man with two faces—the face looking at the cat-man is covered by a mask.

The picture is designed cubistically in pyramidal shapes and forms; the pictorial space is treated as a flat surface: the distant background coming forward to meet with the interior, to form an up and down (rather than a near and distant) pattern of space.

Again you see the adroit, knowing hand of the master craftsman. And you must unstintedly admire the free and fresh inventiveness of the artist, his rich fantasy, the beauty of his organization—binding together the strange and incongruous elements into a harmonious plastic relationship. You must also appre-

Paris Through the Window. Oil. 1913
Museum of Non Objective Painting, New York

Courtesy of The Solomon R. Guggenheim Foundation

PLATE XV

ciate the architectonic of the canvas—what a distance from the "square box" arrangement of his Witebsk "Wedding."

Is there a base of real Parisian life or feeling under this picture? None whatsoever. It is a purely Chagallian fiction.

In a way it is more Witebsk than Paris—though by nothing of its circumstances. One may venture to suggest that the ghost of the dead man of the "Burning Candles in a Dark Street" has appeared here in this picture in the incarnation of the cat-man or in the double faced visitor. But we don't have to speculate that far. One thing is clear: Chagall cannot satisfy himself by the "materialistic," formal plasticity of the canvas. He endeavors to give to the picture not only a pictorial idea, the art soul of the picture, but also an "additional soul."

It is a strange, enigmatic, and mystic soul. In vain will you attempt to make contact with it—it remains morose, dark, and morbidly absorbed in its own mystery. If you persist in your attention, you will be mesmerized by its spirit into a state of melancholy and malevolence—if not misanthropy . . .

Standing in front of the large and beautiful canvas you would like to understand its lore, its strange fascination; but your human appeal to the cat-man who dominates the scene, or to the double-faced stranger who had come to visit him, is unaccepted.

But you know that the artist himself remained on the outside of the canvas, unaccepted and unhonored by the unholy spirits that he had conjured up from some nether pit, the guardians of lost souls.

This secret, that the artist remained alienate from his canvas, is betrayed by the colors, that always carry the confession of Chagall's heart.

Compare this canvas with another one, "Lovers of the Eiffel Tower," painted many years later (1928).

The two pictures are related by their general plan of construction, by the Parisian background, and the Eiffel Tower as seen through an open window.

In the later dated picture you have two lovers standing close together against the Eiffel Tower, preoccupied with the wonder of their love; they do not see the angel that has come to bring them flowers and a message. Here, too, you have a supernatural fantasy. But the spirit here is the angel of love. Behind the canvas you can feel its creator, a man with human sympathy; his heart was in his work and the colors sing.

There were many other canvases that Chagall painted in Paris—but we cannot examine them all. Some were purely cubistic with Chagallian modifications. Others had Witebsk for their subject. They all can be classified, more or less, with one or the other of those we have discussed. We have examined only a few that illustrate best the state of the artist's soul in those youthful "storm and stress" years in Paris.

To sum up, the struggle within the heart and mind of the artist between his Witebsk heritage and the new Parisian influences did not abate. The final victory belonged to Paris—but it was not an easy victory.

He sinned against Witebsk as a recalcitrant and faithless son—but looked back longingly.

He sinned carnally with cubism—but did not love his "materialistic" concubine that had no soul.

The fruit of his sins is a large number of brilliant canvases that are original, unique, and striking; that are characteristically Chagallian, but only for that period. These canvases are a very valuable contribution to our new culture. To this day they hold your admiration by their freshness of imagination, daring, originality, and consummate craftsmanship.

Their influence on artists and the tendencies they have engendered will be noted later.

Hard Times

FOR the young Witebsk dreamer and incorrigible idealist those days in Paris were not peaceful nor joyous.

His pictures found no buyers and no patrons—and the francs were not rolling in.

The artist relates:

"A colleague in the "BeeHive" was manufacturing pictures that he sold in the market.

"Once I said to him, 'Maybe I, too, will be lucky and sell something in the market?'

"He painted pretty women in crinolines that walk in parks. This did not suit me. But to paint landscape in the manner of Corot, why not?

"I took a photograph of some Corot—but the more I forced myself to follow Corot, the further away from him I got and ended up as Chagall."

And the pictures did not sell.

The artist's friend, the poet Canudo, gave him a letter of recommendation to a collector, a certain Mons. Dusso. With this letter and a packet of a few dozen water-colors under his arm, the artist went to present himself to Mons. Dusso with the faint hope that perhaps he would buy a few papers.

The collector left the artist standing in the corridor to wait. A quarter of an hour later a servant came and brought back the packet of water-colors. "We are not interested in the greatest colorist of our time"—the servant announced.

Canudo's praises did not help.

Another time the recommendation of the same poet was more successful. This time it was a recommendation that the artist was just the needed actor for a movie. He was to participate in a scene in which a group of painters go out picnicking, eat, drink, and entertain their girls in row-boats on the river.

In the role of eating and drinking, the artist confesses, he gave an accomplished performance—hungry as he was. The romance with his lady in the row-boat he did not develop so famously—in the art of love-making he was still as amateurish as in Witebsk.

But the few francs which he received for his Thespian labors were very welcome.

"There is no doubt that my first tendencies were a little alien to the Frenchmen. And I looked upon them with so much love. It was painful" —the artist reminds himself.

It is characteristic that the first to appreciate Chagall's art were the poets of the bohemia, who befriended and encouraged him. They sensed the poetic charm of his pictures, in the subject matter as well as in his color. Canudo praised him as the greatest colorist of his day. And the same did Apollinaire, the youngest and best beloved poet of the Parisian bohemia.

One evening when Chagall visited Apollinaire at his home where a large gathering was being entertained, the poet approached a small man who was sitting quietly in a corner, alone.

"Do you know what you must do, Herr Walden? You must give an exhibit of this young man's paintings. What, you don't know him? Why, this is Marc Chagall."

In June of the same year, 1914, Chagall went to Berlin to witness the opening of an exhibition of his canvases arranged by Herr Horwirt Walden, the editor of the periodical publication "Der Sturm" that represented German expressionism. The exhibition took place in the two small rooms of the editor's office in the Potsdamer Strasse. The unframed canvases were stuck closely together on the walls, and a hundred water-color papers were simply spread over the tables. Chagall had been represented before in some of the big exhibitions in Paris. But this was his first one-man show.

As an introduction, the exhibition-catalogue presented Apollinaire's cubistic poem, "Rotsoge."

In Witebsk Again

WHEN in Berlin for the opening of his exhibition, Chagall decided to make a detour to Witebsk for a short visit.

Little did he dream that eight horrible years would come and go before he would see his beloved Paris again. He had no forewarning that the world was on the brink of war.

And I doubt very much if Chagall would have changed his mind even if he were warned.

His ostensible reason for going to Witebsk was that he wanted to be at his sister's wedding. And this was undoubtedly one good reason. But there was another force that suddenly pulled him up from the ground in the "Bee Hive" where he had rooted near his easel.

When he had left Witebsk, Bella was a very young girl. Their love was naive, timid, and reticent.

During the artist's years in Paris, Bella went to Moscow, prepared herself and was admitted to the University. She devoted herself mainly to the history of literature. But she also found time to attend Stanislavsky's school for actors, where she attracted the attention of the director himself and also of the famous actor, Mosquin.

All that time she kept up a correspondence with her dear friend, the artist in Paris. In their letters they shared, one with the other, like two dear loving friends, all the intimate daily events of their lives.

In the years that were passing, the heaps of letters grew on both sides; and who knows how high the heaps would have become. But in one of her last letters Bella mentioned in passing the name of one of the young actors.

Well, now, as far as Marc was concerned, Paris might burn and the "Bee Hive" too, and with it all his unfinished canvases: he was going to ask Bella, yes or no?

Bella was on her vacation in Witebsk when he was in Berlin—Marc, too, went to Witebsk.

With deep emotion, with tears in his eyes, the artist set foot again in the streets of his beloved Witebsk.

He met Bella on the bridge—their old trysting place —and he asked her at once: that young actor?

Oh, no!

Well, in that case, the painter can begin to paint again.

Chagall assures me that he had still time to leave Russia before the borders were closed. But he did not want to go away without Bella.

It was in the summer of 1914.

In that year Chagall created a whole series of Witebsk masterpieces. He painted everything that came under his eye. He painted mostly sitting at the window, disliking to carry about his box with paints.

In Witebsk his fight with cubism ended. Here on the Witebsk soil he knew that Witebsk was in the right. He did not, of course, put aside the discipline that Paris taught him. He was still using some of the means of statement that cubism gave him—but he used them to strengthen and secure the formal power of his images. In no way did his cubistic formalism clash with his Witebsk subjects. In fact, he had lost his wish "to trample underfoot" his Witebsk soul. Far from his Paris friends he did not have to fight with himself, and he felt that here he might follow the loves of his heart. And here he achieved a clarity and surety that benefited his art.

"THE SLUTZK PREACHER"

One day, at home, he found an old humble Jew sitting quietly at the table where the samovar was hot.

Father had probably invited the stranger to tea.

The artist inquired gently: "Reb Yidd, who are you?"

The old man was surprised. "What, you don't know me? Did you never hear them talk about the preacher from Slutzk?"

Well, then, would he please step into the other room?

The artist was afraid to mention for what purpose. But the old Jew walked into the artist's bedroom and sat down on a chair. He soon fell to napping. And Chagall painted his portrait, now world-famous as "The Slutzk Preacher."

In the composition of this picture you still have a vestige of cubism—but only in the arrangement.

The old man sits bent over his knees, holding his hands together between his legs. In this position the body with the hands forms a pyramid, base up. On this pyramid sits a smaller pyramid—his heavy head with its pointed beard. The old man's face with its heavy nose and his creased coat and sleeves are painted as if made up of segments—that far cubism, and no further.

On the left arm under the sleeve you seem to see the cube and the ribbon-like windings of the leather strap of the phylactery—you know it was there every morning (except, of course, on Sabbath and holidays) during the long years of his life, and the artist reminds you of it.

All in all you have on the canvas the portrait of a short old Jew with a bent back, a big powerful head, and an "iron" mind. The mouth is of a speaker, a preacher. One of his eyes is napping, the other, half open, looks as if turned to look into himself, brooding thoughtfully. You see on his face a visionary old wisdom. It seems the old man remembers a time of some four thousand years.

It is characteristic and interesting to note that you never find in Chagall's canvases physically big, imposing Jews. He has no heroic figures—but his Jews possess inner power and strength.

If this Slutzk preacher is not a mountain of a man, he is a rock—one of those Jews that are foundations.

Chagall painted him to make you feel it. Isn't that Jewish plastic?

And one thing more must be noticed—it is important: Chagall does not paint the individual but his stem, his stock of origin: I am a Jew. Not so much the personal portrait of the Slutzk preacher as much as a face processed in fire with the God-imprinted stamp upon it, which the whole world can unmistakenly read: "He is a Jew."

The "impossible" colors, the green face and yellow beard, add to the head an air of super-worldliness, at the same time they do not disturb the impression of the powerful living reality of the man.

Chagall practices here the great art of discovering at once the essential and declaring it simply and powerfully.

I do not know what heritage the Slutzk preacher left after him, but Chagall's art made him immortal.

"A JEW PRAYS"

The artist relates:

"An old man passes by our window; gray hair, a pitiful face, a bag on his shoulder.

"Can he open his mouth to beg for alms?—I am wondering. And in truth, he does not talk at all. He comes into the house, and stops at the door humbly. He stands there quietly for a long while. And if he gets nothing, he walks out, as he came in, with no word spoken.

"Come in—I said to him—come here and sit down, rest a while. It is all the same to you, isn't it? Take a rest, yes? I will give you twenty kopeks, only put on my father's prayer shawl and phylacteries and sit here, yes?"

He submits—and Chagall paints one of his greatest masterpieces, "A Jew Prays."

Only the many centuries of homelessness, the whole history of Jewish exile, could produce and mould such a type of Jewish face.

Chagall raised the pauper from his dunghill, lifted him out of his abject natural existence, carried him over into his canvas, gave him an exalted, an immortal plastic life and made him a masterpiece.

The artist selected this dejected beggar, this psalm-mumbling Jew, who would not dream of pushing his way into the gathering of the learned or the council of the wise—him he selected to represent the Jew among the gentiles, to be the symbol of "the people of the book."

And Chagall was right.

When I say that Chagall selected this beggar, I do not mean by it that he had planned to paint a symbol of the Jewish people and selected this Jew for his model.

No, surely not. But when Chagall began to paint his portrait, he sublimated the picturesque naturalism of the model into spiritual qualities of enduring significance. He dressed him up in the traditional ritualistic symbols, and by this he gave him a grave dignity which, superimposed over his doleful face, created a dismal pathos.

For the rest, the artist added to that face of the depth of his own heart, his pity and love for the lowly—and made him worthy of the transcendental mission.

In this manner he created a figure that stands as a symbol of the Jewish suffering people.

If one Jewish created work can by itself give an epitome of the Jew in exile, it is this portrait. Truthfully, I do not know of one Jewish work, after the prophets, that can compare in this respect to Chagall's picture.

Look again, see the painful, dismal dignity that the artist added by his art to the unprepossessing face; the simplicity of heart and humility of spirit that come through; the patience and endurance that bespeak long suffering; the strength that comes from unshakable faith; the spiritual ardor of piety—all combine to give to the man a tragic pathos, an unassuming heroism, that speak concretely of volumes of Jewish history—and yet, in no way is the lowly man denied in the portrait.

The everyday Jew, the man of the people, poor and ignorant as he may be, bears the sorrow of the Goluth and the burden of a spiritual heritage—in addition to his own troubles—as much as the man of learning and nobility.

Chagall was uncompromisingly right in choosing the lowliest to represent his people.

The Talmud had said: "Their poverty is comely for the Jews, as red trappings for a white horse."

The prayer shawl with its stripes and fringes and the phylacteries with their straps were not added in the canvas to witness the Jewishness of the man, nor for mere adornment—as other artists do when they paint a "Jewish" picture. Chagall made these traditional objects the beginning and end of his esthetic design. It is the basis of the whole plastic—and is therefore a Jewish plastic. And how well he made out of the stripes a pattern that suggests sharp toothed lacerations, a suitable frame for the symbolic figure. The colors carry the mood.

And see how becoming to the pauper is his new position, his acquired dignity, to live as a great masterpiece. Without bragging, without hauteur, simply and bravely—but with what assurance and vitality he enters the ranks of the highest creations of modern times, a Jewish masterpiece of art.

"A JEW OVER WITEBSK"

Another famous picture of that period is called, "A Jew Over Witebsk."

At first glance you would think that you are looking at a landscape. You see a snow-covered city square with one human figure in it, but plastically so integrated that it is a part of the landscape as any other component element of it.

But no—when you examine the canvas thoughtfully, you will discover that the Jew, staff in hand and sack on shoulder, descending from the sky, is not at all a neutral figure in the landscape—on the contrary, the landscape was painted as a setting for this hero that is coming down on the scene.

It is possible that a suggestion for this canvas came to the artist from a Yiddish common expression describing a beggar that goes from door to door begging—"Er geht iber'n shtot"—literally, he walks over the city—and so Chagall painted him. Many of the Yiddish-speaking people who look at this picture immediately meet it with a smile of recognition and acceptance.

But here, as everywhere in Chagall's work, as he concentrates his energies on developing the picture, what might have been the first motive is transcended by a higher and more generalized idea with deeper meaning and greater significance. (See page 6.)

Examine this picture more carefully.

It is a wintry and unfriendly afternoon. The square and the streets are heavily heaped with snow. No sight of a living being—only dead silence and loneliness will meet the visitor. Not a face in a window, not a curl of smoke from a chimney to promise a kind warm corner for the new comer. He is an intruder in a dismal world. It is an unkind day for a beggar to go begging.

At evening-prayers in the synagogue the stranger will be noticed among the poor near the warm stove. Reb Yidd, where from?

He is still cowed and cold. He looks at you with fear.

A stranger, come from far, a wanderer that has no home, never long at rest. God's curse.

And what news from our brothers in the four corners of the earth?

New persecutions, new discriminations and restrictions—new destruction—what else can you expect?

He is the messenger of evil tidings.

He is the eternal wanderer, the Jew without a country, always uprooted from his home soil—suddenly, mercilessly torn up and thrown out, the first victim of all destructive storms—tossed into the air to fall down somewhere, God knows where, in a strange, inclement climate, among hostile men, a cursed intruder.

Jew Over Witebsk. Oil. 1914
Collection of Karl Im Oberstag, Basle
Similar Oil in the Collection of The Museum of Modern Art, New York
Courtesy of the Artist
PLATE XVI

This is the mood of Chagall's canvas. Instead of "A Jew Over Witebsk" you may call the picture, "The Jew Without a Land," or "The Jew Over the World."

Was there not a prophecy, a foreboding, in this picture for the Witebsk Jews?

But as long as this wandering Jew was in Chagall's hands, he was safe . . . See how he lets him walk in the air with no support, and he is not hurt—and neither is the canvas.

Here Chagall's mastery over space and movement is admirable.

He makes the Jew the central moment of the landscape by putting him in an unstable position. The figure of the Jew introduces unrest and movement in the otherwise dormant, restful landscape.

The low houses with their horizontal snow-covered roofs give weight and ballast to the composition—they hold the landscape down. In contrast, the wall-masses and towers of the group of church buildings rise vertically—but are heavy and solid and well-founded at their base. The horizontally running planks of the low fences with their posts help to hold the ground, and by widening the base around the church-group, add to the stability of the whole landscape.

Suddenly, unexpectedly (from the viewpoint of the landscape) the figure of the Jew, as if broken away from the church buildings, falls aslant the horizon. This dramatic action is caught by the eye immediately, and the mind perceives that the Jew is the burden of the landscape, its reason and scope.

This burden is plastically accentuated in the color composition—the dark mass of the figure falling over the white snow.

It is interesting to note that the pack on the Jew's back which seems to be only an "ideological" pack (the homeless wanderer's possession), helps with its weight to push downward the falling figure and increases the dark mass—so that not only does it help the thought but also the design of the picture. Similarly, the staff has its plastic and ideologic functions.

The artist has here created a new reality that, though against the logic of nature, stoutly maintains its own art logic, its esthetic soul. And in addition you have the power and emotion of a Jewish epopee.

"FEAST DAY"

It was a very productive year for the artist, a year of great masterpieces. One of his finest, full of gentle humor and folkloristic inventiveness, is a canvas which is listed under the name "Feast Day" (1914).

A bearded God-fearing Jew, in skull cap and prayer shawl, is approaching the steps of the synagogue. He is carrying an Esrog and Lulov (the ritualistic citrus fruit and palm branch used for the Festival of Tabernacles), and his face is solemn and devout; undoubtedly, his heart has turned to God and the holy services.

But on the top of his head stands another Jew, a minim of a Jew, a tiny old fellow, also in a skull cap and prayer shawl but without the Esrog and Lulov—and he seems to be walking in the opposite direction.

I cannot discover any reason for calling this picture, "Feast Day"—a name which is misdirecting.

If I were not afraid of too concrete a limitation, I would call it, "The Jew and his Doppel-Ganger"—his double is his evil spirit, of course.

In a God-fearing Jew his evil spirit is shrunken and tiny—did not get enough sin on which to batten.

But still "he" is there, small as "he" may be . . . However, a picture, like all reality, has a right of its own being. It can suggest a different meaning to each spectator—or no meaning at all outside its own individual existence. And therefore its name should be noncommittal.

And though this little fellow begs to be interpreted—we will not speculate on his nature more than the above suggestion.

But we must say, "he" is quite droll and most embarrassing to the very serious and honorable Jew. He can't get rid of "him." Must he walk into the synagogue with "him" on his head and thus face the whole congregation?

The picture is full of play and fun—and to a Witebsk Jew it has a rich suggestive humor, a Sholem Aleichem kind of humor.

Though the little fellow with his insecure position disturbs the eye, still the canvas is so finely balanced that you feel the little Jew must stand there where he is—without him an important member of the plastic organism would be missing.

The jest becomes more witty when you observe that the Esrog, which the Jew puts forward for display (a Jew would when he has procured a fine fruit) helps in the composition to hold the little Jew by tension. There is humor for the eye as well as for the mind.

Again you have a Jewish plastic, a Jewish style. Chagall's achievement in this picture, as in the others discussed before, is that in place of the old declarative or decorative line he creates a psychological line, a line conveying emotion and thought. Instead of only a formal composition, he creates forms of psychological patterns.

This canvas not only has invention and original fantasy—it is rich with the sap of a folk vein; though no shoot transplanted from the folk garden, it is racy with Jewish soil and salt. To a Jewish folk style that had up to now found existence in story and in song but not in plastic form, Chagall now gave a visual embodiment, bringing to its Jewish spirit the resources of his genius and of modern art.

Were Chagall's pictures made accessible in popular reproductions, they would at once be recognized and accepted by the Jewish masses as their own, as Goldfaden's folk-operettas and Sholem Aleichem's stories.

In those months in Witebsk Chagall painted many pictures of his family and of himself.

His self-portrait, an oil, (1914) is very interesting. It is done in a free cubistic style. He sees himself as a sort of a knight without armor, a St. George, very handsome, romantic and theatrical, with perhaps just a touch of Chagallian humor. Later he painted many self-portraits, mostly in some humorous mask, as jester, or lunatic, with self-raillery—sometimes with a mixture of tears and laughter.

Bella

CHAGALL had not come to Witebsk to paint pictures—this he did of course, everywhere and all the time, in all conditions, under any circumstances.

But now he had come for Bella.

One day Bella reported to him: "You know, mother says that it is no good, we must get married."

And he agreed.

In "Ma Vie" Chagall relates of his first meeting with Bella. It was before he went to Paris.

"I am in Thea's house, stretched full length on the couch in the office of her father, the doctor.

"I like to lie stretched out on this couch which is covered with black oil-cloth, torn in several places. On this couch the doctor examines his patients, the pregnant women and those sick with bellyaches and weak hearts.

"I lie lazily with my hands under my head and dreamily look up to the ceiling and keep my ear listening to the door.

"I am now expecting Thea. She is preparing dinner, fish and bread and butter. Her big fat dog is always in her way.

"I am lying here waiting for Thea to come to me, and I will take her in my arms. I am already opening my arms for her—when there is a ring at the door.

"I jump up—if it is her father, I must disappear.

"Well? Who is there?

"It is just a girl friend of Thea's. She comes into the vestibule. Her voice rings and sings—she warbles like a bird, as she talks to Thea.

"At first I remain in my place, but then I must see her.

"I walk out into the vestibule, but Thea's visitor stands with her back towards me, and I can't see her face.

"But I am upset—on one hand, I am angry that she had interrupted my love-making with Thea. On the other hand, I feel that this visit of the strange girl with her singing voice—one would say a voice from another world—has moved me deeply. I feel that I fear her, at the same time I am drawn towards her and would like to be very near to her, with her.

"But she now says good-bye, and leaves without showing me her face. Why didn't she look at me?

"Now I and Thea go out for a walk. On the bridge we meet her. She is alone.

"All at once I feel that I don't want Thea—I want to be with her friend.

"Her silence is mine. Her eyes are mine. It seems to me, when she looks at me, that she had known me for a very long time. She knows my childhood, my present life, and my future too, though she never saw me before—as if she had always been watching over me. She looks into me and through me. Her first glance had penetrated into my very being.

"There and then I already knew that this is she, my wife.

"Her pale face, her eyes—how big her eyes are, round and black. Those are my eyes, my soul.

"Thea now became a burden.

"I have come into a new house and cannot tear myself away from there."

That is how their tender, devout love began; pure, and innocent of passion. A kiss and no more.

When he got his own studio, a bedroom in a neighbor's house, Bella visited him.

"Bella comes, knocks at the door with her small, delicate and slender fingers, a little timid.

"In her arms, pressed to her breast, a big bunch of Juneberry, a nebulous green pierced with red.

"'Thank you,' I said, 'thank you.'

"No, that was not the right thing to say.

"She becomes moody. I kiss her.

"A still-life composes itself magically in my head.

"She poses for me.

"She lies nude, white and round.

"I approach her timidly. I confess, I saw a naked girl for the first time.

"Though she was almost my fiancée, I was afraid even to come near her, to come too close, to touch all these riches. As if the blade of a sword were lying before your eyes.

"I made an étude of her and hung it on the wall.

"Next day my mother came into my room and saw that étude.

"'What's that?'

"A naked girl, the breasts, the shadowed places—

"I am ashamed; she too.

"'Take off that prostitute!'—she said.

"'Little mama, I love you very, very much. But . . . Didn't you ever see yourself naked? And I looked and did nothing but make a sketch. That's all.'

"But I obeyed my mother and took off the canvas, and instead of the nude I painted another picture on it—a procession."

Some time later he had rented a room in another house where Bella could come and go as she pleased, not under the eyes of his mother.

One time Bella stayed too long. It was already late at night and she could not leave; the door was locked and everyone in the house was asleep.

How could she get out?

"Listen, I said to her, climb out through the window.

"This made us laugh. But I helped her get out and down from the window into the alley.

"Next morning there was whispering in the yard and in the street.

"'Do you know, she climbs in through the window to get to him and she leaves the same way. That's how far it has gone!'

"Go and tell them that my fiancée remained more chaste than Raphael's Madonna, and that I am an angel!"

These few incidents are worth remembering when you stand before his canvases in which he sings of innocent and tender love.

Now he was back after a separation of four years. Bella said that mother wanted them to get married.

But the match was not to the liking of her mother. Her brothers were against it too. The bride's parents were well-to-do people, the owners of three jewelry stores in the city, and "high class." They can give their only daughter a rich dowry. And she is pretty and educated—why, she could get the finest young man in the world. And who is this lover of hers? What is he? An artist—!

The bride's kin talked and whispered: people say that "he" is famous and that "he" actually gets money for his pictures. But that's what people say. Who knows—can he really support a wife, and such a fine girl as Bashke (Bella)? True, a good name, fame, is something—but then, who is his father? A helper in a herring store! And his grandfather? Sh—sh—better say nothing,—the girl gets enraged.

The bride's mother said:

"Listen, my child, it looks to me that he paints his cheeks; what kind of a husband will he make, this young fellow with pink cheeks like a girl's? He will never be able to give you bread. Why him, of all the young men?"

But what could they do with her?—she was stubborn and had set her heart on him. She wouldn't be talked out of it; she would not give him up!

Her mother and brothers pitied her and shook their heads ominously: she is lost.

Her mother cried over her:

"With him you will perish, my darling. You are throwing yourself away for nothing."

But all their arguments were wasted on the girl. She paid no heed to her mother's and brothers' pleading. She did not listen to what her kin said.

She ran to him every day, any hour, day or night, and brought him all the sweet-cakes from home, and broiled fish that he liked, and hot boiled milk—and what not. She fed him out of her hand.

"I only had to open my window and the blue air, love, and the fragrance of flowers entered with her.

"Dressed all in black, or all in white, she hovers over my canvases a long time since and directs my art.

"I never complete a canvas or an etching before asking her, yes or no?

"What do I care what her mother and brothers say?

"My poor father!

"Come, father, come to my wedding!

"He would rather go to sleep. And so would I.

"Is it really worth all this heartache and commotion to tie yourself with people of such high class?"

But the bridegroom arrived with his father, though much belated—and he and Bella were married in a quiet ceremony, in her home.

It took place in the spring of 1915.

With Bella a new motif entered his life and his art. With his beloved wife near him and with him, his canvases began to sing. His colors become softer, more lyrical, and airy.

With Bella Witebsk was fulfilled for him.

Soon after Chagall reached Witebsk, the Russian borders were closed and the war mobilization of the first World War began.

The artist and his wife could spend only a short vacation in the country where they went for their honeymoon.

He was soon called up for military service.

Thanks to the effort of his brother-in-law, Bella's oldest brother, the artist was freed from active military training and became a clerk in his brother-in-law's military cabinet in Petersburg. His duty was to keep accounts of the recruits that had to clear through his brother-in-law's bureau.

His chief did not spare him. He was afraid that the good-for-nothing artist would neglect his job—and he, the chief, would have to take the blame. Besides, he felt, on general principles, that he must keep an eye on his sister's husband and teach him a thing or two—and every time the artist could not give him instantly a full and orderly report whenever he called for it, there was the devil to pay.

He "bossed" the artist with a hard hand until the artist finally learned to manage not to mix up the accounts of those recruits who came in with those who had left . . . He even learned to make out a full and methodical report according to all the military regulations.

But it was hard on the temperamental, sensitive artist—and at night he complained to his sympathetic wife, who pacified and consoled him as best as she could.

Anyway, they could be together—and he found some time to paint.

War and Revolution

RUSSIA entered the first World War in July, 1914. Chagall left Russia in 1922.

During his enforced stay in Russia he witnessed the war, the revolution, and the civil war that followed. Most of the time he was close to the center of moving events, in Petersburg and in Moscow. But, as his notes of those days show, he did not fully appraise the significance of the world-shaking historic events, and he remained a passive onlooker.

To be just to the artist, we must bear in mind that he was young and that he had no political training.

Busy and completely preoccupied with his artistic growth, devoting to it all his heart and soul and all his time, he had no time nor will for other things. He became aware early, as we have seen, that his calling and business in life was to be an artist—and he bent all his energies to it.

The political mass-movements in the small Jewish towns, the Bund and Zionism, did not touch him closely. The Bund (the Jewish section of the All Russian Social Democratic Party, with a special Jewish nationalistic and cultural program) was active underground among the young Jewish workers—their propaganda did not reach a non-worker like Chagall.

The young Marc did hear of Zionism. His father and Uncle Noah were Zionists and paid their "Shekel." And Marc knew that Zionism is good for the Jews. But he did not join any of the active youth groups of Zionism.

Once, in his young artistic days, he saw Dr. Herzl's picture in a newspaper. Marc was struck with the noble appearance of the leader who looked like a Jewish prince in exile, and he made an enlarged drawing of Herzl. With his father's consent, the artist removed the mirror from its frame and put Herzl there. He gave his Herzl the most honorary place in the house, on the east wall, behind his father's chair. In an early interior sketch of his home, you can see the drawing of Herzl in its place on the wall.

In Chagall's youth Yiddish literature experienced a renaissance, with Mendele, Peretz and Sholem Aleichem leading a whole host of gifted young writers and poets. Later Chagall came close to the Yiddish literature and its leaders. He made illustrations for some Jewish books. But that was later—not in his youth.

Once Sholem Aleichem, on a lecture tour, stopped in Witebsk—and, of course, was the talk of the town. Marc wanted to go to hear the famous Jewish writer who made everybody laugh with his stories—but admission was a quarter—a sum too great for such a luxury.

Marc had another wish, to visit the famous writer privately: first of all, to show him his art; also, there were rumors that the kind Sholem Aleichem had helped a young sculptor to find a patron—perhaps he would do the same thing for him.

But for the shy young Marc it was not easy to get to the famous man, and this wish, too, remained unfulfilled.

This was all the acquaintance with Jewish and world political affairs that Chagall had in his early youth. Later in life he did find time and interest to participate in Jewish public activities; he followed keenly the political life of the world.

Public discussions in books and in newspapers of social questions were prohibited under the Tzar. Only one that belonged to some underground "cell" had access to uncensored literature. In the student-circles in the universities and colleges lively political agitation was going on all the time, under cover, as well as in the factories. But in the art academy that Chagall attended in Petersburg such political student-circles did not exist—and if they did, Chagall did not know of them.

In Petersburg, as we have seen, he was annoyed by the miserable police—but that was on account of his passport. And the worry to keep alive in the big city and keep up his art studies sufficed to keep him busy, with no leisure and no energy for other activities.

In Paris, where he came in 1910, he immediately entered into the art life of the city and became completely absorbed in the problems which then agitated the hearts and minds of the old and young bohemians. He was captivated by all the new theories and practices that he heard discussed in the studios and cafes, and watched what was displayed in the galleries and public exhibitions. I have attempted to show the intensive cogitation that was going on in him during the process of conciliating, mating and fecundating his old Witebsk with his new Paris.

And here it may not be out of place to remind ourselves how much of the whole man genius demands and appropriates for itself. The greater the power of the artist, the more completely he is swallowed up by his work. To develop his faculties to their full strength, the artist must give to his art his entire devotion, the full concentration of his energies, and his determined and assiduous efforts—all this consumes the sap of his bones, and there is no power left in him for any other intellectual activity. It is little wonder, therefore, that when Chagall found himself suddenly in the midst of the Russian Revolution, he could not fully grasp the historic significance of what was happening and remained cold and hostile, an outsider, a chance onlooker that saw only change and chaos.

In his memories of those days he gives no intimation that he had any sense of the historic importance of the struggle that he was watching. He walked on the squares, saw and heard some of the famous speakers of the day, saw the placards, heard the slogans of the parties fighting for the control of the revolution, heard the shouting and shooting—and remained disinterested.

The overthrow of the Tzar and his generals Chagall accepted with gladness; first of all, he was now free from his duties in his brother-in-law's bureau. And now there would be no passports and no discrimination against him as a Jew.

For the rest, he had no heart for politics.

The revolution kindled a passion that caught millions of people in its white heat. The galvanic psychosis of impassioned masses in motion (the elementary dynamic force of every revolution) had, by its magnetic force, drawn hundreds of thousands of peasant lads, villagers, soldiers, sailors, ignorant and illiterate, who would in other times have no interest in politics and no understanding for the ideologies propagated to them. The man of the masses, the common soldier that ran away from death on the battle field, suddenly finding himself in the streets of Petersburg, instinctively understood that it was his fight too, and joined his comrades in the revolution. And later in the civil war he went with the partisan divisions and gave his life voluntarily to safeguard the gains of the revolution.

Looking at the artist from this angle, we cannot forgive him his complete social isolation on the ground of his political immaturity.

However, at a time when the man of the masses identified himself with his social class and sympathetically joined up with it, our artist was completely declassed; he did not feel related to any group and could not identify his own interest with any social stratum—unless artists can be looked at as a social class by themselves. And so we must come again to Chagall's artistic personality to explain his apathy.

He was so fully the artist, first and last, he was so obsequiously devoted to his genius that no other interests could get close to his heart. We know how selfish genius is. He wore his art-consciousness like a mail of armor and could therefore walk through war and revolution without a scar to his soul. Only the world of art was his territory—everywhere else he was an alien, a "tourist"—a disinterested onlooker.

Goethe was right when he said that there is no better hideaway from the world than in art—and there is no better tie-up with the world than by art.

But the young artist must first relinquish the world for his art. Only later, in the mature years when a new love for the world is born out of the travail of the years, then only can he come in close contact with the world again through his art—and that is what happened to Chagall, as we will see later.

Only Chagall could never forget his Witebsk and always kept a close relationship with it. And so we find in his memories of those days the following biting satire:

"I beg of you, Wilhelm (the German Kaiser), be satisfied with Warsaw, with Kovno, don't come to Dvinsk; and particularly don't touch Witebsk —there I am and there I paint my pictures.

"But it is Wilhelm's good luck that the Russians fight badly. And no matter how frightfully they fight, they cannot push back the enemy. Ours are only masters of the offensive.

"Each defeat of the army is an excuse for the Grand Duke, Nicolai Nicolaiewitch, the Commander in Chief, to blame the Jews.

"'Drive them out in twenty-four hours or shoot them all. Or, both things at the same time.'

"The army moves back, and the Jews flee beforehand, abandoning their cities and villages.

"I have a wish to carry them over into my canvases to provide a place of safety for them."

It may not be amiss to score here once again for Chagall's authenticity as a Jewish artist: there is no split in his consciousness between the artist and the Jew; when he thinks as an artist, he feels like a Jew.

I have persisted in looking for a reasonable explanation of Chagall's unperturbed aloofness in face of powerful social passions (that affected people even on the antipodes), first of all, for the purpose of searching out how dominant his artistic genius is in his personality. Secondly, to account for the absence of any artistic recording of events that he witnessed. There is not a sketch, not a paper, not a canvas that carries a fresh memory of those crucial years—and yet Chagall painted many canvases during his years in Petersburg and Moscow.

Our knowledge gained in the study of the artist's personality in the above paragraphs will serve us well when we come to look at these canvases.

There is one canvas, painted many years later, but because it is related in subject matter to the events under consideration, I want to mention here, his canvas called "Revolution."

After working on it for several years, he finished it in 1940 and exhibited it in the Pierre Matisse Gallery in 1942. It was a large canvas, 10 x 5½ feet, and contained about one hundred figures.

It would be to no purpose to discuss this canvas now since the artist, to my grief, one evil day looked upon his unique masterpiece—unique in the whole world of art of modern times—with a disparaging eye and decided to destroy it. All my protesting and pleading did not save the canvas. To placate me the artist promised to paint it again.

I mention all this to save the future historian of Jewish art the heartache of trying to find this canvas—because reproductions of it exist in some books and newspapers, unfortunately in very poor condition and no real appreciation of its art values can be obtained from them. It is a great loss.

I may add, in memoriam and for the benefit of the study of the nature of Chagall's creations, that it was not a historical narrative, but a symphonic poem built on the motif of revolution. Chagall did not give a description of its reality as he saw it in the streets, but a transformation of it into an art creation that contained its substance only in its essence, in idea. It was related to reality only so far as it was a sublimation of it. It was a symbolic creation, not a document.

May its soul trouble the artist's dreams! . . .*

---

* The artist informs me that he has kept a sketch in oils (19½–39½") to which he adhered faithfully in painting the "Revolution." Strictly speaking, it is not a sketch, except that it was the project for the larger painting. It is very fine and the artist is quite satisfied with it. Thus the "Revolution" still exists in its smaller version.

Minister of Art

ONE day all the artists were called to a meeting in the Michailovsky Theater, in Petrograd, for the purpose of establishing a Ministry of the Arts.

Chagall came to the meeting, but took a back seat as a disinterested observer.

Suddenly he heard his name called. He was nominated by the young artists for the position of Minister of the Plastic Arts.

He immediately left Petrograd and returned to Witebsk.

Minister of Art he would rather be in Witebsk.

With the aid of Lunatcharsky, who was People's Commissar for Public Instruction in Lenin's first cabinet, Chagall organized an art academy in Witebsk and became its director. This was in 1917.

Bella, his wife, was very much against it and warned him that no good would come of it—he would only waste his valuable time. He did not take her advice and regretted it later.

Chagall had met Lunatcharsky only once before, when Lunatcharsky came to visit the artist in his studio in the "Bee-Hive," in Paris. Lunatcharsky was then in Paris as foreign correspondent for Russian newspapers. He planned to write an article about Chagall for a Russian magazine and he came to interview him.

Chagall was not very friendly to his visitor. He had heard that the journalist was a Marxist, and Chagall in those days knew of Marx only that he was a Jew with a long beard—as the artist confesses—but he had an inexplicable prejudice against a "Marxist." What relation can there be between a "Marxist" and art in general and particularly with Chagallian art?

The artist had a suspicion that the "learned Marxist" came to question him critically and to demand an accounting for his "strange" art.

He showed the visitor his canvases unwillingly and hurriedly, and admonished him:

"Only don't ask me why I paint my cows green, and why you can see the heifer in its mother's belly. I like it that way. If your Marx is so wise, let him get up and explain it to you."

Lunatcharsky smiled at the naive antagonism of the artist, smiled silently and made notes in his notebook.

Now when Chagall came to see Lunatcharsky about the project of the Witebsk Art Academy, he was apprehensive that Lunatcharsky would remember the unkind reception he gave him in his studio. He must have formed a very poor opinion about him.

But Lunatcharsky received the artist in his office in the Kremlin with a friendly smile, listened attentively to his plans, and appointed him Minister of Art for Witebsk.

Chagall came back to Witebsk shortly before the first anniversary of the October (Bolshevik) Revolution.

Witebsk, like all cities, was preparing to celebrate the holiday by decorating the streets and squares of the city with flags and posters.

Witebsk had many house painters. Chagall called them all to a meeting and gave them his mandate.

"From now on you and your helpers belong to the Academy. You are my students.

"Close up your studios and your smudge-shops. All orders will come in to our school, and you will all share them equally.

"And here is a dozen of my sketches. Copy them on large canvases. And on the day when the workers will come out to march with flags and torches, you will decorate the city and the suburbs with these pictures."

All the house painters, the old Jews with long beards as well as their young lads, went to work to copy Chagall's cows and horses.

On October 25th, Chagall's many colored animals, "blown-up by the Revolution" (as the artist remarks), were floating all over the city and suburbs.

The workers came marching by, singing the "International."

The artist notes:

The Green Violinist. Oil. 1918
Museum of Non Objective Painting, New York

Courtesy of The Solomon R. Guggenheim Foundation

PLATE XVII

"Seeing that the workers were smiling at the canvases, I was sure they understood me. But their leaders, the Communists, were displeased.

"'Why are your cows green? And why do your horses prance in the sky?'

"'And how are your animals related to Marx and Lenin?'"

In a hurry they issued orders to the young sculptors to make cement busts of Marx and Lenin.

When the Minister of Art saw what kind of Marxes and Lenins they put up in the squares and parks, he was ashamed.

The artist was certainly right in ordering the city streets to be decorated with his pictures in honor of the Revolution.

To celebrate our national holidays, we dress up in our finery and march in the streets with our wives and children and carry flags and flowers.

But that is not enough. We must celebrate it by displaying our cultural achievements, exhibiting our pictures, reciting our poetry, performing our best plays, singing and dancing in the parks and public places. Certainly, the artist had the right spirit.

At fault was only his sense of timing. He came with his program a hundred years too early. But then, that is the sin of all great artists, they come before their time—though by their coming they bring the future nearer.

At fault was also his Utopian belief that the revolution had with one stroke changed the minds of the ignorant masses and endowed them at once with a highly cultivated taste and an enlightened mind to appreciate the refined Chagallian art. He had expected it, at least, of the leaders.

And he was also guilty of not understanding that the Witebsk tailors, shoemakers and bakers came to the busts of Marx and Lenin not to satisfy their art needs, but with the same inner needs that moved the primitive religious man to kneel and worship the stone and stick if the spirit-gods had chosen the stone and stick to dwell in. Not what they found in the blocks of cement with the name of Marx and Lenin on them, but what they brought in their hearts to them made the glory of the busts.

It may well be that Chagall perceived this and found love, if not respect, in his heart for these simple workers—and, indeed, that may be the reason why he gave himself, heart and soul, to his academy and worked without rest and ran about tirelessly to solicit and demand endowments for canvases and colors and money and things for his teachers and his school.

"What do you think, Comrade Chagall, what is more important, to repair the bridge or spend money for your academy?"—argued the chairman of the regional Soviet.

Comrade Chagall had no doubts that the priority belonged to his academy and insisted on it.

For whom was he putting himself out?

He had no illusion that he would make great artists out of his lads—and yet, when he could not obtain any help from the local authorities, he applied to the higher-ups.

He thought that maybe Gorky would help him—and he went to see Gorky. But unexpected disappointment awaited him in Gorky's home. In his waiting room on the walls Chagall saw such atrocious pictures, that the artist looked about to make sure that he made no mistake and came to the right place.

Gorky received the artist lying on his sickbed—he kept spitting, now in his kerchief, now in a spit-box. He listened with surprise to the artist's projects and accepted them all without discussion—trying all the time to recall who this Chagall might be, and where he came from.

But Chagall forgot meanwhile what he came for.

However, Lunatcharsky never failed him and gave him the necessary maintenance for his academy.

We must keep in mind that there was a scarcity of money and materials.

His constant material worry was not the worst for the artist. His greatest heartaches came from his professors.

Chagall confesses that he had the weakness to invite everyone who asked for it to become a teacher in his school. It came out of his desire to have in his academy a representative of all the different tendencies in art.

The director soon discovered how ungrateful men can be. While he was away from the school soliciting patronage, importuning bureaucrats and busy commissars for aid to provide his professors with salaries and supplies, these professors continued their libertine ways and bohemian manners, which gave the school a bad name. They still considered their individual indulgence above the welfare of the school which was maintained from the public treasury.

And when the director demanded discipline and

more attention to their duties as teachers, they became his secret enemies—though they openly flattered their chief and begged for favors.

When Chagall first discovered their antagonism, he blamed himself, his own impatience. He knew that he was not too gentle with them, that he did not pat their vanities and did not connive at their neglect of duties.

They began to plot against him. And though they were always grudging one against the other and often brought their squabbles to the director, in his absence they united against him and won the students over to their side. And one day when Chagall was once again in Moscow, waiting in the offices of his influential friends in order to procure bread and canvas and money for his professors, they held a meeting, passed a resolution, and issued a decree, all behind his back, to throw him out of the academy within twenty-four hours.

Among the leaders of the plot were some of his best friends, his colleagues of many years; he had brought them into his school, given them their positions, and provided them with bread. From some of them he bought canvases with government funds with a view to establishing an art museum for Witebsk.

The chief conspirator against him was the artist Malewitch. His ostensible reason for ousting Chagall was that Chagall's art was not revolutionary enough for the times.

Malewitch belonged to the group of Supramatists who declared that the artist "must penetrate into his sub-consciousness, select there his material, circumscribe it with a line, and color it." Malewitch insisted that the Revolution can only be painted "supramatistically" and in no other way. And in the name of the Revolution he insisted that the "academecian" Chagall had no right to be the head of an art school.

There was confusion in the heads of the artists as in the heads of other groups of people. A "revolutionary" phrase could cover much nonsense.

It is interesting to note here that when Lenin, in 1922, in a manifesto called upon the artists to throw away their "leftist" silliness and first rebuild themselves and then put their energy to help rebuild the country, like the other people, this same Malewitch gave up his painting altogether and made himself useful by designing patterns for pottery and textiles.

After ridding themselves of Chagall, the professors began to pirate the school, each one helping himself to what he could, taking back the canvases that were bought from them; and abandoning their students, they dispersed, each following his own nose.

Some time later when Chagall was in Moscow, he received a letter of regret from the students, begging him to come back and take over.

The soft-hearted Chagall took his family and returned to Witebsk and the academy, but it was too late—he did not succeed in reorganizing it, and after a while he gave up.

New Creations

ECONOMIC conditions in the country were very bad and growing worse. The artist and his family —his daughter, Ida, had been born—lived in want and misery.

There was no milk for the infant, and she refused to be fooled by sweetened water. She screamed with hunger and drove the sensitive father to despair.

In Moscow they had a difficult time finding living quarters. The family straggled from place to place without a home.

Here they fell into a house that was formerly used as a clinic for contagious diseases. The walls exhaled nauseating odors of medications, and in the corners could be found bottles with poisonous liquids and jars with disgusting salves.

And later the family had to live with a woman who bragged about having slept with a dozen soldiers, one after the other, in order to get a sack of flour.

In another house the landlord kept two street-girls who carried on their trade on the premises—"because otherwise he could not exist."

Again, the family moved to a house where the walls and the ceiling were so wet that drops dripped into the baby's cradle, and the canvases on the walls mildewed.

The artist ran his legs off to get a cart of wood for the stove. But it couldn't be left lying in the yard; it would be stolen the first hour—and the logs were too heavy for the artist to carry up to his rooms.

Fortunately, a few Red Army men passing by, sympathized with the helpless artist and volunteered to haul the logs up.

The wood was wet and would not burn. The wily peasant who sold him the cart of wood had deceived the artist, assuring him that the wood was dry. It had to stand around the walls to dry—and smoked and spluttered and spread a sickening fume over the house—but refused to burn.

The next apartment turned out to be worse—its roof was so damaged that one morning the mother found snow in her baby's bed.

Conditions became worse.

One day the artist's wife went to the open market to sell her rings, gifts from her father's shops, that she still possessed but now was forced to sell to get some milk and butter for the baby—and she was arrested.

Her father was completely ruined. The revolutionary committees had confiscated his shops and all his possessions at home and left him destitute.

The artist received belated tragic news from home: a sister died, his mother died, his father was killed in an accident, his brother was killed on the front.

A sorely needed friend in those difficult days was Dr. Eliashof—better known by his pen-name, Baal Makhshoves, the celebrated Yiddish critic and essayist. The artist relates:

"His friendship was a joy to me. We got acquainted in Moscow, at the home of the art collector, Kagan-Shabshoi, where impassioned discussions of art were nightly occurrences.

"This collector bought a few of my canvases with which to begin a collection for a Jewish Museum of Art in Moscow.

"Coming out late at night from Kagan-Shabshoi, Baal-Makhshoves and I used to walk home together. Walking rapidly through the Moscow alleys, he kept on talking, letting his eloquence flow out before me into the night. When he turned to me, his eyeglasses would flash in the darkness. His small black mustache and his penetrating sharp look would catch my eyes and hold them. Skeptic and friendly at the same time, he would listen, talk, dispute, gesticulating with his hands and limping slightly.

"We became attached to each other. And when it happened that I had to stay overnight at his house, he never stopped talking to me until dawn, all night under the glimmer of the small night-lamp that stood near my bed.

"He would speak of writers, of the war, of art, of life, of the revolution, of his nephew, a People's Commissar—and most of all, of his wife who had left him.

"He married her when she was still very young. She was a rare beauty: big black eyes, a pale complexion, tall and graceful—always silent and cold. Nothing touched her, not his literary work, not his celebrity, not his love. Indifferent and cold she accepted his devotion, until one day she left him for another man.

"'Out of necessity'—he would try to explain—'you know, she needed a husband that could satisfy her fully. Look at me, one side of me is paralyzed, and when I talk I slaver, the spittle driveling over me.'

"He was practicing his medical profession but accepted only those patients he knew he could help—and free, taking no fees. He was busy with his sick people every morning, and the afternoons he would spend at his writing table.

"More than once in that period of hunger and cold he would share with us his own ration of horse-meat. We would regale ourselves with it sitting in his kitchen, his young son playing near us. The father took care of him as best he could.

"A glass of tea in his trembling hands, he kept talking on and on. His tea spilt over, but it was hot no longer. I sipped mine, and he kept talking, and while talking, with one hand adjusted his eyeglasses that almost dropped into his tea— but his tea was now cold in his frozen hands."

We have here a picture of those difficult days.

Another friend of that time was Dr. Sirkin, the well known Zionist. He valued Chagall's art highly and often came to its defense.

Could we expect much creative work from Chagall under such inauspicious circumstances?

In 1915, when Chagall was invited to exhibit in the Moscow Art Salon, he contributed 24 canvases to that year's exhibition.

The following year, when he exhibited with the Petrograd group of artists known as the "Tchervony Valet" (Jack of Diamonds), he was represented by 50 canvases, all painted since his return from Paris.

The artists of this group were all of the "left," united under the call: pure form! The group represented the tendencies of art of Western Europe: Parisian cubism, Italian futurism, and German expressionism.

For these artists and art critics who were all hot with the belated European extremism, Chagall's Witebsk masterpieces with their reserved tempo and disciplined form were too conservative—especially as they could not package them under one of their labels.

A year later, with the onrush of the revolution, Chagall's restraint, that came from peace of heart and mind, was shattered.

While not implicated in the revolution, neither politically nor emotionally, he could not escape the accelerated dynamic rhythm of the times. The canvases that he submitted in 1918 were all fully acceptable to the extremist left.

By now we should not be surprised to discover that in the canvases of this period there are no records of the distressing experiences endured by the artist and his family at the time he was doing them.

Were we to judge the artist by the work of this period only, we might think that the artist consciously escaped from his harsh reality into the painless world of fantasy.

But that would be a false conclusion. Neither did he in days of happy and pleasurable living bring into his canvases the factual reality of his existence.

We will repeat that a picture of Chagall does not represent one detail, one episode, not even one sequence, of his experience—a picture of his is a summation, a distillation of experience.

When he gives us later a picture of the terror that overpowered the Jewish towns, it is not one story, one actual incident—but a representation that symbolizes the tragedy of the Jewish people.

When he paints a pair of lovers, you don't see an individual pair but a picture of young lovers of a certain class, the class of small-town innocent Jewish lovers. And also their background—the sky, river, flowers, cows, candles and flute players—though the artist might have borrowed them from the Witebsk landscape, you feel it is not a local landscape, not a real landscape, but an ideal setting for lovers.

Even when he had sitting in front of him a real model, an old Jew, that he painted as a portrait, the model is transfigured by his art into a symbol—as in his picture, "A Jew Prays." (See page 36.)

In a canvas where he wants to tell of his happiness with his beloved Bella, you can't feel a personal emotion, the transport of a moment of love; the tale becomes transformed into a Jewish idyll. (See page 5.)

When we have in mind this characteristic of Chagall's formative imagination, we may approach his new creative works with understanding.

Material want, hunger, cold, insecurity, homelessness, disillusionment, even bitter failure—as in his Witebsk Academy of Art—all these "trifles" do not affect his art. In his art he transcends the plane of every-day living.

Chagall's art motifs have a spiritual source of origin. The roots of his art are nourished by the same food that sustains his soul. This was true even in his first Parisian period when his attitude to his Witebsk soul was negative and destructive, when he felt like trampling his "old" soul underfoot.

The canvases of the Russian period that remained and reached us show that the artist had been developing his constructive powers.

One of his greatest canvases, his "Promenade" (1917), we have already discussed. (See page 5.)

"THE CEMETERY"

Another canvas of the same year is called "The Cemetery." What made him think of the subject was probably the death of his parents. He greatly deplored that he could not be present at their funerals, having learned of their deaths later. He visited their graves.

Here again Chagall found a subject that he could transcend.

You still see Chagallian cubism—but never before was cubism used for such a purpose. Instead of re-enforcing the physical aspect of things; instead of stressing the spatial extension, the body, which is the essence of form; instead of denying the relevancy of the spiritual in plastic art since the spirit has no spatial dimension (the cardinal principle of cubism), Chagall, on the contrary, uses cubistic means to manifest the spiritual world.

Of course, he does not paint ghosts or devils in this picture—and yet, looking at the picture you become aware of the commotion of unseen activity; you sense the influence of an animistic world, a world of spirits.

What you see visible is a gathering of tomb-stones, monuments of poor people, slabs of stone with a few lines in praise of their virtues, not very impressive, what you would expect in a Witebsk cemetery. There are a few mortuary tents for the dead "rich," some in ruins, old ones—their children gone, nobody remembers them.

It looks as if a meeting of all the dead had been called, and all the dead came and they all brought with them their grave-stones—so that you may know who

was who. And there is a restlessness in them, an agitated movement. And all stand awakened, with their faces up, bent backward as if turning away in fear or in awe from the face of the "Just Judge" that they can see—though you cannot.

The commotion among the stones is caused by the agitated rhythm in their arrangement on the canvas—and by the play of light and shadow over them, a ghostly light that comes from an unknown source. The color patterns add to this effect. The colors, muted greys and soft pale reds, carry the mood. The air above the gravestones is formed in thick layers and concreted into air-textured figures. For a moment you seem to believe that you can see a face in the air, but it evanesces into a nebulous light that comes from an invisible source. A no-man's-land mystery is pressing its forbidden presence on the borders of the living world.

Yet, the picture has body and mass and material substantiality that can satisfy even one who is skeptical about ghost stories. The daring and successful handling of such tenuous material in terms of plastic structure is to be admired. You have here again the creation of an art reality, contiguous to the reality of nature.

A year later the artist painted another canvas of the same character, "The Gates of the Cemetery."

"INSPIRATION"

Another picture of 1917 is related to the above two, though differing in subject, by the method of work and by the spiritual quality which the artist gave to it.

This picture is called "Inspiration." A gentle young man, a poet-painter, sits in front of his easel, ready with his brushes to begin—but he has turned around to face the opposite wall where his "inspiration" has appeared. It is a young woman with an extended arm, who seems to have alighted here from above to rest a moment, ready to lift herself up and disappear. She seems to have wings, but when you look again you begin to think that it is only her garment spread out by her arm—though it assumes the appearance of wings. You can distinguish in the room a table and chairs, but half veiled. The mystic emanation that comes from the figure fills the entire room with a dreamy, visionary, nebulous light.

The whole canvas is composed of buoyant, airy spheres, circles and arcs hovering one over the other, giving the picture a lightness of mass. Also the variously shaped segments, ribbons and strips of which the figures are made do not rest in their place, but fly in airy patterns. There is no heavy-bodied solidity and repose in the whole picture. We get the feeling that the flat, light, transparent figure of the "Inspiration" stands upheld by her wings. The softly bright and shadowy colors add to the effect of the immateriality of the room—the colors passing from high light to dark shade in thin translucent planes.

The picture is particularly interesting for its grey light of which the body of the angel is composed, and which it spreads around itself. It is not a color but a mystic luminosity—a light without a shine, a light which has not the corporeal quality of our terrestrial lights—the light of a disembodied spirit that the sun cannot make warm. This effect the artist creates by the beautiful toning of the light qualities of his colors in their relation of one to the others.

This canvas possesses a richness of lyrical tenderness, softness, dreamy youthfulness—which appears for the first time in a canvas of his. It is often displayed, later on.

How does a canvas like that fit with years of war and revolution, of hunger and deprivation?

Did suffering soften the pride of the artist? How did he admit tender feeling into his art?

To the set of "spirit"-pictures belongs also his "Blue House" of 1920—a house where you feel the "soul of misfortune" is caged and cannot leave its confines—and pain, fear, and gloom cover the walls of the house with a blue despair. A mood created by color only.

"SELF PORTRAIT WITH A WINEGLASS"

Entirely of a different nature, of a more earthly content, is his canvas called "Self Portrait with a Wineglass," also painted in 1917.

In this canvas he painted himself sitting on the shoulders of his wife and on his head their little daughter, Ida. In the background, the distant Witebsk buildings, the river and its bridge.

Bella steps forward carrying her burden of husband and child very proudly. The artist holds a glass of wine raised triumphantly, and his face is beaming with happiness—alas, we know it was only a pictorial happiness.

Mr. James Johnson Sweeney, in his fine appreciation of Chagall, suggests that this picture might have been derived, unconsciously perhaps, from an eight-eenth century engraving attributed to Hogarth, "A Man Loaded with Mischief." In that picture a man is carrying on his shoulders a woman with a wineglass and monkey.

It seems Mr. Sweeney is not acquainted with Chagall's picturesque mother tongue, Yiddish. It would have saved him the trouble of looking so far back to find an inspiration for Chagall's canvas. There is a very common colloquial expression in Yiddish for a wife who is devoted to her husband; they say: "Si trogt im oif di hent." (She carries him on her hands.) Chagall made use of the people's picturesque speech in a few of his canvases. (See page 37.) Here it gave him an idea for a brilliant picture.

This canvas is a victory of Chagall's organizing powers. The two figures with the child above them lift themselves up in a vertical height to the top of the canvas. They move forward in the pictorial space without the support of any horizontal ballast on the sides—and yet keep their balance.

The whole composition is striking, original and daring.

The lines are soft and flowing; the colors are brilliant—but unwarmed by emotion, which is a true sign that not the heart but the head informed the hand of the master craftsman. It is sheer virtuosity—but a plastic energy, quivering within the composition, quickens the canvas into significance and vitalizes the lines and colors to be more than an organized heap.

Did the distant breath of the revolution touch this masterpiece?

"THE GREEN FIDDLER"

The same suggestion can be made about another of his canvases, "The Green Fiddler," painted in 1918, now owned by the Guggenheim Foundation of New York.

From the point of view of its conception, this picture belongs with the pictures of his Paris days when the artist aimed at smashing the rational sense of the picture, depending entirely on its plastic logic.

The "Fiddler" sits in midair. Only one leg of a stool can be surmised, but his position is that of a seated figure, playing a violin. Two small roofs placed in the lowest foreground of the canvas serve as foot-stools for the "Fiddler's" feet. His head reaches up to the clouds. The head with its vizored cap is framed by two small houses arranged in primitive perspective on the top of the canvas. A little man floats in the clouds over the head of the "Fiddler." The middle ground is faintly indicated by a man throwing a violin up in the air.

In proportion, the "Fiddler" looms gigantic over the whole canvas even in his sitting position.

The "Fiddler's" figure is made up of two separate vertical halves that are united by his ritualistic four-cornered garment. Each part is composed of differently shaped segments, variegated in color. The legs of his trousers are unmatched; his shoes not of the same pair. The whole figure is flat, with some weight to the head. The lines of the patterns have a hard precision, unusual for the artist. The canvas has a graphic quality.

The face with its wild eyes is crooked; the nose is twisted to one side and the mouth to the other. . . .

And yet, the whole figure has a strange charm—even a certain refined elegance. From the point of view of design it is a rare masterpiece of unusual power. And no matter how opposed you may be to accepting the figure as a natural being, you cannot deny its visible vitality and its own powerful reality. It possesses a living energy that demands recognition and a place for itself. It is, of course, the power of the Chagallian art that you feel—no small tribute to the artist.

But it is a power tainted with Satanism. And you can turn to admire, but not to love the creature there on the canvas, between heaven and earth.—You usually turn with sympathy to Chagall's Jews.

What is most striking is this: in a canvas where nothing is natural, how easily the artist could have lost the authenticity of the "Fiddler"—yet, deformed, distorted, cut up, patched up as it is, you recognize the Jew, the Witebsk musician; so uncompromising is Chagall in his Jewish feeling.

The artist painted a number of variations of the "Fiddler."

Two other canvases of that period go back to the Paris days.

One is called "Anywhere in the World"—actually a Witebsk street, one side of it, houses and all, rearing its terminal end sheer into the sky. Parallel to the vertical street, a very tall man stands against it; half of his head cleanly sawed off—the cut-off part lying aside, looking up with one blind eye at its body.

The other canvas is a picture of a human figure rolling along the street like a wheel in motion—called, "Going."

Slowly Chagall was making headway with the art-loving intellectuals. Many articles began to appear about him. In 1918, a book by two well-known Russian critics, Efross and Tugendhold, appeared in Moscow; each contributed his own appreciation of Chagall's genius. Later this book was translated and published in Germany.

It was Efross who called Chagall to come to the Moscow State Jewish Theater.

The State Jewish Theater of Moscow

IN THE spring of 1920, Alexander Granovsky brought his "Jewish Theater Studio," then one year old, from Petrograd to Moscow.

Granovsky's ambition was not only to have a theater for Jewish plays, but to create a National Jewish Theater with a histrionic style originally and characteristically Jewish.

He was not satisfied to bring to the stage Jewish figures in their home setting. By a generalized stylization of Jewish generic manners and folkways, he tried to create a Jewish theatrical art that would serve him in all his productions.

Out of the Jewish gesticulation, intonation, sing-song talking, grimacing, walking, posing; of the Jewish beard and ear-locks, hooked nose and crooked back; of the Jewish garb and ritualistic garments; of the Jewish home and synagogue—of these he would extract formal elements and create of them a theatrical style: a style of acting, stage-setting and decorations that would be typically—even if grotesquely—Jewish.

In directing, Granovsky's method was not to permit the actor free will. Every move, every intonation, every expression, was planned and prescribed by the regiseur himself. He therefore could force upon the actors and upon the stage the stylized Jewish make-up and mimicry and the formalized stage-setting, and thus create his new Jewish theater.

But before everything else, Granovsky wanted to have a Jewish painter make the stage sets for his new theater and decorate the walls of the auditorium.

There was no lack then of Jewish painters in Moscow—but he was looking for the most Jewish one, and one that was at the same time new and daring. Chagall was the choice.

Chagall had just become free of entanglements with his Witebsk academy.

The artist has this story to tell:

"About 1919, there came to our city from Petrograd a Jewish Theater Studio with an unknown director. He came to our city most likely because his wife was from Witebsk. His "Studio" consisted of a company of old and young amateurs.

"After the performance, I found myself moodily loitering in the foyer of the City Theater in the company of my old teacher, Judah Pen, who always annoyed me with his cold skeptical smile—nobody knew whereat . . . Finally, I stumbled upon the director himself.

"Alexey Granovsky, blond, tall, and swaying, looked to me somewhat gentile. He seldom opened his mouth, perhaps because of his bad teeth. He could talk with his mouth closed. His eyes smiled with a casual pleasure that came upon him suddenly, unexpectedly, attacking him like a fly. And he always looked at you and at somebody else on the side at the same time.

"'I really need you, Chagall,' he said suddenly—'you know, I have a play . . . just for you.'

"For myself I was thinking that it was high time that I got into a Jewish theater.

"Something had to "explode" to open a way for me. But here now, why was I so little attracted to Granovsky?

"Shortly after, my friend Efross called me to come to Moscow to paint the walls of the New Jewish Theater and also to make the stage sets for the first performance of the troupe of players that was being organized.

"When I came to Moscow, I found the manager-director, Granovsky, in bed. He liked to coddle himself and capriciously play sick-in-bed. He carried on all conversations while lying in bed. I showed him sketches that I had prepared in Witebsk.

"And while we were talking, Michoels came in. Gently, cautiously, he came over and with great respect said something, listened, and walked out with the self-assurance of the future soldier-general (of the theater).

"Granovsky would make some short and smiling remarks, that would immediately be picked up by the nearby actors as something very precious; they would carry them out and laughingly spread them over the long corridors:

"'Did you hear? Granovsky said this, and Granovsky said that.—Do you hear? Granovsky is laughing. Sh-sh—Granovsky is asleep. He has a visitor. He is declaring himself in love. He—.'

"'Only my romance with him did not clinch' —he said.

"Why?

"I really had no luck at all with directors. None with Wachtangoff, who at first did not have any feeling for my art nor for my sketches for "The Dybbuk" that I had made for the "Habimah"—and yet later asked his own painter to make it "Chagallish," without me.

"Nor did I have better luck with Tairof, who was sick with "constructivism." And the same with the Second Studio of the Moscow Art Theater, that was still drowning in psychological realism . . .

"All of these, and others too, first asked me to make sketches for their plays but were frightened when they looked at them.

"And here now Granovsky. True, a man that was searching for something. But he spoke Russian in the Jewish theater. He did have talent, perhaps an eclectic, but with charm. Only he was still straying on the paths of his German teacher, Max Reinhardt, with his theories of mass-scenes that were then in vogue.

"Granovsky was trying to find something new; not with the ardor of a Jewish soul, but slowly, as if in books. He was trying to rid himself of the German decorative method and was looking for new Jewish forms that had already begun to show up here and there in the Jewish plastic world.

"I happened to be the first painter in the New Jewish Theater. But Granovsky did not talk to me—he satisfied himself with a smile; and I, with my "character," also kept silent."

Chagall did not have any real experience in theater work. However, as he himself said, he had been dreaming for a long time about getting into the theater.

The art critic, Tugendhold, had written as early as 1911, that Chagall's paintings showed such vigorous vital energy that he could make powerful decorations for the stage. The same Tugendhold had sug-

gested to Tairof to get Chagall to make stage sets for Shakespeare's "Merry Wives of Windsor." But nothing came of it.

In 1917 Chagall painted a few curtains and a stage setting for the Gogol celebration, carried out by the experimental "Hermitage Theater" of Petrograd.

The theater that Granovsky obtained from the government was small—actually a re-built drawing-room of a private house that the Revolution had confiscated from a rich owner. Because of its small size, beside its formal name, "The Moscow State Jewish Theater," it was also known as the "Kammer (chamber) Theater," or because of Chagall's paintings, "The Chagall Hall."

Granovsky did not mind its small size—he was much more interested in organizing and developing a company of actors.

Chagall, too, was contented with the small wall-space that he was called upon to paint. His dream to work in a Jewish theater was now to be realized—and he threw himself into the work with all his heart and soul.

Neither Granovsky nor Efross set any conditions. Chagall was free to do what his heart desired.

He tells us that he had decided, once and for all, he would not permit "sweat and garlic" in the new Jewish theater. He must now break the tradition of the naturalistic theater.

One side-wall of the auditorium ran in a continuous stretch, without intersection, from the door to the stage. Here Chagall painted an allegory that was to serve as an introduction to the new theater. He first painted himself being carried by Efross from Witebsk to Moscow and once again, Efross bringing him to the door of the stage. A little further along the wall he painted Granovsky with his star, the young Solomon Michoels, in the role of Hamlet, around them a whole troupe of acrobats, jugglers, clowns, musicians, and dancers—meaning thereby to point out the free and folk spirit of the new theater that was going to do away with the tradition of naturalism which Stanislavsky had established everywhere.

Perhaps I should add here that all the characters the artist introduced to the public on his walls were busily showing their tricks, fancy free, without reserve. Not one of them was left with his natural appearance—and how fantastic Chagall can make them

The Bride with Two Faces. Oil. 1927

Courtesy of the Artist

PLATE XVIII

look we have seen previously, his "Green Fiddler" being a good example.

To return to the theater—the opposite wall was cut up by three windows; and here Chagall painted four panels that represented the forebears of the Jewish theater, namely, the Scribe (of the Scrolls of the Law), representing literature; the Wedding Jester (Badchen), representing the actor; the street musician; and a lively buxom "Aunt," dancing.

(At Jewish weddings there was always somebody's "aunt," usually an older lady, but lively in spirit, who would go dancing in front of the bridal couple as they were led in procession from their nuptial ceremonies, performed usually in the yard of the synagogue under a canopy. There were special dances that the "aunt" would carry out by herself or with the help of others —and there were also folk-songs for her—hence her importance for the folk theater.)

Above the windows, in the long and narrow frieze, Chagall painted a table full of all kinds of foods for the wedding feast.

On the third wall, opposite the stage, which had two doors, the artist painted a modern young pair of lovers dancing gaily.

The artist made his sketches sprawling on the floor of the auditorium.

Efross relates that Chagall locked himself in and admitted nobody, except him (Efross) and Granovsky —and he even kept them at the door, not permitting them to go further in. He watched at his door "as a sentinel standing guard over a powder magazine."

And the comparison was not far out of the way: what the artist was doing on the walls had plenty of explosive stuff in it.

When the artist finally opened the doors and the actors came in, they looked wonderingly at the smeared artist on his ladder, at the figures on the walls, and shrugged their shoulders.

We will let Chagall relate it himself.

"I based my hope particularly on the magical Solomon Michoels, who did not, like the others, roam about in the corridors. Everywhere there were pieces of lumber, boards, old newspapers, dirty rags, and laths still lying about. The corridors were always busy—one was carrying a piece of black bread, another a bottle of diluted bluish milk, to his room. Some were gossiping. And I was on the ladder, busy with my murals. The watchman, Ephraim, a young wild animal, would bring me my portion of straw-bread and watery milk, and meanwhile stand and gape with amusement at my paintings. Sitting on the ladder and painting, I had a desire to paint myself and my villages and towns into the walls.

"Bella came to comfort me and brought with her the little angel, Idotchka, as big as half a yardstick. She moved about on the floor and looked up at 'papa' on top. He was too high up for her.

"Meanwhile 'Mama' went away to get a lesson in Yiddish from her teacher, Michoels. I could hear her voice from a distance as she recited, "Little bells are ringing . . ." (from a poem of Peretz Markish). And I sat and thought of the new art in the new theater, without pasted beards that frightened me like devils . . . I thought of the Purim-Players (the amateur performers of the story of Queen Esther and Haman, based on the story told in the Book of Esther); of the beggar with his green face and his bag on his back where he carries his Sidur (prayer-book), pieces of bread, and a herring. And here I could see him at night in the moonshine with his beard, shaking like a tree in the park—and I wanted to paint him and take him up on the stage too.

"In my heart I was praying quietly to a dead distant relative who had once painted—what a piece of good luck—a synagogue, praying for him to help me!

"I felt that there was one, a young Jew, who could help me. If he were only to come to me and open his mouth—perhaps he too would become a different person.

"This was the young Michoels—young and strong, though small in stature; lean, but muscular; practical, yet visionary, with a logic that is blended with emotion; his Yiddish tongue sounded as if coming from our old holy books. He could help. He could lead himself out, and perhaps also help the director.

"A long time I was sitting there on the ladder in the hall; around me my wall-paintings and also the sketches that I was preparing for the Sholem Aleichem plays.

"The doors I kept locked. Only rarely would Granovsky come in to talk about art and the theater and about the coming performance.

"One day Michoels came in to me with his small steps and veiled yet understandable words: 'Marc Zacharewitch (the artist's Russian patronymic), lend me your sketches that you have here. I want to study them. It must not be like that—you here alone and we there, each for himself . . .'

"And really, I could have sat there for a long time, finished working, gathered up my bundles and disappeared.

"The open comradely approach of Michoels was symbolic of the new type of Jewish man and artist at the beginning of the Revolution.

"I can't forget yet how a few weeks later I suddenly heard Michoels' voice coming from the distance, calling me loudly: 'Chagall, where are you? You know, I understand . . .' And then he rushed in and approached me on my ladder, my sketches in his hands: 'Now I understand! See, Chagall!'—and his eyes filled with happiness, with a smile that covered him to his toes, he began to pose, move about, and speak Sholem Aleichem's text.

"And there was no doubt, Michoels had discovered something: found the true intonation, rhythm and expression—that is, the form, the content, the new spirit, the new actor. It was a new world!

"I was satisfied and continued working. They would soon open the new theater. Granovsky threatened with a smile that they would take me off the ladder by force, and they would have to call two doctors to keep me quiet when they would hang my big canvases on the walls.

"I was waiting to see what would happen. The rehearsals of Sholem Aleichem went on in the same old style, that is, the old psychological realism.

"I imagined that only Michoels would show up in the midst of the whole company of actors—and all of them, including Granovsky himself, would wonder and ask: What had happened that Michoels had suddenly broken away from the chain, and we are not at all prepared?

"I sat thus on the ladder meditating and speculating. Suddenly I heard steps approaching, hands opened the door, and all the actors came in the hall, all together saying:

"'Chagall, Michoels sends us to you. He has changed completely in his role. We ask him what had happened to him, and he says, 'I don't know, go to Chagall, he will explain it to you.' So, here we are, all of us. Please, tell us what to do that we may become like Michoels.'

"After hearing them, I became sad. I had been hanging there on the ladder before their eyes for a long time, but only when Michoels changed, had they come to me to change them. And where was their director? I told them: 'Go back to Michoels, he can explain it to you better than I can.'"

In vain did Chagall wait for a miracle to happen, that all the actors would change and an ensemble finally result, the whole theater unified—the paintings on the walls in the auditorium, the sets on the stage, the actors, all entering into a full harmonious mise en scène.

In those days money was not abundant and there was a shortage of materials for costumes and stage-settings. The very last days before the opening they brought to the artist old and wornout sets, and he repainted them in a hurry.

The theater opened with three short pieces of Sholem Aleichem: "Mazl Tov (Good Luck)," "Agents" and "It's a Lie."

Chagall relates:

"On the night of the opening, before the curtain went up, I was so pressed for time that I hardly had a few minutes to run up on the stage to put a few daubs on the accessories. I could not bear to see any naturalism on the stage.

"Suddenly a clash.

"Granovsky hung up a real hand-towel.

"I cry out with pain: 'A real towel!'

"'Who is the director here, I or you?'— Granovsky said coldly."

Efross relates that Chagall wept bitterly.

"The very last minute—Efross relates—Chagall got hold of Michoels, who was wanted on the stage, and began to paint him up, putting birds on his hat, little animals, sticks and stones—and all so small that the audience could not see them even with binoculars.

"We had to tear Michoels out of Chagall's hands by force; they were waiting for him on the stage."

Chagall remarks with a smile that he was imploring the actor to let him gouge out one of his eyes, to make his mask perfect.

Naturally, the first performance did not accomplish a perfect ensemble, according to my opinion. But my task was done"—Chagall said.

It is very hard from afar for those who have not been in the "Chagall Hall" to adequately evaluate the aim and scope of the artist's work. The little theater lost its existence years ago; a larger and more imposing building now carries the proud name of the "Moscow State Jewish Theater." We do not know whether Chagall's paintings were saved. Chagall tells me that he had used double canvases and the paintings could have been taken off from the walls in good condition.

Full reproductions were never made. In his book on Chagall, published in Leibzig in 1923, Karl With included some black and white reproductions—which can hardly give us an idea of the full and rich effect of Chagall's colored fantasies. Chagall's colors are much more than costumes—they are the emanation of the souls of his creations.

Furthermore, we must bear in mind that Chagall had conceived the whole theater, the auditorium with its painted walls full of action, the stage with its curtains and sets, the actors in their costumes, all as one plastic whole. His painted world was not completed until the curtain went up and the actors appeared on the stage.

The miracle of the Chagall theater happened, or was supposed to happen, when the curtain went up and his figures on the stage began to move and talk. The same Jews that on the frescos were silent and stationary, there, at the extension of the frescos on the stage, attained speech and movement.

Unnecessary and intruding was only the public in the auditorium . . . Could the artist have painted and colored the people in their seats, he would perhaps accept them as part of his composition. As they came in from the street, unchanged and unadapted, they were merely naturalistic things which the artist could not bear to see . . . And Efross relates that Chagall complained disconsolately when they began to put the seats in the auditorium. Chagall, too, mentions how chagrined he was at the thought that outsiders would come in and throw their carcasses into the chairs and obstruct the view of his paintings on the walls. The public did not belong in *his* theater.

Chagall, the painter, was not interested in plays and in a play-house. A theater, yes, a painter's theater; a new kind of plastic art that resembles a play-house

only inasmuch as a part of the whole, one part of the design of the ensemble, consists of moving and talking figures, costumed and colored to unite harmoniously with the painted curtains and scenery on the stage and the painted figures on the walls.

You must not keep your eyes only on the stage where there is motion and sound—take in, in your view, the whole house, the moving people on the stage and the painted but no less animated and performing people on the walls, in order that you may perceive the whole pictorial panorama.

From our practical and realistic point of view it is hard to understand Chagall's visionary creative idea.

Impractical as it was, he did approach his task as a great imaginative painter, not as a theater manager. As in his other pictures, the impossible became a new and daring reality on his canvas. From the point of view of pure art, his "theater" was a great original and creative act. Impractical as it was, the fact remains undeniably that his fantastic theater had a widespread powerful influence.

Efross relates that the public came to be surprised at Chagall's paintings more than to see Sholem Aleichem's plays. And Efross often found himself constrained to come out in front of the curtain to talk to the audiences about Chagall's art rather than about the aims of the new Jewish theater.

Efross came to the conclusion that Chagall did hurt the young Jewish theater in Moscow.

Perhaps Efross was right from the immediate outlook and from the narrow theatrical angle. Against the powerful Chagallian fantasy and intensity of the colored life he created on the walls, the actors and director found themselves helpless and had to step back to second place. But we cannot ask of a great artist to give less than his full strength—even if it dwarfs smaller men.

Now, looking at it in historical perspective, we can see that Chagall's achievement in the Moscow Jewish Theater can be counted as a positive gain in the cultural development of the Jewish theater.

First of all, Chagall's art had, as we have seen, a moulding influence on the young Michoels, who later became the leader, star and director of the Moscow Jewish Theater, as well as professor of a large school of Jewish actors—and thus Chagall had indirectly contributed to the forming of the style of many young actors who are leading in a number of Jewish theaters in the Soviet Union. The well-known star, Suskin, one

White Crucifixion. Oil. 1938

Courtesy of the Artist

PLATE XIX

of the outstanding personalities in the Jewish theatrical world, perfected his ideas of the theater working with Michoels.

Again, Chagall with his critical attitude against naturalism on the stage and also with his own examples of super-naturalistic creations, helped to direct the theater away from naturalism, his influence spreading beyond the limits of the Jewish stage door.

It is a great cultural and historic loss if Chagall's famous paintings are lost.

The Hebrew theater, "Habimah," in Moscow, proposed to Chagall to take into his hands the mise en scène of "The Dybbuk."

Chagall could not readily decide. If his "romance" with Granovsky did not succeed, he was still farther apart from Wachtangoff, the regiseur of the "Habimah," who was at the same time an actor in Stanislavsky's theater.

Wachtangoff's own mise en scène was then still unknown. It was difficult for Chagall to find a common ground with Wachtangoff and a language of artistic communication between them.

Nevertheless, when he was called to the first rehearsal of "The Dybbuk," Chagall went.

Wachtangoff kept himself distant and cold. The two artists watched each other suspiciously and antagonistically. There was a long and hard silence.

"Assuredly, he reads in my eyes the chaos and disorder of the Orient, an art incomprehensible, strange—," Chagall was thinking.

(Wachtangoff was not Jewish).

Finally Zemach, the director of the "Habimah," broke the awkward silence.

"Well, Marc Zacharewitch (Chagall's patronymic), what do you say; according to your opinion, how shall we put on 'The Dybbuk'?"

"I think we should first ask Wachtangoff's opinion" —Chagall suggested.

Wachtangoff, who was holding books with reproductions of Chagall's pictures, continued to turn the pages silently. After a long while, he said:

"All your deformations are alien to me. Only Stanislavsky's line is the right one."

"And I do not see the Stanislavsky line in the renaissance of the Jewish theater"—Chagall insisted.

And to Zemach he said:

"In spite of all, you will eventually put on "The Dybbuk" according to my ideas, even if I would not be there. There is no other way."

On his way home, Chagall relates, he remembered that he met Ansky, the author of "The Dybbuk." Ansky, after embracing him, said joyfully: "Do you know, I have a play, 'The Dybbuk.' You, only you, are the one to put it on. I have been thinking of you."

Baal Makhshoves, who was present at the conversation, nodded in agreement with the author.

Later Chagall was told that Wachtangoff spent hours in front of Chagall's painting in Granovsky's theater.

And Zemach himself admitted afterwards that they had ordered their painters to make it "Chagallish."

Chagall remarks:

"And I have heard that at Granovsky's, too, they are doing it "Chagallish"—more Chagallish than Chagall himself."

We can see now that the impractical, "naive" Chagall was right in following his powerful artistic instinct to give himself fully in his work. Had he been "wise" and adapted himself first to Granovsky and then to Wachtangoff, he would have made no original contribution to the culture of the theater.

It is a tribute to Wachtangoff's genius that in spite of all, he did come to study Chagall's paintings. Being an Armenian, not knowing Jewish life and Jewish folk tradition, he finally came to understand that Chagall's artistic expression contains essences which are vitally important for a Jewish Theater.

Speaking of Michoels, Chagall gives his view on the development of the Jewish theater as he would like to see it.

"What is the art of Michoels?

"This is almost the same question that one can ask about the dreams and tasks of the new Jewish plastic art.

"Goldfaden, Peretz, Sholem Aleichem and the others are for the actor what nature is for the plastic artist.

"The artist does not copy nature; but standing in front of it, creates it. In this way both the artist and the actor create a kind of a new nature. And only this approach can be called respect for dramatist and for nature. Otherwise, it is sheer copy, photography, illustration and not art.

"And once the Jewish theater had, in a rare moment, accomplished a soulful synthesis with a Jewish plastic, it came to life and showed its soul to the world. But when the theater kept itself at a distance, it remained, with its casual actor-talents, a "local" affair. I do not have in mind here the "decorative" help of the invited artist. This is often of small importance.

"It is not enough to speak about the history of the Jewish theater from the point of view of the literary, psychological and reading-plays and their roles produced in the past; we unquestionably had and still have scores of fine and great Jewish actors—born talents. I had the good fortune to see a few of them at different times. Just as there were, in the history of art, solitary greater and lesser artists; yet of a higher value were those artists who could understand and unite with the whole epoch of art. As in the French schools of the plastic arts of recent times, and as in the case of our own Jewish literature the classic writers of the new epoch who created a style—so also the Jewish actor in the new theater.

"And so Michoels, too, endeavored to create a new Jewish actor in the new Jewish theater, and a new Jewish style.

"And when one comes to sense in oneself the important meaning of the technical material, one can at the same time perceive in oneself the whole man."

"And thus Michoels opened wide the road on which he could by his own powers enlarge and deepen his theatrical art. Michoels was one of the rare fortunate ones who had succeeded in "reaching" such a road, had understood its importance and pointed it out to others.

"I later saw other actors in the Moscow Jewish Theater, particularly Suskin with the melody on his thick lips, going the same way.

"I later saw the regiseur, Wachtangoff, sit in the hall in front of my murals and, like one on fire, lead the troupe of the "Habimah" with Rovina and others in "The Dybbuk," on the same road,—though at first he was opposed.

"Thus while studying art, Michoels came to see life. And as on the theater stage, so on the stage of life, he brought his analysis to the problems of our great and tragic time. Time too is of the materials with which we breathe and work in our art.

"And that proves how ridiculous is the opinion that there is such a thing as "pure art"—an "art for art's sake."

"On the contrary, that art that you call "pure" art is very often "soiled."

"And if Michoels—as he had said—had once learned from me, I should now learn from him.

"And perhaps then I would not drown in my doubts as in a pot of paint that paints the Jewish face and soul in the colors of fear and sadness."

Chagall wrote the above in the summer of 1943, on the occasion of Michoels' visit to the United States together with the poet Feffer as delegates of the Soviet Jews to plead for unity in the fight against Hitler.

Now Michoels is dead, killed in an automobile accident in Minsk.

Chagall's mood here is rare and indicates how much the appalling tragedy of the Jews affected him.

PROFESSOR OF ART

After he completed his work in Granovsky's theater, Chagall was invited by the Commissar of Public Instruction to become Professor of Art of two children's colonies near Moscow.

Chagall accepted the position.

These were colonies of orphans, victims of the war and civil war, who had no kin to claim them.

To get some conception of who these new pupils of Chagall were, you have to remember that the Government had picked them up in the cellars, attics and streets of Moscow. Clad in tatters, unwashed, full of vermin, ill-fed and frozen, these unclaimed waifs roamed in groups, living by what their hands could get. Demoralized and even degenerated, they at first refused to accept the home and food the Government offered them, valuing their undisciplined freedom above food and shelter. Under the supervision of the best pedagogues they were gradually brought to live together in children's colonies and guided to become useful men and women.

In the two colonies that Chagall was teaching, there were about fifty children distributed in small houses. To study, they were called together in one hall.

Chagall recalls with love those unfortunate children who carried in their souls the burns of their experiences.

"Their eyes could never smile—," their professor noticed. "They threw themselves on colors as wild animals on meat—," he relates. "From every corner their eager voices came to me, one out-shouting the other: 'Comrade Chagall, Comrade Chagall' . . .

"When I think of them my heart contracts with pain up to this day."

He busied himself with them until he left the Soviet Union.

"MA VIE"

One more important task he undertook and accomplished before he left the Soviet Union. He wrote a series of autobiographical sketches which he completed in 1922.

They were written in Russian, and the manuscript, still in the author's hands, remains unpublished. In 1931 his wife, Bella, prepared a French translation, which appeared in Paris as "Ma Vie."

These sketches are of a high literary value. The images are free and palpitating with life; his impressions picturesquely transmitted. His remarks are racy with a fresh and folkloristic humor and pungent unequivocal satire—sometimes playful, at other times deeply serious. Chagall's poetic fantasy and inventiveness are everywhere evident. The plastic artist comes through, though the medium is language. The sketches are drawn so boldly and in such pronounced relief that nothing of it is lost in translation. Most important of all, it gives an intimate revelation of the sentiments, moods and character of the artist—a valuable supplement to what he reveals of himself in his canvases.

The artist promised that he would find time to continue to tell the story of his life and bring it up to the present.

While giving me "Ma Vie" for my information, the artist warned me that there is in it not only *Warheit* but also *Dichtung*.

IN BERLIN

One day standing in front of the Kremlin in Moscow, Chagall reminded himself that he had a friend there, the poet Demian Biedny. Chagall had known him intimately at the time both of them worked in the military bureau of Chagall's brother-in-law in Petersburg.

With the help of the poet and Lunatcharsky, Chagall obtained permission to leave Soviet Russia.

On his way to Paris the artist stopped in Berlin.

His old friend, the poet Rubiner, had written to him from Berlin:

"Are you alive? Rumors circulate here that you were killed in the war. Do you know that you are famous here? Your pictures have created our Expressionism. They sell here for high prices. However, do not expect to get the money that Walden owes you. He will not pay you because he thinks that your glory is sufficient for you."

In 1914 Chagall had taken his best oils and water colors to Berlin, and Walden, editor of "Der Sturm," exhibited them in his offices. Chagall left them there and went to Witebsk. Now, eight years later, Chagall found only a few of his pictures unsold. But due to the fallen value of the mark, the sum of money that Walden owed him amounted to very little.

But Rubiner did not exaggerate about Chagall's fame. In the years that he was in Russia, the younger generation of Berlin artists became acquainted with Chagall's pictures, admired them greatly, and were influenced by them, as their own works show.

Karl With wrote:

"What Chagall could represent in his person to the intellectual life of Germany, only he can understand who can penetrate with sympathy and understanding into the abysses and catastrophes of the soul. I shall not be accused of exaggeration in saying that Chagall's name sounded legendary. It was painful for us to come to believe that Chagall can be met in Berlin—so accustomed were we to forget that this artist is a man of our own time, like ourselves, and not some magician practicing the art of enchantment somewhere between earth and heaven."

Chagall's influence reached to other European art centers as well.

The now famous Surrealist, Max Ernst, recalls how struck he was when he first saw a reproduction of Chagall's picture, "To Russia, Asses and Others." (See page 30.) And when he came to Berlin in 1916, he went directly, on leaving the train, to the offices of "Der Sturm" to see if anything was left of Chagall's exhibition.

For some time thereafter, Chagall's influence was noticeable in the canvases of this artist.

In Belgium too, Chagall's work found admirers.

Chagall remained in Berlin for eight months. During all that time, he did not paint one canvas. But he made a series of engravings to illustrate a German translation of "Ma Vie," that Paul Cassirer was to publish. Later Cassirer changed his mind and published the engravings without the text; he issued them in a portfolio under the name of "Mein Leben." Besides this portfolio he also published other engravings of Chagall.

The illustrations that were later published with the French text did not come from the Berlin series but from earlier drawings.

In Paris Again

IN THE spring of 1923 Chagall and his family came to Paris. They lived in a studio at 110 Avenue D'Orleans. Two years later they settled in their own home in Boulogne-sur-Seine.

Each year on their vacation they would go to different parts of France.

France had now really become his home.

Chagall had stated before that in France everything, nature, the people, the very air is conducive to art.

After the distressing experience and cheerless life in the years of war and revolution in Russia, now here in the mild and sunny air of France, in the free and tolerant climate of the art capital of the world, Chagall found the repose and peace of heart and mind that was necessary for him to continue his creative work.

There began for him a period of quiet joy, smiling and serene days, rich with fruitful living. First here he began to feel the warmth of a home with a tender and devoted wife and a close and helpful companion, such as his beloved Bella was for him.

"For many years my art felt her love-influence"—the artist said later.

Now ended his youthful period of storm and stress, of revolt and destructive Satanism. There ensued a period of trustfulness, gentleness, of warm and tender song and fluid melody.

And the leading motif was love and love's young dream.

Chagall was always a master of brilliant colors—from the very outset. But now his palette sprouted as a May morning with a fresh and fragrant effluence of tender and sparkling colors. His canvas became enriched with a world of new tones and nuances,—became more intimate and personal, more tender and soulful in mood, softened by human sympathy, suffused with spirit and light, lyrical instead of dramatic. It became airy without losing solidity. He achieved a refinement of tone and an ethereal transparency that has no equal in the whole world of art.

And as if he had discovered a new sense in himself, he now felt the sensuous quality of textures—and painted with pleasure the flesh of young girls and flowers and the warp and woof of leaf, bark, and feather, of sky and distance, of textiles—but he did not paint gems and jewels.

His former sharp and angular lines became rare now and soft contours and flowing curves took their place. Instead of the cut-up, turbulent, and sometimes brutal rhythms of his cubistic days, as in "A Soldier Drinks Tea" (1912), or "The Poet" (1911), "Dedicated to My Fiancée" (1911), you now find a peaceful lyrical harmony.

Even in such a brilliant canvas as the "Green Fiddler" (1918), there still is a stiffness and resilience in the planes, as of sheet-metal. True, it is purposeful and plastically concordant with the spirit of the canvas—but that is precisely what I want to point out, the change of spirit in the artist. In his magnificent canvas, "Self Portrait with a Wineglass" (1917), you can hear the cry of triumph—but not the song of love. I do not mean to undervalue this picture, or the others. It is unnecessary to repeat that these are works of art in the full glorious right of their excellence, that do not yield their high place to any other canvas of their kind. But I want to stress the change that took place in the artist's heart and soul when he took up his work again in France.

"THE BIRTHDAY"

From this angle, it is very instructive to examine his canvas, "The Birthday," which carries the double date, 1915–1923 (Witebsk-Paris).

The meaning of this picture becomes clear to us from Bella's account of it in her autobiographical story book, "The First Meeting."

Bella discovered the date of the artist's birthday, which he never cared to remember. On that day she came to him with flowers and colored shawls and strips of colored silks that she brought from her rich home to decorate his bare room.

She relates:

"Quickly I took apart my colored shawls and hung them up on the walls; the bed I covered with the bedspread that I brought with me; I covered the table—and you, you went to the corner and began to sort your stretched canvases; you picked one and quickly put it on the easel.

"'Don't move! Remain standing there as you are!'—you commanded. The flowers were still in my hands. I could hardly keep quiet. I would have liked to put them in water, to prevent their wilting. But soon I forgot about them. You attacked the canvas with such energy that it trembled under your brush.

"You daubed with your brushes, you gave color, red, blue, white, black. You pulled me along with the stream of colors. Suddenly, you tore me up from the floor and pushed yourself up with one foot, as if there were not enough space for you in the small room. You swooped up in the air, stretched yourself out full length, and flew up to the ceiling. Your head had turned aside and you also turned mine. You crept up behind my ear and whispered something to me . . .

"I listened to you—as if you were singing a song to me in your deep soft voice. Even your eyes expressed the song. We lifted ourselves easily—together—above the decorated room and floated; we came to the window and wanted to push through. From the window the light clouds were calling us, and a patch of blue sky—

"The walls with the colored shawls began to whirl around us and made us dizzy. We flew over meadows filled with flowers, over sleeping houses, roofs, yards, churches . . .

"'How do you like my picture?' You suddenly dropped to the floor on your feet. You looked at the canvas, you looked at me, you walked away from the easel, and came back.

"'Is there still much left to be done? It can't be left like that, don't you think? Tell me, where do I have to do more work—'

"You spoke to yourself and waited, fearing what I might say.

"'Oh, it is very good. You flew away so beautifully. We will call it, "The Birthday."'"

"Your heart was quieted.

"'Will you come tomorrow? I will paint another picture, and we will fly again.'"

These intimate lines suggest the meaning not only of this picture but also of other pictures of flying lovers.

As happens to other artists, Chagall is sometimes not fully pleased with a canvas and he goes back to work on it again.

And that is what happened to this canvas, not only as the dates on it indicated, but as intrinsic evidence in the color-texture tells the tale.

Every other detail was probably completed in 1915. But the colored shawls and the flowers with which Bella decorated the room were repainted in 1923—no canvas prior to this year shows the artist's keen interest in texture contrasts.

This new interest in texture brings a scintillating richness and sensuousness to the canvases he now paints—as in "The Trough" (1925), "The Circus" (1926), "The Bride with Double Face" (1927), "Lovers in Flowers" (1931), and many others.

Chagall, who loves to paint flowers, paints them readily, with a warm sentiment for them, paints their fervid brilliance and rich opulence, or delicate and tender refinement, aware of the variety of their sensual allurement—he first found this love in the sunny South of France. In his Witebsk he did not know flowers, not with the infatuation that he shows now in his painting of them.

"LOVERS IN FLOWERS"

But Chagall's gift of singing, fragrant colors came into its plentitude of power only when he began to paint his pairs of lovers.

This is a perennial subject for him and he comes back to this leit-motif again and again up to this day—and each time he creates one more imaginative, new, and original canvas that is lyrical, tender, and fresh with the blood of eternal youth. When you stand before one of these canvases, like "Lovers in Flowers," you sense at once even in the form of the picture, a disarming simplicity and innocence, a flowing, glowing softness that his former canvases did not have—and yet the composition is now no less daring, no less original and fascinating than in his former diabolic smashing canvases.

Look at this picture, "Lovers in Flowers." The very act of placing a pair of human lovers in a bush of flowers, as a pair of love-birds in a nest in the bush, shows an inventiveness that is both psychological in effect and plastic in consequence. The comparison between a pair of human lovers and a pair of birds is developed in the delicacy and tenderness of the two diminutive youthful human figures nesting together.

Plastically the artist harmonized and contrasted the textures of the nude body of the girl with the fragrant flesh of the flower petals. Something of the sweetness, freshness and delicacy of the flowers entered into the texture of the naked body lying among them. The eye visiting the lilac blossoms, like a bee, gathers with delight the color nuances of the blossoms and coming to the nude body, brings over to it some of the fragrant freshness of the petals and mixes it into the texture of the flesh—and the white flesh-tones of the nude girl among the lilac shades scintillate with a dewy fragrance as of the blossoms around her. The two young round faces of the lovers and the small white round breasts of the girl in the lilac shadows, as the two round white moons, one in the sky above and one in the sleeping river below, light up the young May night with a somnolent radiance. And the young spring night breathes upon the lovers and upon the flowers its dreamland enchantment, moist with dew and the breath of the river.

The colors are undoubtedly French—but there is an exotic, an oriental flavor in this picture. It reminds me of a picture in verse by our bard of the 12th century, Judah Halevi, which has a similar theme and oriental spirit.

"Amid the Myrtles." *

"The bridal pair stand amid the myrtles,
Sending forth pure myrrh on every side;
The myrtle desireth the sweetness of their fragrance
And spreadeth his wings like a cherub above them.
The myrtle thinketh to cover their fragrance,
But the sweetness of their spices overwhelmeth his scent."

I know that Chagall will sometimes, in a mood of negation, say deprecatingly, it is all a question of chemistry.

That is to say, it is only a problem of the chemistry of colors, of the science of match-making, of mating colors on the canvas and making them consort one with the other in matrimonial happiness forever after.

Yes, undoubtedly, chemistry!

But questions come to the mind that cannot be answered by chemical analysis.

I want to ask the artist: What leads the fine chemist Chagall to search for and find the purest,

* From the Hebrew by Nina Salaman.

tenderest white, blue, and lilac for his pair of lovers in the flowers—what and why?

And what makes the artist know and not stop until he gets the blue as pure, as tender, and as chaste, as ethereal as the first innocent dream of love of the young lovers in his canvas, "The Red Cock at Night"?

And what, if not the same sensitive poetic imagination, leads the hand of the master to draw with such touching delicacy, so lovingly and tenderly the head, neck, and bosom of the child-woman in the same picture? And what dead chemistry could give birth to the naive, gentle and youthful head of the chaste lover that comes out of the blue of the night and out of her dream, only to touch her hair, to touch it adoringly?

It is the same sensitive poetic imagination that led the word-chemist, Heine, the tone-chemist, Schubert, and the color-chemist, Chagall, to look for and find the words, tones and colors for their love songs.

In old France, the singer of love songs was called "Trouvere," or "Troubadour"—that meant the finder of sweet words and melodies to express the pains, longings and dreams of the lovers.

Chagall is our modern troubadour, the finder of the purest, richest and tenderest colors with which to paint the forever young lovers, the eternal youth of humanity.

It was in the dark Middle Ages when the religious mystics ruled over the imagination of the people, when tears, groans and pains, when putrid sores, scurvy chorea and epilepsy were the evidence of saintliness—then it was that the woman's body was despised as a vessel of shame, uncleanliness and sin; and love was looked upon as the snare of the devil, the eternal sworn enemy of mankind. But that was in the gloomiest and darkest time of human history when human dignity was lower than dirt, when the world was a "vale of tears," a place only for penitence and prayer, and the greatest virtue, to mortify the body.

The first signs of the coming renaissance, of the birth of the new man, was the joy with which men and women turned their faces to life, to the sun and to the rich earth—and before all it was the artist. And the first harbingers of the new era, the apostles of the new gospel of the proud free man, were the troubadours, the minnesingers—the singers of chivalry and love. With the new songs in the tongue of the people, with the poems that exalted the beauty of woman and the love of her, they opened the enlightened epoch in the history of our culture.

The Three Candles. Oil. 1938.

Courtesy of the Artist

PLATE XX

Only once did a sweet singer of Judah bend his devout heart to the Goddess of Love, and the gracious Goddess was good to him and smiled upon him with her ambrosial lips and with that gave immortality to his verses and to his girl, Shulamite.

It was in the Hellenistic epoch, under the influence of the Venus-cult, that the Jewish love poem was composed, the immortal "Shir Hashirim," "The Song of Songs"—and see how refreshing it is to come upon the ever blossoming rose of Sharon among the yellow tear-stained leaves of the old and new Lamentations. Through the long black night of exile, they heard the voice of the young king as he makes haste, leaping as a roe or a young hart upon the mountains of spices, skipping upon the hills of spikenard of Judah, to come to his beloved shepherd girl, the dusky Shulam-ite—and the Jewish hearts stirred with memories, and they dreamed again of youth and renewal.

The Jewish sage, Rabbi Akiba, who had been a shepherd in his youth and had experienced a great romantic love, thought so highly of the beautiful verses that he said the poem is an allegory describing the love between Israel and God! "Eternity is not worth more than the day on which this great poem was given to Israel. For all the books in Scripture are holy, but the Song of Solomon is the holy of holies."

A wise general said: "You let me write the love songs of the people, and I will let you win its battles . . ."

The one who writes or paints the love songs of his people keeps his people from getting old.

Woman, according to the biblical legend, was God's last piece of work: with her He completed His plan of the creation of the world. Six days He worked, each day its task accomplished, until the heavens and what is in them and the earth with all its host, cattle and creeping things, and the beasts after their kind, and man in the image of God, all were created and ap-pointed—and then God made woman.

Not before He achieved artistic maturity, only after His varied experience gave Him full mastery, did He attempt to make her, Eve—not from the crude ele-mental mud, but from the most precious material, of Adam's finest Carrara, did He fashion His masterpiece, woman, with all the beauty of her sculpture and the fascination of her pictorial nudity.

And that is the reason why, as all men know, woman is the eternal inspiration of the artist. And as God

Himself, many of the greatest artists won their crown of glory by creating the nude woman. It is the test of highest mastership—every artist tries, only the great succeed.

The last great masters of the nude were Degas and Renoir. It is a great loss for modern art that Cézanne could not remain serene at the sight of a nude girl and he painted apples and pears instead. This is one of the reasons why our modern art is intellectual, material-istic, and loveless. The modern artist approaches woman as a still-life.

In his approach to woman, the artist reveals not only his religion, his philosophy and his personal taste, but also the culture of his time and his national-ity. Witness: Phidias, Titian, Rembrandt, Rubens, Goya, Gainsborough, Rodin, Renoir.

How does Chagall paint woman?

I know of only a few canvases of his with nude figures.

Chagall is not a realist. He never paints nature as is. He does not aim to portray the physical aspect of his subjects. He limits himself to generalized, sim-plified forms. He does not describe but suggests. He paints less of the body to paint more of the spirit that lives within or with it. He paints the significance that an object gathers into itself by associating with the world of the soul. We must bear in mind that a pic-ture is for him first of all a state of the soul.

And therefore, we cannot expect of him the perfect drawing of the nude—though I do remember one nude of his, "Nude Over Witebsk," that is magnificent with its beautifully realized forms.

But mostly he does not draw the female figure for its beauty. On the contrary, it often seems to me that he purposely mistreats his female figures and leaves parts mis-shapen—but see what a world of tenderness he creates about his women.

In his attitude to his lovers, Chagall is Jew. There is no pagan joy in his lovers, no earthly flame, no inebriate passion. Nor is his small-town Venus a madonna. She is painted with a purely human tender-ness and modest innocence. His lovers stand pressed together, clinging to each other, lost in the mystery, in the wonder of their love. No tale of lure and pur-suit, none of coquetry and conquest. The lust of the flesh is never a motif in any of Chagall's canvases. Love for his young pairs is fate. Their match was made in heaven. The wonder is that the mates found each other on the multitudinous living earth—and they live in the wonder of the miracle. They are preoccupied with the seriousness of their emotions—a seriousness that deepens into sadness, for his lovers are sad. Or is it the Jewish sadness that always appears on Jewish faces at times of great rejoicing?

And for them, above them, and about them God created a young and radiant world. No, not God but Chagall made it for them. And it is a Chagallian world, a world of sweet singing colors, blue skies and green earth, of angels and flutists and fiddlers, of moons and candles and lamps hanging in the sky. If in God's world everything grows old, fades and withers, Chagall put them into his canvases where they will always be young and in love.

And again we ask: does Chagall do it all with the science of chemistry?—alchemy?

CHAGALL'S JEWISH LANDSCAPES

The artist, recalling his childhood, tells us of his roaming about with a comrade in the open country around Witebsk and also of his visits with Uncle Noah to the neighboring villages.

But in his canvases you will not find the plowman, neither the freshly turned over earth, the field with ripe wheat and rye, nor the song of the reapers. Neither sheep nor shepherd. He loves horses and cows, but not in the pasture.

The Dvina runs through Witebsk. The artist tells how he liked to play in the river and on its banks, to swim and float on rafts—to dress and undress again and sport in the water.

But in his canvases there is no remembrance of his youthful joy in the river.

Later, when he painted his pairs of lovers, he portrayed the river with young pairs nesting on the banks. The river appears again and again in his pictures. You can tell that the Dvina lives in his memory and comes to consciousness in his imagination—but always as a background, as in his "Lovers in Flowers," "Self Portrait with Wineglass," and others. He also paints the river as a symbol—as in "Time is a River without Banks" (1930), "Crucifixion" (1938), and others. You will not find in his canvases the beauty of the sunny river, nor the flashing of wet naked bodies.

The Witebsk landscape did not find in Chagall its poet—indeed, Chagall is hardly the poet of nature. When he comes to the Witebsk landscape, he changes it, turns it into a legend, to make of it a backdrop for his heroes.

I know only of three landscapes of his that may truthfully be called landscape painting: "Ile Adam" (1925), "Peira Cava" (1930) and "In the Mountains" (1930). And even these landscapes are not nature studies. We would not expect it from Chagall's brush.

In these landscapes as in his other compositions, you will find, first of all, Chagall the tender lyricist. He gives you nature as seen with the eyes of innocent joy, a joy fresh and pure as man before he knew of sin. He paints mood, spirit, emotion, here too, here expressed in the landscape as in other pictures in different compositions.

He is painting the landscape of his own vision. He is as subjective in his approach to nature as the old Jewish poets were. It is characteristic that none of these landscapes is without a human figure.

In the canvas, "In the Mountains"—a French landscape—he paints a young pair leaving the steps of their cottage to go to the distant mountains, riding on a young deer-like animal. The human pair and the animal are as young and as pure as the fresh day and the sunny landscape that wait for them.

The verses of "The Song of Songs" come to mind:

> "My beloved spake and said to me,
> Rise up, my love, my fair one and come away,
> For, lo, the winter is past, the rain is over and gone,
> The flowers appear on the earth; the time of the singing of birds is come, and the voice of the turtle is heard in our land;
> The fig tree putteth forth her green figs, and the vines with the tender grape give a good smell.
> Arise, my love, my fair one, and come away."

This is not nature poetry for its own sake. The Jewish poets, like the singer of "Shir Hashirim," must have man in the center of nature—only man's spirit gives it its real meaning and full value. This is in the tradition of the Jewish poets of all time.

Isaiah (X-14):

"And my hand hath found as a nest the riches of the people: and as one gathereth eggs that are left have I gathered all the earth; and there was none that moved the wing, or opened the mouth, or peeped."

How careful Isaiah is to complete his realistic picture of lowly nature—to give full meaning to his sublime message!

"—— as the light of the morning, when the sun riseth, even a morning without cloud, as the tender grass springing out of the ground through the clear shining after the rain—." This discerning and painstaking drawing King David brings not to give an etude of nature, but to give a picture of the just ruler over men, ruling in the fear of God, how he shall be— (II Samuel xxiii: 1–4).

Isaiah (lv: 12–13) declares:

"—— the mountains and the hills shall break forth before you into singing, and all the trees of the field shall clap their hands.

"Instead of the thorn shall come up the fir tree, and instead of the brier shall come up the myrtle tree."

Nature is interested in man and morally bound up with him—so wills the poet.

"The vine is dried up, and the fig tree languisheth; the pomegranate tree, the palm tree also, and all the trees of the field, are withered"—why?—"because joy is withered away from the sons of men"—says the prophet Joel (I:12).

This is much more than the "pathetic fallacy" of the Western poets.

We find it beautifully expressed in Judah Halevi's poem which describes the lull after the storm, in his poems of the sea:

"Then in a moment the waves are stilled,
Like flocks spread abroad upon the field;
And the night, when the sun hath come down the steps
Of the starry host, captained now by the moon,
Is like an Ethiopian woman in raiment of gold
And blue inset with crystals.
And the stars are confused in the heart of the sea,
Like strangers driven out of their homes;
And after their image, in their likeness, they make light
In the sea's heart, like flames of fire.
The face of the waters and the face of the heavens, the infinity of the sea,
The infinity of night, are grown pure, are made clear,
And the sea appeareth as a firmament—
Then are they two seas bound up together;
And between is my heart, a third sea
Lifting up ever anew my waves of praise." *

The heart of the poet must be in the center to give praise.

This is the Jewish approach to nature—through man.

When you stand before Chagall's purest landscape, you feel that you are not looking with your eyes at a picture of nature as it was put there by the hand of God. You are seeing through the eyes and emotions of the poet painter. You feel it is his spirit that entered into the image of nature and purified and refined it for you; and the spirit in Chagall's canvases is Jewish. You breathe here the rare mountain air of exalted human creation.

As we have noted before, the artist transformed a Witebsk city square into a dramatic tale symbolizing the eternal wanderer, the Jew in diaspora. Chagall's landscapes, "Cemetery" and the "Gates of the Cemetery," he transmuted into a spiritual reality, a super-reality. The same is true of his "Blue House."

Chagall, as we have seen, is not satisfied with the natural landscape, but must humanize it. He makes it the background of human emotions, moods and visions—sometimes folkloristic, sometimes idyllic but always Chagallian. Art for him is first of all "a state of the soul."

---

* Translated from the Hebrew by Nina Salaman.

Chagall's Illustrations

TWO MONTHS before Chagall left Paris for what he then thought would be a short visit to Berlin and Witebsk, his friend, the poet Cendrars, helped him to arrange a contract with the art dealer Malpel, in which the art dealer agreed to pay to the artist 250 francs monthly for seven small canvases.

After Chagall was gone and was cut off from Paris by the war, Malpel opened the door for himself to Chagall's studio in the "Bee Hive" and helped himself to his stock of canvases there—with the good intention of paying the artist for the canvases according to the terms of the contract. Some good neighbors followed Malpel's example and they, too, made themselves free with Chagall's canvases. On returning to Paris in 1922, Chagall found himself robbed of all his old paintings. Many of them Chagall never saw again. Some turned up years later in museums and private collections.

The art critic Gustave Coquiot, not knowing how Chagall's canvases came to the market, bought several of them. And it was at Coquiot's that Ambroise Vollard, the art dealer of the Impressionists, of Cézanne and Renoir, saw Chagall's work for the first time and became interested.

Vollard was also a publisher of art books and he wanted Chagall to do illustrations for him. He immediately got in touch with the artist who was still lingering in Berlin.

As soon as Chagall came to Paris, Vollard asked him to illustrate a Russian classic. On Chagall's suggestion Gogol's "Dead Souls" was selected.

Chagall began at once to work on a set of etchings which took him five years to do. The set was completed in 1927, and though the illustrations were printed, the book was not published. Due to various business complications Vollard kept delaying its publication and when he suddenly died in 1939 the book still did not appear.

"Les Ames Mortes" with Chagall's 96 etchings, 11 vignettes and initials for chapter headings, and an 11 page index to the plates finally appeared in Paris in 1948, published by Tériade.

It was exhibited in New York by Knoedler and Co. in March, 1949, and again by the Museum of Modern Art in November, with other etchings of Chagall in the Museum's collection.

Nicolai Gogol's "Dead Souls" appeared in 1842. Russian life had changed completely in our half of the century. The remotest village of Gogol's country had undergone a complete transformation as a result of the wars and the revolution. If Gogol's book still holds our interest, it is because Gogol, laughing hilariously and sardonically at the Russian men and women of his own day, created living human beings that are to be met everywhere and at all times, though in changed garb and in different circumstances.

His hero, Tchitchikov, the cunning, indefatigable, petty egotist, with his self-assurance and self-righteousness, vain and cowardly—who gets to the softer side of all who can benefit him, by flattery and self-abasement—he is not limited to Russia and the last century. Neither is Manilov, the ineffectual sentimentalist who wastes his days in nonsensical day-dreams, nor the miser Plyushkin, the crafty Sobakewitch, the arch liar and cheat Nosdrev. Gogol, as a great artist, had cast them all in a national Russian mold. But they are types not limited to Russia and the last century.

This fact becomes evident even to a casual reader of "Dead Souls." And this is the conclusion one must come to on examining Chagall's illustrations. He does not give a history of the manners and fashions of old Russia, but a presentation of an all too human comedy.

There is one thing, though, we must bear in mind in comparing the illustrations with the text. Gogol was a reformer who held a mirror up to his countrymen. Chagall is not. Chagall is vastly amused depicting the comportment of Tchitchikov and his friends. Their rascalities, absurdities, and sordidness do not move Chagall to indignation, but to a Rabelaisian laughter. The Russian poet Pushkin, friend of Gogol, said: "Behind his (Gogol's) laughter you feel his unseen tears." There are no tear stains apparent in Chagall's illustrations. He seems to delight in watching this "comedie humaine" as it appears to him in his imagination—and he helps his characters to their most revealing, if most ridiculous, appearance in his papers.

As a means of exposition Chagall uses exaggeration and caricature. He does not limit himself in his portraiture to the facial mask. Going to the psychological core of his heroes, viewing them from that point of vantage, he can apprehend the motives that move them to action, and he translates these motives into visual expression, bringing all the parts of the body into play—so that looking at Chagall's papers you can see the most characteristic gestures and postures of the actors in the revealing moments Chagall picks for his telling.

And he tells it with a truthfulness that comes from

To My Wife. Oil. 1934–44
Musée d'Art Moderne, Paris

Courtesy of the Artist
PLATE XXI

deep knowledge of Russian types and life and close observation of human behavior—but converted imaginatively into something beyond reality, into fictional extravagance, explosively humorous.

Though he is not a fighting moralist, Chagall's figures are as uncompromising in their characterization as Daumier's cartoons, and no less persuasive. But not being a crusader, he approaches his figures, first and last, as an artist, and his papers have a saving artistic charm which wins, for even the most vulgar of his characters, a smile and a laugh.

LA FONTAINE'S FABLES

Before Chagall had completed his set of illustrations for "Dead Souls," Vollard commissioned him to make illustrations for La Fontaine's "Fables."

Vollard wanted Chagall to make colored engravings for the "Fables." In preparation Chagall painted a hundred gouaches.

When Vollard exhibited these, it brought a storm of protests on his head. How dare he call on a foreigner, a Russian, a Jew, and a romantic to the bargain, to illustrate such a specifically French classic as the "Fables"! It was called unpatriotic and insulting to the French genius of La Fontaine.

Vollard answered his critics by saying that, to begin with, the "Fables" come from oriental first sources, from Aesop, from Arabian, Persian, Chinese and Indian story-tellers from whom La Fontaine borrowed not only the themes, but very often the whole frame and atmosphere of his fables. And, therefore, no other artist can give them such a suitable plastic translation as the artist who, because of his ancestry, has a natural sense for its oriental atmosphere. Again, the "Fables" have a universal spirit that transcends national boundaries. La Fontaine has become a world genius whose influence has spread everywhere. He inspired the poets of other countries who found in his "Fables" sympathetic motives and adapted these in their own national tongues. And so did the Russian Krilov recreate the fables in the Russian language; and his fables are as classically Russian as La Fontaine's are classically French.

Vollard added: "And when you ask me, 'Why Chagall'? I answer, 'Precisely because his esthetics seem to me to be in a certain way akin to La Fontaine's, at once heavy and subtle, real and fantastic.'"

Vollard was sure that he was right and was not frightened by the attacks of his critics.

He had a special studio built for the work and engaged the famous engraver Maurice Potin to supervise and direct a group of carefully picked workmen. They made many experiments with color reproductions—but found it impossible to do justice to Chagall's beautiful tones and Vollard was not satisfied with the results obtained. He then decided to give up the colored illustrations and commissioned Chagall to prepare plates for black and white engravings.

Even now the project did not proceed smoothly. Vollard was not easily satisfied. He changed his engravers three times, destroyed one complete printing together with the plates and set Chagall to do the plates over.

With the new plates the work was finally accomplished in 1931, after four years of trials. The final results were rewarding for all the efforts.

And yet this book, too, La Fontaine's "Fables," was, for various reasons, unpublished—and to this day only a few of the papers have been shown to the public.

Chagall had an old familiarity with the "Fables" through Krilov. Krilov's fables are as popular in Russia as La Fontaine's in France. And Chagall possesses that imagination that can easily bring down the wall that separates man from beast and bird. He entered with La Fontaine, as with Krilov, the forest, field and barnyard and met the fox and the wolf, the sheep and the ass, as a neighbor and kinsman, with kindness and understanding. Animals and birds have found inhabitance in Chagall's canvases before. They are part of his population, the domestic animals are. And I want to say that Chagall did not come to the animals to steal from them the homilies of the fabulist. Again, not as a moralist, but as an artist did he enter their world; and when he came, he found an abundance of forms and a rich living world for picture-making.

La Fontaine remarks, not without pride: "With a new language I made the wolf speak and the sheep answer; and I did even more, the trees and the plants became through me creatures that talk. And who would not call that enchantment?"

One would say that it was this enchantment that was truly the important thing to the poet La Fontaine, the magic of imaginative creation. And it is this enchantment that I find in Chagall's "Fables," sparkling with pictorial beauty.

Once again Vollard came to Chagall with a commission—this time to make illustrations for the Bible for a Vollard edition. More about these later.

Illustrations of Jewish Books

BESIDES the large series for Vollard, Chagall had made illustrations for many books.

I want to examine a few of the illustrations that he made for Jewish books. I have some at hand.

Chagall's illustrations in these books may easily be divided into two categories: pictures of Jewish folk ways, where tradition had established definite forms; and pictures of free imaginative creation, of a generally human or Biblical content.

Chagall shows a deep love for the "old-fashioned" Jew and his life. He knows well his ways and customs, his walk and talk, his grimacing and gesticulating. He knows well the Jewish face with all its expressiveness. He can fix on his paper a spiritual countenance with a few wispy scrawls; or sketch a devotional mood by the run of a scanty few strokes and dots. He has made figures no bigger than a "peanut"—how big can the head of such a figure be? And yet one can tell at a glance that it is a Jewish head with a Jewish expression. Chagall knows how with a twist of the earlock, a curl in the beard, and a crimple in the man's hat to give you a type recognizable at once. With sparingly few touches of his knowing pencil he can light up a face with the inner radiance of the wisdom of an ancient Talmudic sage.

It gives me unending delight to study the papers where Chagall had displayed his brilliant short-hand improvisations of Jewish traditional types. As I look at his wise dots and dashes, I do not wonder that the Rabbis find so much to elucidate in a single letter or dot in the holy Scriptures . . .

Here is Chagall's illustration to Liesin's poem "A Funeral." * On a page of the usual book format you will find thirty-five human figures besides a group of cottages with their chimneys and window shutters, a horse and wagon that carry the dead man, and the driver with his whip—and enough space for a wide street with its sky, not forgetting a tree on the side. And you have enough clarity within the picture to see the mise en scène of a Jewish funeral, with its lamen-

tations and expostulations, hair-tearing and chest-beating, dragging mourners and straggling kinsmen, busy alms-collectors with their "Charity saves from death" collection-boxes. All are there, the old Jew hopping on his wooden leg, too. Faces and gestures indicated by a few dots and scanty scrawls, but you know the Jewish types, men and women.

And here now look (in Vol. I of the same edition) at the picture of a synagogue full of Jewish scholars who remained after the evening prayer to study. Again on the page of a book Chagall draws an interior of a synagogue with the holy shrine ornamented with two lions, the cantor's desk, a chandelier, tables with lamps and candles, and a score of Jews sitting about with their books—and there is enough space for two windows with a peep of the landscape outside and the crescent moon, enough room for air and spaciousness, and enough for free margins to frame in the picture. Yet you can clearly distinguish the types of scholars and their habits of study. Here is one who isolates himself, standing alone by the window—a recluse. Here is a man ecstatic with a mystic vision. Here is a student in a heated discussion with his fellows at the table, arguing with his hands over an obscure passage. Here is a man proving to an appreciative neighbor his talent of speculative acumen. Here is one with a flaming face of enthusiasm, kindled by the sudden flashes of "light" upon his mind, which opened to him a pass to the treasury of sacred mysteries locked in the small Cabalistic volume in his hands.

A movement of the hand, the position of the head, the inclination of the body, characteristically tell the story where you can hardly see the face.

Look at the "Sabbath Jew" (in Bella Chagall's "Burning Candles"). You see a dignified, venerable, well-to-do Jew. How did Chagall draw this figure? He made a circle—but mark the effect of the few curlicued strokes that make the beard. Not only does the beard complete the head, but it also defines and accomplishes the drawing of the figure. Cut off the beard and you have left only a circular line with no indication of a human figure. And by the direction of the beard you

* Vol. III of Liesin's Collected Poems, published by the "Forward Association," New York, 1938.

get the inclination of the head and of the whole body; and you know that the Jew sits comfortably, in dignified repose, leaning on the table that you don't see . . .

How many times have Jewish artists "sinned" with the Jewish beard—stuck it on everywhere, and often made it carry the whole Jewishness of the Jew? This "beard" of Chagall redeems all the beards of their uselessness. Here it is needed not only to show the Jew, but plastically in the drawing; without it there would be no face and no body.

Again, a few tiny strokes of the pencil placed with consummate knowledge not only suggest the eyes, nose and mouth of the man, but they also suggest that the face that they make up belongs to a god-fearing man, "a son of the Torah"—and complete the impression of a personable and dignified figure of a Jew.

Look now at "Blessing the Sabbath Candles" (in Bella's book).

Mother and young daughter are standing in front of their lit candles, their faces covered by their hands, saying the prescribed prayers to welcome the Sabbath. (The mother would say her blessing slowly and the child would repeat the words after her).

You see at once that the young girl is the daughter, not only by the suggested story, but plastically—her figure is a chip of her mother's which it so markedly resembles. There is an intrinsic relationship between the two, pictorially as well as psychologically. And watch the play of white and black patches in their dresses—it suggests the flickering of the burning candles.

Notice the third candlestick. It is smaller and of a different design; it is the child's; you know it, though it stands on the other side. It gives a moment of contrast. The artist purposely moved it to the other side to have place to display the full face of the girl, but also for better balance. However, the eye knows at once where it belongs and goes from the candlestick to the child and back, creating a dramatic moment.

And what gives you the notion that the child keeps her eyes closed tightly under the cover of her hands? You feel that to her the ceremony of blessing the candles is very important, and her whole soul is in it; the mother takes it more perfunctorily. Thus the artist succeeds in telling you the inner story—as well as making a beautiful picture of Jewish home life.

Now follow for a moment the figure of the Shames

(the beadle) carrying the Lulov and Esrog (the ceremonial palm branch and citron).

All you see here is a hand, a pair of walking feet, and the flying line of his back—the parts that function; the rest of the body is not needed here. He is rushing, the back line indicates that—and you know that he must visit many houses to let the women and children who stayed home hold his Lulov and Esrog and say the blessing after him.

The artist did not forget to show you the new hat that the Shames bought for the holiday, bought on the credit of his prospective income from his Lulov and Esrog service; his hat is still stiff with newness and its crown is as yet uncrumpled . . .

And look at his whiskers and earlocks—the artist made them look like the twigs of the myrtle that adorn the Lulov . . .

And here is another important functionary, particularly for the Purim Festival, the "Scroll Reader." Watch him read the Scroll of Esther; look at his throat and mouth. One would swear he is the "champion" scroll reader of the world. Chagall built him so that the terrible Haman, the son of Hammedatha the Agagite, and his ten horrible sons would not get stuck in his throat but come rolling out successfully, with the proper intonation according to the prescribed ancient chant—especially that he must do it in a hurry, you know, because he must bring his scroll reading to many women busy at home. Here now, watching him, you can almost see the words gurgling through his throat carried on the waves of his sing-song and tumbling out over his lips safely. You can see the artist standing and watching him with his amused smile.

And here is one, a lesser dignitary of the Purim Festival, but no less indispensable—the "Purim Gift Messenger." A typical Chagallian figure, a bird-like creature with the strange name Pinya. "Can you whistle, Pinya?"—Bashke, the little girl of the story asks him.

You don't see Pinya the whole year round. On Purim-day he suddenly appears, has come to do his mission, to carry your Purim gifts on your plate, covered with your especially embroidered Purim kerchief, to all your kinsmen and friends. And safe they are in his hands, no matter how tempting a cookie, tart or marmalade may be—he will carry them gently and deliver them with proper respect, announcing the name of the sender ceremoniously—you don't have to teach him that—and he will bring back the exchange, untouched by him, you may rest assured. Just look at him, it's Pinya! You know him at first glance.

How well Chagall knows his Pinyas and how little he has to do to make them appear alive on the paper.

Turn now to the "Matzoth Carrier." He has grown in dignity the last few weeks before Passover. He is now the most important community functionary. Now he is Reb Yankel! He has grown taller, towering over the snow-covered huts as he passes them by with the crates of freshly baked matzoth on his back. He plods heavily, bent under the pack on his back—but he seems to carry a heavier burden on his mind: the pack of worries of all the poor of the town who have no wherewithal to bring in the expensive holiday into their destitute homes, and he must by-pass their doors.

How lovingly Chagall recorded all the familiar traditional Jewish types—as if forewarned of their disappearance together with their communities; he made memorial tablets of them—you can hardly call them monuments, these papers of Chagall; but they will be the only ones to carry to posterity the memory of these once very familiar figures. Chagall, with the touch of his art, gave them immortality.

In the "Seder," Chagall brings the whole family together, around the festive table. There are also a few guests, invited because they are strangers in town and have no Seder of their own—two of them are Jewish soldiers, (stationed near the town with leave for the holiday; they had waited in the synagogue to be invited to a Seder), and two are poor men. They all follow the father in the rites and ceremonies, but each with his personal life about him. The artist individualizes his figures physically and psychologically.

Of great interest is Chagall's illustration to Liesin's poem, "Rejoicing of the Drawing of Water." It was a very gay and joyous occasion in the days of the Temple—now its memory is celebrated by some of the more devout Jews with singing and dancing in the synagogue.

In the drawing, following the suggestion of the poem, there is a bottle of liquor standing on a chair in the middle of the room. The celebrants must have tasted some, or got drunk by looking at it; they are now merry and are dancing, presumably a choral dance—but each one is performing the dance in his own inimitable manner; all together, but each for himself.

In the poem they sing and dance rapturously repeating the verses:

"He will hide us in the shadow of His hand,
Under the wings of His Glory."

Chagall made a wonderful illustration for it. There is a great deal of truth and beauty in the drawing.

The old religious Jew had learned to control his gaiety and cannot abandon himself even when under the effect of intoxicating drink. His drunkenness is an exultation of the spirit, and his orgy is an ecstasy. And Chagall found the means to transmit this inner transport through outer movement—a movement which on the paper can only be a pose. What is even more marvelous, Chagall uses the momentary pose to display each individual type of the revelers. By a few broken contouring lines he describes them with psychological conviction. Many Jewish artists remember photographically; Chagall knows his Jews inside out. With the crooked line of the back, the tilt of the hat, the angle of the beard, a few dots for the fact, he gives you a Jew in a merry-making mood, and you can tell the type. The movement of a hand, a foot, the lift of a shoulder, the bend of a knee, the position of a shoe—and you have the dancing, and the character of the performer, too.

Chagall has done the same with his dancing Jews in his illustration to "Simchath Torah" (The Rejoicing at the Law) in Bella's book, and again a "Wedding" (in Feffer's "Homeland").

Fully preoccupied as Chagall is with his individual figures and the details of his exposition, he never forgets to create a unified effect of the whole page. As he unites in expressive relationship the dots and lines in the design of the single figure, so he composes all figures into one design in the space of the page. Chagall's illustrations are therefore true decorations for the pages and please the eye as well as the mind.

Chagall's graphic art in the Jewish books is a Jewish graphic, not only because of the subjects it describes, but because he loads his lines with Jewish meaning and character, with Jewish emotion and rhythm.

Around Her. Oil. 1945
Musée d'Art Moderne, Paris

Courtesy of the Artist

PLATE XXII

Chagall's Illustrations to the Bible

WHEN Vollard commissioned Chagall to make illustrations for a Vollard edition of the Bible, Chagall began to prepare himself by visiting Palestine, Egypt, and Syria. This was in 1931.

Coming back he prepared about twenty studies and began to work on his plates.

But he was not satisfied. In 1932 he went to Holland to get a closer knowledge of Rembrandt and his Biblical oils, etchings, and drawings. And in 1934 he went to Spain to study El Greco's religious paintings.

In 1935 Chagall visited Poland to get a fresh contact with the Jewish "old fashioned" fathers and grandfathers—to reawaken in himself their spirit which he felt he needed in his work on the Bible. He was not permitted to visit his Witebsk.

In 1937 he visited Italy to study the Italian primitives and their religious art.

He was trying to get the spirit of those artists who were not corrupted as the moderns by the mechanical civilization of our time.

Later he said:

"I felt, and even saw, that there is no difference between our fathers and grandfathers and, for instance, the ancient Egyptian, Assyrian, and other sculptures in the museums of Alexandria and Athens—the former and the latter have the static and dynamic expression of humanity, of naturalness, untouched by the mechanical spirit, as in our own transitional time."

His visit to Palestine left a lasting influence on him. The Palestinian landscape, its sun and air stimulated his imagination and emotions and he felt more at home with the Biblical people.

"The air of the land of Israel makes one wise"— we have an old tradition.

"In the East I unexpectedly found the Bible and a part of my very being"—he said.

During his travels his work progressed slowly but with great artistic success. He enlarged and refined his technical means and accomplished a great mastery in his new etchings.

In July 1939, when Vollard died suddenly, Chagall had made one hundred and five etching and dry point plates with Biblical subjects.

The artist begins in that first process of receiving impressions, collecting them, and preserving them in memory as material to be useful to him in his future work—a process that is principally unconscious. But his art begins to manifest itself when his imagination goes to the store-room of his memory for raw materials and begins to assort and select them, throwing off the impurities and refining the remains until what is left is the very finest matter for his art.

His imagination also brings to the artist a ready plan for organizing his material, a plan that the imagination found in the artist's memory together with his material—for the plastic artist this plan is the wrapper of spatial form in which the material first entered into his memory and which kept it there in preservation in its entirety—a plan that the artist may now change, cutting out parts, or adding parts here and there; but essentially the plan will retain its original pattern of design.

Here you have an artistic imagination that principally depends on a faithful eye and good memory.

This sort of imagination is of a lesser rank and of a lower category than the imagination that has the power of intuitive vision, of spontaneous image formation.

Somewhere, some time, at the very beginning of its conception, perhaps, and even later, this nobler imagination, too, in the deep unconscious darkness of its womb, nourishes its embryo from the rich sources of memory. But when its image is born, it is so complete in all its organic parts, that it makes you believe in a virginal birth, born out of nothing material, by the fiat of a mysterious power—intuitive creation.

In his pictures of Jewish genre Chagall shows that he has great powers of observation and an "iron" memory. He saw truly and deeply and remembers well what he saw. And though Chagall here depends on his memory—and in pictures of traditional folk-ways this is a very valuable, indispensable qualification—he does not satisfy himself by merely writing down his memories. He brings to his picture his wisdom, his judgment, and above all, his great craftsmanship. He gives it a living breath, a soul, a Jewish soul.

"MOSES"

But only when you come to his creations of the second category, to his works of art conceived by inspiration, born of his intuitive imagination, do you come to an artist of kingly rank.

Work of this category, too, can be found among Chagall's illustrations: such are his etchings of Biblical subjects and others, where he did not have to follow traditional forms.

One can see evidence of Chagall's inspired creativeness in the fact that he often creates a few different figures of the same Biblical personality. He has more than one Moses, one unlike the other, to take the first example.

Looking at it superficially it may appear as a weakness of the artist, an inconsistency, proof that to the artist Moses is not a real man, not a historically determined individual, but an invention of a fickle imagination.

You must remember, however, that Chagall is not writing history. Instead of hardening one image into a cliché and duplicating it when needed, imitating himself, Chagall creates a new figure as the vision comes to him; a new personality according to the need of the occasion, stimulated by the new inspiration to true creativeness.

Now look at his "Moses" of "Then Sang Moses" (Liesin's Vol. III). What a radiant poetic conception! Chagall is not a faithful follower of the text. Chagall's type here is not the Moses who, in his anger, killed an Egyptian, brought ten plagues on Pharaoh, and with stubborn will, with Jewish obstinacy, overpowered the Egyptian potentate, and by deception freed his six hundred thousand slaves and made them into an eternal people. Chagall did not give us here the Moses of "Then Sang Moses" for whom the Lord is man of war, whose right hand is glorious with power, for with His right hand He dashed to pieces the enemy.

The figure that Chagall has given here is a tender, radiant man, a poet, a sweet singer. Perhaps he is one of the masters of the Psalms, who instead of a sword

holds in his right hand a Shminith (an instrument with eight strings), one of the music masters that sings a psalm with the accompaniment of strings. It may be the singer-king himself (Chagall made him a crown and a brocaded royal or priestly mantle), David, singing his "Psalm, Song for the Sabbath Day."

"It is a good thing to give thanks unto the Lord,
And to sing praises unto Thy name, O, Most high;
To declare Thy loving kindness in the morning,
And Thy faithfulness in the seasons of the night,
With an instrument of ten strings and the psaltery;
With a solemn sound upon the harp.
For Thou, Lord, hast made me glad through Thy work,
I will exult in the work of Thy hands.
How great are Thy works, O Lord!"

You can see the Jewish pure piety, the restrained rapture in the lifted noble head. And it looks as if the whole body sings the psalm. A Sabbath grace and spiritual radiance falls over the whole figure.

See how the crown helps in the structure of the head and adds to the dignity of the figure, not only to its decoration. Also the loose cloak helps to give softness and stateliness to the figure—a convincingly Jewish figure. And whoever it may not be—you have here the work of a noble faculty; a product of a highly poetic imagination—art of the finest quality. And altogether it is only a lightly scrawled sketch.

Here we have Jewish art, a Jewish plastic—even if you don't accept the figure as a "Moses," or a "David." Call it by any other name, gentile or pagan—it still remains a Jewish image.

In a second place Chagall had made only the face of a "Moses"—and there you have a face of a man of God; a face that beams not with sunlight, not with song, but with wisdom, with divine law. Looking at the face, you say to yourself, Yes, God spoke mouth to mouth with this man and left upon his lips a sublime message.

This Chagall accomplished with a few scrawls, leaving it as a scanty notation only, not more than a suggestive idea, not fully outlined. And it is in this stopping short, in not attempting a fuller realization, that one can see the integrity of Chagall's artistry. The image initially suggested can only be seen in a flash, not long enough to rest your eyes upon it for a full view—the power to behold God is not given to man's eyes. The old masters represented God as a man, and rightly so. Man cannot make a being higher than himself—at the peril of his art.

Had Chagall followed the initial plan and built up the figure in full, it would have forced him into grand eloquence and bombast—which as a true artist he always avoids.

Chagall followed his true artistic instinct, not only the wisdom of the old masters, and he made the heroes of his Bible as human as his Witebsk ancestors—to his glory.

But sometimes Chagall treats legend as legend. And thus he made a third "Moses" who comes down from heaven with the Tablets of the Law in his hands and rayhorns on his head—for a Jewish family on the Pentecost Festival (the season of the giving of the Torah).

He has another "Moses," the magician, who turns his staff into a snake. (It was Aaron who turned the trick—according to the Bible). Here you see sheer virtuosity. Chagall's imagination will give him anything he asks of it.

He has several other figures of Moses. Not all the plates were published.

"ABRAHAM"

Of father Abraham, too, Chagall made several representations, each differently conceived. And again you can say that Chagall is not an historian.

Chagall told me an anecdote apropos of that and I think it worth retelling, to prove some points.

When the artist was in Tel Aviv, at the time he went to Palestine for his Biblical studies, he paid a visit to the famous Hebrew poet, Bialik. He took a number of his sketches to show to the poet with the hope of getting some inspiring comment.

Who, if not Bialik, the great master of his own art, who made the heritage of the creative Jewish spirits of all times his own nourishment and inspiration; who, if not the national Hebrew poet, Bialik, would appreciate another Jewish poet, though his medium of expression is different—especially in creative work inspired by the Bible?

After examining Chagall's papers, Bialik found a fault in Chagall's interpretation of the Bible: the cloak which Chagall had "Abraham" wear, is one with sleeves—while the Hebrews of Abraham's times wore cloaks without sleeves, similar to the abaye still worn by the Arabs of today.

As if Chagall had gone to Bialik for a tailor's diploma.

The artist left Bialik with shame in his heart for the great poet who could not rise above historical literalism and got entangled in Abraham's sleeves.

Bialik's understanding of plastic art was not more developed than Gorky's. (See page 47.)

It would have helped little to point out to Bialik that the greatest painters disregarded factual history.

You might as well reject Raphael's Madonnas because he used Italian girls for models; or Titian's Venuses, because he placed them in the surroundings and atmosphere of Venice.

The greatest offender against history, as is well known, was Rembrandt, though he was the first one to take a Jewish model for the Christ. And, alas, in his magnificent painting "Abraham's Sacrifice," his "Abraham" wears a cloak with sleeves.

It is rather anomalous for Bialik to look for veracity in an illustration of the mythical part of the Bible. I do not know how orthodox Bialik was in his piety—but I imagine that he did not believe all the legends of the Bible to be historically authentic: did he for that reason reject any of them?

At the subsequent banquet given in Tel Aviv to honor Chagall, Bialik was chairman and warmly expressed his esteem for the great Jewish artist.

Bialik also invited Chagall to collaborate with him on a book.

If I have brought up the story of Bialik's criticism of Chagall's neglect of historical truth, I did it not to disparage Bialik's greatness as a poet, nor is it merely for the sake of gossiping. I mention it because it is typical of the censure I have heard many times of Chagall's "unfaithfulness to history"—mostly coming from literary people.

The artist today, particularly the modernist, cannot create the illusion that the works of his hands are documents that came down to him from the distant centuries—with sleeves or without. At best he can only demonstrate his scientific research—and who wants that?

The painter who went to Palestine to copy the workshop and tools of the still primitive Arab carpenter, with the aim of giving a more faithful representa-

Self Portrait with a Clock. Oil. 1947

Courtesy of the Artist

PLATE XXIII

tion of the life of the Holy Family, did in no way enhance the spiritual effectiveness of his canvas, nor the greatness of his interpretation of the story. The primitive painters who, to show their love and honor of the great Lady, dressed her in gold embroidered robes, with a crown of jewels, were more effective because they were more truthful; they communicated not a science but a sincere religious emotion.

Rembrandt's painting would not have gained in any quality as a great work of art if he had painted Abraham in a cloak without sleeves.

No one forgets, or wants to forget, in standing before a piece of art that it is fiction, invention—that it is the spirit of the artist communicating itself to you through his work, and not the ghost of the historic or allegoric figure, that came to live on the canvas, or in the statue. That blessed delusion was only vouchsafed to the fetish worshipers.

As much as the prophets of Israel are a living influence today they are our contemporaries. Their appeal is of today, not of the past. We honor in them those values that are of all time—that is, what has value also for us, today. And is it not that which the poets and painters want to convey when they invoke by their art the spirits of the prophets?

That is what Chagall attempted to do in his illustrations. The artist did not imagine himself and us living in the wondrous time of long ago—but that the wondrous long ago is still enduring, is still here for him and his Witebsk folks of today.

However, above all we must have in mind that Chagall is a great artist who conceives his fantasies in plastic terms, in pictures. And the picture comes first. Approach him through his pictures and you will not miss Chagall, and he will not fail you.

And now look at his beautiful etching, "Abraham and the Three Angels."

At first glance you will see that the picture is of the angels, and not as much of the angels as of their shining wings.

You remember the story as told in Genesis: Abraham was ninety-nine years old when the angels came to announce to him that his wife, Sarah, would bear him a son.

The artist made his "Abraham" and "Sarah" thin, fragile, wasted, and pathetically old—though not without a winning old-age charm, especially the homely grandma "Sarah," the mother of all grandmothers.

The artist made them so, first of all, in contrast to the eternally young and vigorous angels. Secondly, to embody the miracle of the annunciation that out of the loins of this frail, aged couple will come forth a son, a nation, and many nations. Grandma Sarah did not believe it possible.

In the etching the old people stand aside, in shadow. The three angels that were invited to the table for food and drink, occupy the center of the picture. And not so much the angels as their wings which spread a softly-white light against a dark background.

The wings with their light, these are the angels. Their heads and faces are of no great interest. You do not see their figures; they sit with their backs to the spectator, and you see their wings. Though the angels sit at rest, partaking of the food, their wings did not fully close on their bodies, as you would see on resting birds. The angels' wings are still stirred up with the energy that moved them in flight, the momentum has not completely subsided. As they sit in the open air, under the sky, it may be the tease of the air and the call of the sky that do not let them rest calmly. You have a feeling, while you look, as though the wings will fly open and rise with power and lift the bodies up with them.

The artist did not plainly show the feathery nature of the wings, but suggested it through their soft, shining texture.

Here is a new reality, not experienced before, appealing to your eye with its convincing realization. You have here a beauty of surface unequaled. And the whole picture is of an exquisite beauty, archaic, idyllic, strange and familiar, as a chapter of Genesis.

In a second etching of the series, "Abraham and the Angels Approaching Sodom," "Abraham" is the picture.

Chagall shows a poetic figure of a saintly Rabbi, transparently pure and gentle, full of kindness and sadness, sorrowing over the sinful city and its people that God wants to destroy.

This is a rare and noble figure; you can hardly find its equal in the whole world of art—outside of Rembrandt's etchings—a figure possessing a spiritual eminence, and yet simple in its humanity; compassionate and sorrowful, but refined, not ostentatious before the Lord.

Only a great Jewish artist could create such a saintly Jewish man, the primal ancestor of the "merciful sons of the merciful" (attribute of the Jewish people).

The Morning of the World. Oil. 1948
Courtesy of the Artist

PLATE XXIV

This is surely a Jewish contribution to the gallery of great types of men.

And here, again, is another image of Abraham, in the etching "Abraham's Sacrifice."

Here, if you wish, you have further evidence that Chagall is inconsistent: the "Abraham" of the paper where the angels come to announce the birth of a son to him, is much older than the man who is now bringing the same son as a sacrifice . . .

But the artist is justified in following his inspiration and doing for each picture what he deems important, according to its inner needs, its own life.

There are two compositions of the same subject—one is a drawing and one an etching.

In the drawing the dramatic story is scantily sketched. But before you have seen the etching you think the drawing sufficient. The few lines and scrawls are so masterly chosen and placed, and so uncompromisingly do they delineate the essential features, that you can grasp at once the type of man chosen for the representation of this story—Abraham, God's sublime fanatic, the zealot who will not step aside from his path of duty. His God told him to—and he is all prepared, knife in hand, to slaughter his beloved son, child of his old age, his heir—and you see that he will do it.

The head is in profile, and you see only the outline that marks in passing the mouth, nose and forehead; a few dots for the eye—but you have a portrait of this type of a man.

However, only when you do see the etching can you get the full maturity of Chagall's conception and realization of the portrait of the father of a stubborn people . . . His face in the etching is full of the flame and exultation of the God-chosen, God-intoxicated idealist who comes to proclaim a new religion. For him his calling is more important than his life or the life of his beloved.

The angel of the drawing pleases me more than the one of the etching. In the drawing, before he had time to bring his feet in line with his head, he had already stopped Abraham's hand with the knife and is pointing to the ram. His wings are spread out, but the onrushing movement of the angel is seen not in his wings, but in his legs.

In the etching the angel takes up less space and gets less attention—but the composition of the etching must be different than that of the drawing. It only proves that Chagall has the attendance of many angels, and the one whom he calls is the one who comes.

"YOUNG JOSEPH"

A creation of loveliness and charm is "Young Joseph." It is Joseph the dreamer before his father distinguished him by making for him a coat of many colors and set him off to dream of glory, power and supremacy. Chagall's "Joseph" is still wearing a goatskin coat and is a shepherd lad like his brothers. This Joseph did not yet dream that his sheaf stood upright in the field and the sheaves of his brothers made obeisance to his sheaf. He did not see himself in the sky with the sun and moon and eleven stars bowing to him. This young fellow did not know as yet the deadly poison of brothers' envy and hate, of duplicity and betrayal. He was still innocent and unaware of the seductiveness of a passionate Potiphara, and even the Princess Asenath was a young dream of the night that did not disturb his sleep.

But looking at the broad-shouldered youth with his majestic head lifted high, you can foresee his ambitions and temptations and you know he will fulfill his dreams.

Meanwhile he still is crowned with purity and golden innocence as the sheaf of wheat in the sun, and he looks at the world with his round, trustful wide-open eyes, full of hunger and wonder. And the world is young with him, green and golden, full of good tastes and smells. The good God creates it for him every morning, for him and for his goat that is in love with him and follows him around. And whatever his eyes behold is his, his father's possession. And what he wants he will get, as it is promised to him in his dreams.

The "Young Joseph" is Joseph the poet, the visionary who keeps the world fresh and young, forever new.

Looking at the "Young Joseph" as Chagall made him, you can tell that his youthful dreams and visions will never leave him, even in his kingly days. And often, alone on his couch, the royal robes removed, he will remember the young Joseph, the shepherd in his goatskin cloak, followed around by his beloved goat— for a while he will dream again those young innocent joys, his life as clean and as golden as the sheaf of wheat in the field—and wake up and wonder: was it all worth while?

This is the "Young Joseph" of Chagall's etching.

"THE PROPHETESS DEBORAH"

Only at the beginning of the Jewish national life were there women prophetesses in Israel—Miriam and Deborah.

In the epochs of high cultural attainments there was not one woman in place of leadership, neither in learning nor in wisdom nor in prophecy.

In primitive times when greatness depended purely on intuition, on the gift of nature, then there was the possibility of a woman judge and prophetess in Israel.

And that is how Chagall imagined his "The Prophetess Deborah."

She is "a mother in Israel"—a mother also of prophecy and poetry.

The song of victory that is connected with her name is the most magnificent dramatic poem we possess in the Jewish folks' rich treasury. Its poetic dynamics is that of an explosive force of nature, as the leaping of a stream down the mountain crags—and yet the song shows the experienced hand of a master maker of songs.

In Chagall's etching "Deborah" sits on the ground under a spreading fig tree. The tree and "Deborah" are the product of the same nature; both are nourished by the same soil and the dew from heaven—the tree with its fat figs and "Deborah" with her verses. Chagall made them so.

He did not give "Deborah" the refined and spiritual air that he gives his intellectual Jewish men. She does not have any physical or spiritual beauty. There is not a touch of the heroic in her appearance, a woman of the people, of the common people—but a prophetess.

Full of humor and Chagallian charm is the man, "Deborah's" companion in the etching. Is it Lapidoth, her husband? Far too unheroic for Barak whom Deborah picked for her field marshal. As the husband of a prophetess there could be no better choice than this quizzical fellow.

In contrast to Chagall's treatment of the prophetess, I am thinking of Michaelangelo's Sibyls in the Sistine Chapel. No possible point of comparison. And yet Chagall seems to be right in his own way of interpretation, his own (Witebsk) vision, and his own realization.

"DAVID"

Among Chagall's most important and finest Biblical creations, "David with the Head of Goliath" stands out preeminently.

It is interesting to compare Chagall's "David" with the "Davids" of other great artists.

The two Renaissance sculptors, Donatello and Verracchio, chose to represent David standing victor over the severed head of the Philistine.

David was but a youth when he brought down the giant. Both, King Saul and Goliath, taunted David with his youthfulness.

Donatello's "David" is young, gentle, and almost girlish. Not at all visible in him is the young strength that "smote the lion and delivered the sheep out of his mouth"—as David boasted before the King. Looking at Donatello's "David" you can not be convinced that he felled the gigantic man of war with his sling—except by the help of God . . . And it appears that he is not pleased with the bloody deed: he is sad and thoughtful. No joy of victory for him.

Perhaps Donatello had in mind David the musician and sweet singer. No intimation in the statue of David the king and warrior, of the man of bloody hands and hot passions.

Verracchio's "David" is even younger, a mere lad, though manly. He seems to have the will and energy to do great deeds. He smiles, with his sword in hand, over the head of the slain enemy—but it is a smile of youthful vanity rather than a joyful hot-blooded excitement after a fight. Also in Verracchio's statue there is no indication of the richly endowed sanguine nature of the Biblical David.

Michaelangelo's giant marble statue of David represents the hero in preparation for combat. The sculptor, as it is well known, modeled with consummate knowledge and mastery the anatomy of the nude male figure of a young athlete, making the head too heavy and the limbs too long for the still unmatured torso—which is the natural state of a growing young man before reaching full physical development.

The tense dramatic moment before the fight is fully expressed in the pose of the young man. The figure is animated with the quickened emotions and thoughts of the coming encounter. The face and brow are filled with restrained energy, forethought, and determination. His hands are loaded with force, controlled for the moment, but ready to explode in action. The body rests on the right foot, with the left extended forward. The whole body is poised before a change which your eye begins to anticipate, foreseeing its direction and vehemence when he will suddenly leap to the aim.

Michaelangelo is thus completely preoccupied with the psychological animation of his marble. All parts of its anatomy are quickened in unison with the same impulse that runs from the will and the emotions, translated into suspended action, controlled but enlivening the stone.

The sculptor did not essay here to give a character portrait of David as he did and superbly succeeded with the prophets.

In his painting "David and Goliath" on the Sistine ceiling Michaelangelo is again interested in dramatic action, only more violent than is permitted in the medium of stone. Here again is suspense before the climax. "David" stands astride the fallen "Goliath" who lifts his head and tries to rise. But "David" has seized the giant's head by the hair and raised the sword to strike.

Again it is action and not portraiture that is the motif here.

(Rembrandt has images of "David"—but in different episodes, except one small plate of the combat.)

Chagall like Donatello and Verracchio picked the moment after the decapitation. His "David" stands holding the giant's bloody head by the hair.

Chagall's hero is much older than the David of this episode in the story of the Bible. But this permits the artist to indicate in the maturer man his rich nature as we know him from his later exploits.

Chagall gives him a long body and limbs—though you don't see him in full length. His handsome manly head stands proud and self-assured, high over his shoulders. He smiles—and his smile is hot with the sensuality of the bloody deed. He gets a physical pleasure in spilling blood. The cutting off of the head was a passionate act with him. He is the David that goes out with his men at night and brings back the foreskins of two hundred dead Philistines instead of the hundred that King Saul asked of him for giving him Michal.

He is the David whose hands will be steeped in blood from his constant warring; and God will refuse to let him build the Temple because of it.

It is the David, the sensual and handsome man, whom the women love, whom the women of the people will come out to meet, "singing and dancing with tabrets, with joy, and with instruments of music."

And he can at once win the heart of the King's son and daughter, and they will be faithful to him against their King and father.

He is the David, the King David, who cries and tears his clothes in an hour of affliction before the eyes of the whole people, and goes jumping and dancing with the common folks before the Shrine—until the well-bred Michal, his wife, will upbraid him and scold him for lowering his Kingly dignity.

He is the sanguine, hot, lustful man who, when he sees a beautiful woman bathing, will not refuse himself and must possess her and make her pregnant—and to cover up his deed, will cause her husband to be killed in battle. And he will be truly repentant and bend his heart before the prophet who comes to reproach him for his wantonness.

You can also see in Chagall's "David" the musician and psalmist, whom his lyre wakes at midnight and he gets up to improvise a psalm and sing it accompanying himself on the strings.

This "David" of Chagall's can be both, the warrior and the "sweet singer of Israel."

I do not know whether Chagall had thought of these and other traits of the Biblical David when he worked on the etching. But look at it carefully and you will agree that this is the only type of man who would possess all the possibilities of developing the character of the sanguine, many sided Biblical hero. No one of the greatest artists have done any better.

He has made a number of other representations of David, still unpublished.

"ELIJAH"

An etching as full of grace as a beehive with honey is Chagall's "Elijah Meets the Widow who is Gathering Sticks." According to the stories of the Bible, Elijah was a fierce, angry and fiery man of the desert. And, symbolically enough, he was taken up to heaven alive in a chariot of fire.

But in the legends of the Jewish people Elijah appears as a kind, benevolent, dear old man. No other prophet was reborn in the tales of the Jewish grandmothers and mothers. No other prophet is talked of in their folklore with so much love and affection as Elijah. No other prophet came back to earth to mingle with the people. Elijah came back and comes back any time—not to prophesy or to chastise with his fiery tongue, but to participate in the festivals and joyous events of the common people. He is the harbinger of good news; and one who is deserving will get his help and succor in need or in sickness.

He had been assigned to come with the Messiah, son of David. And when the sages could not find a solution to a problem of Jewish law, or an answer to a question, they said it must wait for the Tishbite.

It is Elijah who comes to drink the cup of wine set aside for him at the Passover Seder table. And a chair is set in his name at the rite of circumcision.

In their prayers at the departure of the holy Sabbath, the Jewish grandmother and mother ask God: "Send us Elijah the prophet into our house." And grandfather and father after their consecration of the cup of wine, in the ceremony of ushering out the holy Sabbath, sing an ode to Elijah, extolling his attributes, his qualities, and his acts—ending in: "Blessed is he who sees his face in a dream; blessed is he who gives him the greeting of peace and he answers him with the greeting of peace."

In the old Jewish home which Chagall knew as a child, Elijah was a familiar holy man, whose name was often invoked.

And Chagall pictures him as a familiar lovely old man, tall and airy, with soft kind hands. His whole being is light. He seems not to walk but is being carried by an inner force—and he carries with him a spiritual grace.

He is the holy old man whom a sick Jewish child would meet with beaming eyes and feel at once the flush of returning health.

The whole etching conveys a Biblical atmosphere of simplicity and elevation of spirit. You are brought into the land of legend and of distant ages. And yet you feel that you have known this old man, a remembered figure in your own experience; was it in dream or in reality? But you know that you are in the presence of a holy man.

Here you have an original art creation of a refined and rare spirit.

You see again that Chagall is not only the light-hearted singer of love and love's sorrows, of innocent fantasies and dreams. He can feel deeply, think profoundly—and still sing.

The light in this etching is pure painter's melody.

"THE END OF THE ROAD"

Chagall's art embraces all phases of life, and he is the poet all the time. To follow the range of his vision a little further, I would now like to point to his drawing, "The End of the Road."

An aged man in a hairy cloak sits on the ground, his feet bare, his head bowed to his knees around which his long thin arms are encircled.

Near him on the ground lies his empty water jug and his wanderer's staff. Above him in the sky hovers a young angel, pointing to the last piece of road ahead.

The aged man is very old, almost bent double—but not broken; he is back at the beginning, close to the earth again, soon to become part of it.

A soft light radiating from his wizened face flows over his beard and on his hands.

A soft wise smile touches his mouth. Is it the satiety of earthly days that he feels, and is now ready to be gathered to his ancestors? Is it faith? Hope? He is not disappointed in the place that he will soon be leaving, and he is not lost: a guide from heaven waits to lead him on.

This is the traditional account of life's travail, its sum total.

Is this the view of the artist too? I hardly believe it, and for evidence I look to the angel.

And here, now, get acquainted with another one of Chagall's angelic tribe. This one is a dear, young and lovely—only he is frightened. He certainly is not the horribly ugly Angel of Death. He seems to be frightened of the Death that waits for the old man. In his eyes there is great fear: he may be beholding the horrible Angel of Death standing on the boundary of the beyond. He points with one hand to the road ahead—but he averts his head from there; and in his turn of the head and in the position of the body, he expresses compassion and sorrow.

He is a dear, good angel, and I believe in him.

He belongs to Chagall's finest creatures.

I am wondering, is it really true that, had the angel been made with two noses, he would have had greater art value?

"THE SAGE AND THE DEVIL"

And for contrast again, now look at the drawing, "The Sage and the Devil."

Liesin's poem, which this drawing illustrates, is called, "The Sage and Satan"—but I take the liberty to doubt that, after a scientific investigation, a reputable demonologist would accept Chagall's little devil with his curled up short tail and goatee for the king of all black spirits.

Be it as it may, a devil (even if Satan, still a devil) came to a sage who was sitting late at night before a burning candle, poring over a volume of sacred lore —to tempt him and lead him into sin.

In the ballad the devil almost succeeds: he shows the sage a castle and there sits the most beautiful of human daughters:

"She sings to him, winks to him, beams to
him, and smiles,
And draws him and pulls him with devilish
guiles—"

The sage feels he is lost, his saintliness can hold out no longer, and he tears his eyes out.

But thank heaven, this does not happen in Chagall's picture.

Perhaps because in Chagall's drawing it was not Satan himself (as I still maintain), but one of his lesser serving devils—and what avail the tricks of a minor devil against the saintliness of such a sage? And it may well be also because Chagall made a strong sage, as if made of steel, a giant, a stubborn man. So, nothing happens to this one. He sits over his sacred book and delves in its treasures.

It is true, he had already noticed the uninvited visitor that stands on the table over his head—but he does not get panicky: he only pulls his prayer-shawl over his head and ears, bends his head lower over the book, and forces his thoughts to turn away from the tempter. He continues his holy occupation, only with more assiduity.

Maybe later, at midnight, when he will get tired and weaker—but meanwhile there is no sign of weakening in him.

I suspect, as I suggested before, that the artist came to the aid of the sage by making him an old ascetic. There is nowhere in him a mark to show that he ever indulged his flesh. He looks as if he had more than once met a devil in battle and vanquished him. His tall slender body, one can see under his white linen robe, is bony and dry; he did not pamper himself.

As little and as sparingly as Chagall used his pencil, he nevertheless succeeded in creating a noble figure of a Jewish sage—and it is not by his beard that he is a Jew.

And also the devil is a novel creature in modern art. There is humor and charm in the sensual creature. He is a fine, nimble fellow, really. You must like him. If he does not belong to Chagall's hierarchy of angels, he is surely of a higher order than the artist's horses and goats . . .

And not only is the sage Jewish, but his devil also is Jewish—I would stake my beard and earlocks upon it! Look at him again, does he not possess all the seven charms of a Jew?

(And who, I beg you, if not a Jewish devil would creep into a book of Jewish poetry—and of an unpopular poet, to the bargain?)

Chagall and Rembrandt

IN ALL the above mentioned of Chagall's pictures —and in the many more unmentioned, too many to be mentioned—you have Jewish works of art, not only because of their subjects, but essentially because they have a Jewish spirit. All Chagall's Jewish figures and images are Jewish not only by their Jewish appearance—they have a Jewish soul.

Chagall is Jewish in heart and soul, and that influences his work—because being honest with himself, as only a great artist can be, his work does represent him honestly. And when he gives expression to his artistic ideas, his Jewish imagination becomes active and his soul becomes communicative—and influences the formation of his figures and the mixing of his colors.

"If I were not a Jew (with the content that I put into this word) I would have never been an artist or entirely a different one—" Chagall states.

Chagall is consciously Jewish and warm-heartedly so, and the Jewish feeling and spirit in his work is not an accidental phase of his art.

Many of the greatest artists of the world used Biblical material for their works of art. When you compare their works with Chagall's you first realize how intimately Jewish in spirit Chagall is, and how alien and gentile the others are—to a Jew. The only exception is Rembrandt and some works of El Greco.

Always, when I speak of Chagall's Jewish art, I am immediately confronted with Rembrandt.

—Take Rembrandt! . . .

The argument seems to be very simple. Rembrandt was not a Jew, but many of his works of art with Jewish or Biblical subjects could be readily accepted as Jewish art. Therefore there is no Jewish art.

Yes, I will take Rembrandt—with great satisfaction and honor. But let us first look close at him.

All his childhood years Rembrandt knew only one book, the Bible. Even before he could read himself, the world of the Bible was opened to him—a child with a hungry imagination—by his mother.

His father was a miller and the mother, a baker's daughter. In the devout Protestant (Calvinist) home, religion was the only comfort, and the holy book the only spiritual food. Every day Rembrandt's religious mother would read to her children some choice pages of the only book in the house, the family Bible.

Rembrandt painted his old mother with her eyeglasses low on her nose, bent over the heavy volume on her knees, with a happy, pious, and intent face, reading the wrinkled page, as if someone were listening to her reading. Watching her lips for a while it begins to seem that the old woman's open mouth moves slowly, spelling out the precious words carefully that the children may not lose any.

It surely left a formative influence on the young mind of the future genius. The lad knew the heroes of the Bible—and the Old Testament with its Jewish heroes was a part of the Bible—before he knew the neighbors in the street.

And this familiarity with the Bible continued all his life, to his last day. When Rembrandt died, the only book found in his possession was the Bible.

One brother of his was a baker, the other a shoemaker. But Rembrandt, because he showed early great intelligence, the family sent to school.

In school Rembrandt became acquainted with worldly classics—but religion was the main subject of study in the schools of those days—and every morning the classes opened with the study of the Bible—then there was the singing of psalms.

All his life Rembrandt was interested in painting, etching or drawing from the Bible. That means that he knew the Bible by working on it—for a great artist that means knowing it with all the powers of his imagination.

In Holland the Jews had the right of citizenship. In the big commercial city of Amsterdam, where Rembrandt came to live when he was twenty, the Jews lived in friendly relations with their Christian neighbors. And though the Jews lived separately in their own quarters of the city, it was because of their religious and community needs; it was not a ghetto. Christian neighbors did not abandon the Jewish section and had tolerant and friendly intercommunication with them.

When Rembrandt came to Amsterdam he lodged with an art-dealer in the Jewish quarter. Seven years later, after marrying Saskia, he bought for himself a fine three story house in a Jewish street. Across from him lived Rabbi Menasseh ben Israel. Rembrandt painted his portrait in 1654, and made an etching of him. He also made four small etchings to illustrate a book of Menasseh. Other Jewish notables were Rembrandt's neighbors and acquaintances, among them the poet and physician, Dr. Ephraim Bonus, of whom Rembrandt painted a portrait and made an etching.

Rembrandt lived among Jews twenty-five years of his life, until his house was sold in bankruptcy. There remained only ten years of his life, and though he lived away from the Jewish quarter he still came there to visit friends and acquaintances.

After Rembrandt's death there were left thirty-seven portraits of Jews, some of these he painted in his later life, and belong to the finest portraits he had painted. There are many other pictures where Rembrandt used Jewish models.

In this connection it is very important to remember that Rembrandt was the first artist to use a Jewish model for the figure of Christ.*

"Rembrandt used Biblical subjects in 160 paintings, 80 etchings, and more than 600 drawings, or a total of 850.

"The market value of drawings was negligible. Religious paintings generally were little in demand in Calvinistic Holland. It was Rembrandt's own choice.

"It was Calvinism in particular which drew attention to the Old Testament and opened a more just consideration to the original Biblical people.

"But in addition to all the historical circumstances which fostered Rembrandt's interest, there remains the indisputable fact that the artist's attitude to the Jewish people was unusually sympathetic."**

---

* Thomas Craven states about Leonardo da Vinci:
"He roamed the Milanese ghetto, notebook in hand, for expressive faces—observed condemned men about to be hanged—for his drawing of Judas, and after two years of searching, *found a suitable model for Christ in a princely Jewish youth.*"
Professor Arturo Castiglioni of Milan, in a letter of March 20, 1950, writes to Mr. Willy Aron of New York:
"The assertion of Thomas Craven seems to be fantastic. I have questioned the director of the Sforza Museum, an authority on Leonardo, and consulted all biographies of Leonardo. There is not any proof that he might have lived in the Ghetto in Milan, and at least as far as we know there was no Ghetto in Milan . . . the story of the princely youth as model for Christ is unknown to the Italian historians . . ."
** Jacob Rosenberg, "Rembrandt."

There can be no doubt that Rembrandt visited the homes of his Jewish neighbors to witness their weddings, circumcision rites, and other ceremonies which were of interest to him and understandable from his knowledge of both Testaments. His pictures show evidence that he was not unfamiliar with Jewish customs.

One more fact we must bear in mind, that Rembrandt was one of the greatest masters of portraiture with the genius for researching the refinement of personality. He was the painter of man, and by selection the painter of the soulful, poetic, visionary man. His supreme gift, which is rare even among the greatest portrait painters, was his high sensitivity to the spiritual demarcation of personality.

What wonder then that Rembrandt was able to discover the specifically Jewish sensitivity of spirit in his Jewish friends whom he painted and his Jewish models. He had an old standing familiarity with the Jewish spiritual soul—in his beloved heroes of both Testaments.

This aspect of the soul of the Jew, his particular kind of spiritual sensitivity, his highly spiritualized intelligence, this is the Jewish character that you recognize in Rembrandt's paintings; this distinguishes Jewish from other spiritual faces.

To change a former painting of his of a Jewish young man into a picture of a Christ, Rembrandt had only rarefied its realism and heightened its spirituality in the copy—following the lead of his Jewish countenance—without altering the likeness of the model.

When Rembrandt bent his mind on the face of the Jew sitting for his portrait, or as a model, and to him the man was pre-eminently a Jew, he was searching to give expression to the Jewish attributes of the sitter, to those supertones of his personality which make his face spiritually Jewish.

Now, if Rembrandt found it, found the specific Jewish mold of the human soul—and could hold it with his pencil, burin, or paint brush, then it is a thing in existence and not a fiction of Chagall.

And if Chagall has his Jewishness by inheritance, by absorption in early environment, and by observation, and he can put it into his works—it only proves that he is a great artist; for it takes a great artist to transmit the psychic patterns of nationality. In fact, only the very great artists and poets leave in their work the cast of their national complexion.

The national Jewish spirit found expression formerly

Hatikvah. Oil. 1948
(Dedicated to Israel)

Courtesy of the Artist

PLATE XXV

only in the Jewish (polyglot) word; we now find it expressed in Chagall's art.

Yes, let Rembrandt testify, and El Greco also—if you need two witnesses—

Chagall himself said:

"I want to speak so very little of myself; I have never said to myself that I have accomplished something, or reached somewhere. The only thing that I wanted in my life was—not to get near the great masters of the world like Rembrandt, Greco, Tinteretto, and others—but to get close to the spirit of our own fathers and grandfathers, to be of their essence, to mingle myself among their folds, as if lying hidden in their garments—with their souls and sorrows, with their worries and rare joys."

There are people who do not know the full range and manysidedness of Chagall's artistic nature, and they classify him as a folk artist. They see him as a highly gifted but simple-minded, even naive, man of the people. They take his great achievement of simplicity for the innocence of a "big child."

Chagall certainly is in many of his works folkloristic. But that does not mean that Chagall's, and Peretz', art is folk art—which is a primitive art. Chagall was too much man and artist of the world, too refined and too knowing, to be a naive creator.

Chagall said of himself:

"I had the good fortune to be born of the people; but popular art, although I always liked it, did not satisfy me. It was too exclusive. It excluded the refinement of civilization. And I have always had a decided taste for refined expression, for culture."

Chagall had not merely accepted the lore of his people and transcribed it on his papers—out of the elements of their folklore he made great works of art and created in them spiritual values fully in the best tradition of the builders of Jewish culture, old and new.

His Biblical creations show that Chagall had the strength to rise to the loftiness of thought, nobility of feeling, and purity of vision necessary to meet the challenge of the creators of the Bible in any serious attempt to follow them.

With true-hearted dignity, with deep-going seriousness, with largeness of range and purity of vision Chagall entered into the world of the Bible—and in his illustrations remained faithful to his fathers, close to the heart of the lowly, with the simple grandeur and warm humanity that made the Jewish Book the Book of all the world.

The very fact that Chagall conceived the Biblical heroes in the norm of his own people, in the image of his Witebsk Jews, is the best evidence of the artist's Jewish intuition.

Master Etcher

TO GIVE visual reality to his exalted visions no great artist would borrow a method of work, or use the idiom of another. As he creates he invents a language for his images, intimate and plastic and yielding to his needs. And that is what Chagall did for his creations of the Bible.

With the Gogol book Chagall began to develop his art of etching; in La Fontaine's "Fables" he improved it further; in his Bible plates he reached such magnificent mastery that it placed him at the very top, among the greatest graphic artists of all time.

In his oils and water-colors it is color that sings his tenderest melodies; in his etchings he makes light do it: light has become for him the carrier of emotion.

And here, too, every figure comes with its own atmosphere, with an individual pattern that develops with the spiritual character of the figure.

The rich modulation of light and the spiritual grace that it spreads airily and palpitatingly over the papers are of exquisite refinement and rare beauty.

In contrast to the light and, of course, the genitor of the light, is the black color—sensual, corporeal and shimmering with its own glory.

And between the two, the twilight child of the two, is the mystical gray that floats over the paper unpalpable as an unembodied soul.

The sheer surface beauty of Chagall's etchings is unmatched in modern art.

The Sun of Lovers. Oil. 1949

Courtesy of the Artist

PLATE XXVI

Foreboding

BUSY AS Chagall was with his work for Vollard, he found time to do a number of oils that keep their place among his masterpieces.

A few of the canvases with the motif of love I have mentioned before.

Two other canvases remind me of his pictures of Jews that he had painted in Witebsk.

"Lying in the Snow" (1930–1931)—a man holding a violin lies in the snow on a field, the city in the distance.

The hairy, overgrown Jew in the field is painted almost realistically except that his figure is unproportionately large against the landscape. By himself he looks small and hunched; against the landscape, because of the distorted proportions, he looks like a giant. In his blue trousers, green coat and red fur cap, lying in the cold snow, under the dark blue sky, he looks lonely, an outcast, sad, forlorn and silent. But watching him steadily for a while, you become aware of an inner stubborn strength in him, some mysterious, primitive force; his glowering eyes give you an uncanny feeling.

It is one of Chagall's figures that is eloquently silent. When your eyes first rest on him, it seems to you that he has many tales to tell you; but as soon as you try to understand the ominous meaning of his communication, he becomes silent. When you try to take your eyes away, he holds you back and again he seems to be talking, confiding something of utmost importance—so full of suggestiveness is this picture.

"In a Russian House" (1931) could be a companion canvas to the above.

A Jew with an open prayer book is sitting at the Sabbath table, his wife nearby, half aside; both have Russianized faces, peasant type, but the Jewish stamp is indelible on them. They are Jewish villagers. Two roughly hammered-out characters, people with the history of unremitting toil on them, that molded them solid, elemental, and unbreakable. Daumier himself would have been pleased with such character drawing.

But we have here Chagall and not Daumier—and Chagall is not content with realistic portraiture.

In this canvas the proportions are reversed: the man looks small against the house, with the face of a dwarf. In addition, the artist distorted his face by leaving the nose unmodeled, which leads to the impression that the two squinting eyes in the flat face are too wide apart. The whole small face is ugly—but it possesses a rare naive purity. You are not sure that he can spell out the words of the prayer book—but you are convinced of the chastity of his heart.

The canvas is magnificent with its simplicity and warm contrasting colors.

Chagall very often uses the following method: he makes his invented, fantastic creatures as real and as solid as if they were natural beings; and, on the contrary, he treats real things as fictitious, adding to the natural the fascination of the imagination, turning the factual into a legend, without permitting, however, the reality of being to be completely lost. He thus merges life with illusion and fantasy with reality.

"The Bridal Chair" (1934) is a canvas that he painted at the occasion of his daughter's marriage. The chair is empty, covered with white and decorated with fresh white flowers, standing amidst white flowers.

Here the artist displays his tenderest and most delicate nuances of white, white against white, that irradiated a purity—but not a white joy. On the contrary, you sense a soft sadness exhaled by the flowers like a perfume.

It may well be that the artist here gives an intimation of the sadness of his heart that began to be troubled by forebodings of evil days to come.

The first joyous years have passed. Though in his personal life the artist had much to be contented with, he was upset by fear for his people. Doubly sensitive as Jew and Artist, he began to be affected by the oncoming storm long before its deadly terror struck the world.

As early as 1933 he painted *"Solitude"* (see page 6)

showing the Jew alone and friendless in the world.

In 1923 he began to paint a fantastic vision, *"The Fallen Angel."* He did not complete it then but put it aside. In 1933 he went back to it and made it a symbol of the coming cataclysm of the world.

The angel falls head down in a pool of blood. The Witebsk cottages are threatened by flames. The kind cow with one human eye stands with her head raised to the sky—but in the sky there is confusion and frightfulness—the sun and the moon, both, are drowning in the clouds of smoke. The synagogue Jew had snatched the Torah out of the flames and he runs with it—he had rescued his most precious possession, and he has something to hold on to—though it did not save him later from Buchenwald and Tremblinka. There is another Jew in the picture, the worldly Jew, thrown up into the air; torn out, roots and all, from the soil that he thought was his, and there he is now, in the air—where will he land? He is not the Chagallian Jew walking in the air, the wanderer who for hundreds of years has learned to exist in mid-air—this Jew is scared to death.

In 1938 Chagall painted one of his most touching lyrical canvases, *"Three Candles."* It is one of my favorites; every time I come across it in a reproduction I am touched by its tender and sad beauty.

A pair of lovers, young, delicate, and fragile, pressed to each other, holding on one to the other with a movement as if to protect the other from something threatening. With a foreboding of disaster they are frightened and shrink and retire backward—though their own world is still rich with flowers; and cherubim are still about; and the flute player is still playing his song of youth, spring, and love; and the white candles burn with a festive glow.

The composition is magnificent, original, new, daring—asymmetric and yet balanced; the color is subdued, fresh, and fluid; the rhythm soft and lyrical; it is altogether of a sad and lyrical beauty.

The background is Witebsk.

"Snowing" is another canvas of those days (1939) with Witebsk as a background.

In the center of a wintry square, the same square that the artist painted in *"Jew Over Witebsk"* (see page 37), a gigantic figure, holding a little fiddle. This one is not a Witebsk musician. He is a stranger. His head with its peaked cap rises about the rooftops and the church towers. Above him hovers a monster on two spread wings—with a head of a donkey and long ears, and an eye and hands and feet of a man.

Again it is a picture that gives you an uncanny feeling.

CRUCIFIXION SERIES

In 1938 Chagall painted his *"White Crucifixion."*

A white Christ is nailed to a cross. Over his head is a glory and in Hebrew letters the legend: "Jesus of Nazareth King of the Jews."

Around the "Jewish King" is a pogrom. A synagogue is in flames. Some cottages have been turned over, their possessions scattered and owners killed. In a corner is a conflagration of Jewish books and sacred scrolls. Jews flee in all directions, a group in a boat. One group is up in the sky, in violent lamentation. The organized band of assassins with flags and weapons are still threatening.

The Christ here is strongly traditional, though the cloth on his loin has white and black stripes, suggesting a Jewish prayer-shawl.

In 1940 Chagall returned to the same subject in a canvas called, *"Martyr."* But here it is a young Jew tied with ropes to a post in the middle of a square. Around him destruction and conflagration. The martyr is enveloped in a prayer-shawl and on his head is a Jewish cap—but more than that, his Jewishness is fully, even if delicately, expressed in his face; a face in no way reminding you of a Christ—though it is full of sorrow and resignation, but lit up with a sensitivity and spiritual grace which is Jewish. The eyes are closed as a dead man's—and yet you are aware of a living thoughtfulness behind the face which moves you to stop and think with compassion.

What helps in reminding you of a crucifixion is the Madonna-bride who stands all in white at the feet of the martyr.

The composition of the two figures and their plastic relationship to the whole canvas is excellent.

The panic and tragedy that surround the two figures help in developing the symbolism of the "Martyr." The artist's cry of pain and pity over the destruction of his people in a Christian world is most touchingly expressed here.

And in 1943 Chagall again painted a *"Crucifixion."*

In his first canvas of this series (1938), the crucified

is a Christ in the tradition of Christian painters. In the second canvas (1940), the "Martyr" is a Jew but not nailed to a cross. In the third canvas (1943), it is a Jew on the cross, a crucified Jew, with the head-phylactery still tied on his head, and on his arm the marks of the winding of the straps of the other phylactery as if it had been just removed.

You would have no doubt that the crucified here is a Jew even without the phylacteries—a Jew without the traditional long beard, but God's image on his face is of a Jewish cast. And his pain is Jewish, without Christian mysticism, as the great painter himself felt it when painting it; the pain that all Jews carry in their hearts for their six million brothers and sisters tortured and murdered. And though the artist painted a glory around the head of the crucified, in the manner of the primitive religious painters, its agony is of our own time and clime.

It is a beautifully drawn intellectual head and face of a modern Jewish type that you may find in many universities.

Near the cross, occupying the other half of the canvas in the same plane, is an unrolled, open scroll held in mid-air, without hands holding it. A sad-eyed angel lights up the scroll with a burning candle blowing a shofar (a ram's horn) at the same time.

Where there is a scroll, as you know well, it tells a tale of Jewish woe. It is interesting to note that Chagall painted here an old scroll with the old lines of script rubbed out—the scratches of the old letters are visible. There is only one word newly written on it, "Witebsk"—Chagall's symbol for all the Jewish ruined cities and villages—as if to say, the new chronicles of horror take the place of the old ones, and the new suffering is greater than ever before in the tragic annals of the ancient people.

Under the cross and the scroll there is a sea in which Jews are drowning.

A Jew with a ladder is close to the cross—he had come to take off his brother from the cross, but fell, himself, into the abyss of disaster.

In the foreground a mother and her baby are running away on a deep-blue horse. In the background is a poor village street. Throughout are groups of Jewish refugees in panic.

In this canvas you note again the import of colors in Chagall's work. Each new picture carries new color-emotions (not only sensations). Chagall is tireless in developing new color tonalities to express spiritual and emotional states—besides their plastic and esthetic values.

Look at the white color of the crucified; it cuts itself painfully into your awareness. The green of the scroll is not the color of old parchment, but of misfortune. The open scroll with its own tale is as tragically effective as the crucified. And so is the angel. The blue horse does not remind one of the horses seen on the panicky roads leading out of the devastated villages. The best painted torn or frightened war horses would not have communicated the appalling fear which the little blue horse suggests.

It is very interesting to note the exceptional composition of this canvas—altogether new and daring. The cross with the crucified stands on one side (usually it would be in the center) and is counterposed by the open flat piece of parchment that has hardly any mass—and yet the picture holds its balance.

Chagall returned to the subject in two other canvases painted later.

One is called "Descent from the Cross"—again a magnificent Jewish intellectual head. This time the crucified is clothed in his ritual four-cornered garment. But the meaning of this canvas is entirely different. Here it is not a symbol of the Jewish people's suffering, but a statement that Jesus was a Jew. The mood here is archaic and mystic.

A big bird with the body, hands and feet of a man lowers the dead Christ from the cross. At the foot of the ladder a Jew holds up a burning candle to give light. Two women assist (the two Marys?). An angel that looks like a bird hovers over the scene with a sad and frightened face.

This canvas has no story of our own days—but is interesting as a work of art with its archaic charm.

The motif is as primitive as the pictures found in the catacombs.

It is well known that the Church accepted the four creatures of the vision of Ezekiel as representing the four evangelists. For that reason the primitive Christian painters painted the evangelists with the heads of the four creatures of Ezekiel—the face of a man, the face of a lion, the face of an ox, and the face of an eagle.

In the ancient sculptures of Egypt, Assyria, Chaldea, their gods were represented as beasts and birds. In Homeric poetry the Greek gods assumed the forms of animals and birds.

Chagall brings to this canvas a taste of naive primitive poetry.

Another canvas shown at the same exhibition with the above was called, "The Yellow Christ." (Gauguin had painted a Yellow Christ.)

Again a different mood and a different spirit.

In this canvas Chagall painted himself sitting in front of his easel painting a Crucifixion—he turned his head to watch an old bent Jew approaching, leaning heavily on his walking stick. The artist in the picture seems to be thinking not of his picture but of the old man. He probably thinks of what the old grandfather would not do to him with his stick, catching the artist making Christian images . . .

The Jesus on the easel resembles an icon of a Russian village, carved by a primitive native artist who presented his masterpiece to be put in a shrine on a cross road—and the peasant girls embroider loin cloths for Him and adorn His head with wreaths of daisies.

Again the touch and breath of simple primitive life.

The "Martyr" Chagall painted when he was still in France. In 1939 the artist and his family moved to Gordes above Marseille. And when in September of the same year the war began, Chagall continued to work undisturbed.

In February, 1940, he held a big exhibition of his works in Paris.

When Hitler entered Paris, Chagall and his family became fugitives for a whole year, until they finally reached New York.

In a letter from Lisbon, dated 1941 (May-June), written to his friend, the well-known Jewish novelist, Joseph Opatoshu, of New York, the artist gives a glimpse of his grim humor of those days:

". . . Finally I arrived here and can write to you a few calm words.

"The Director of the Museum of Modern Art of New York has invited me to come to an exhibition. It is indeed very nice of him; he worked hard to arrange it—and he is not Jewish . . .

"Even here in such a bright and dumb city it looks to me all muddled: I am going, and who knows, though I am invited, I still seem from afar (and may be even from near) 'somewhat' like a man without a country . . .

"Here in the harbor near the ship I discovered about a hundred of my Jews with their staffs and packs. I have never seen such a sad case when an author and his heroes take the same boat . . .

"But I am not taking the boat yet. I am sitting here waiting for my pictures that for some unknown reason got parted from me and in their boxes and coffins straggle somewhere in Spain. When will they get here?—the boat is still waiting for me . . .

"Well, I have faith in God that He will not keep me too long stranded at the Gibraltar.

"As in Palestine I once rejoiced to see our land, in the United States I will rejoice to see my own people. And one more thought: to work . . ."

An exhibition of Chagall's representative masterpieces could not really be thought of with the conditions then prevailing in Europe. The invitation to the artist to come to an exhibition in New York was a ruse to get the Vichy government's permission to take out from France the pictures in Chagall's possession. The Museum of Modern Art first gave Chagall a one man exhibition in 1946 when it collected his works from many countries. About that later. (See page 117.)

In the United States

ON JUNE 21st, 1941, Chagall and his family reached New York. It was a much needed haven of rest. They made their home here.

A year of precarious living—fugitives, with Hitler's murderous hordes at their heels; the calamitous events of the war; the subjugation of his beloved France under the iron boots of Hitler's militarism; the increasing destruction of Jewish cities and villages and the annihilation of millions of his brothers and sisters in the Nazi extermination camps and torture chambers —all combined to exhaust the artist and depress his spirit.

However, to work was as much a necessity for him as to breathe. At all times, in all the trials and tribulations of his life, he found respite at his easel. Now, too, he could not keep away—but his canvases showed his tired mind and low spirits.

Then, unexpectedly, came a reprieve. Leonide Massine, the ballet master, asked Chagall to make costumes and stage sets for his new ballet, "Aleko," and to supervise its production in Mexico.

This happened in the beginning of 1942. The artist saw an opportunity to tear himself away from the gloom of reality and busy himself with purely artistic fantasies, and he eagerly accepted the commission and plunged into work at once.

In Mexico, where the war had only a faint reverberation, the sunny air, the novelty, freshness and dissimilarity of life; the color, pattern, and form richness of the landscape—that and the stimulation of a definitive plan and concrete aim of work had a revivifying effect on the fatigued powers of the artist.

Coming back from Mexico he brought a number of gouaches, a series of impressions of Mexico, and exhibited them at the Matisse Galleries.

Chagall saw the picturesque, the gay, and playfully childlike ways of the Mexican peon and he painted them with sparkling humor.

Also in Mexico Chagall did not copy what he saw, but of the Mexican elements created Chagallian pictures—his impressions of Mexico.

Chagall was interested in the simple people, who always appealed to him. Though richer in color and in many ways different in their dress and manners, they are essentially, humanly, the same as in the Russian village.

Chagall made the Mexican lover too carry his sweetheart up in the air; in Mexico, too, he put lovers in a flower bush. The Mexican moon is no less romantic than the Witebsk. The young night, the moon, the flowers, the young lovers—the same idyllic, lyrical song of life everywhere. Surely in Mexico, too, young hearts spin and weave the golden dream of youth and love as in every country. And Chagall, the tenderest and most lyrical of artists, painted this love dream also in the land of Mexico—only with brighter colors.

All simple people are not much different in their domestic life. In Chagall's Mexico the cow, donkey, and little horse are as much a part of the peon's household as in a Russian isba. There is an intimacy and understanding between man, animal and bird: the cow looks up with sisterly solicitude to her Mexican mistress; and the horse turns back its head to watch its master and talk to him—it even smiles at its master's foolishness—but when the family goes to the fiesta, the little horse can dance most elegantly.

The artist found a pair of lovers hidden in the tail feathers of a Mexican hen—and she did not say a word about it. He saw in Mexico a goat holding an open fan, like a real lady. He met a cock all dressed up like a young gentleman, carrying a guitar—going to serenade his lady love? The curious artist also discovered a hen with a human head, wearing a sombrero.

He painted a village street, a Mexican landscape, a fiesta—but also the night-rider, the moon-horse.

The critics came to see Chagall's Mexican canvases, and some demurred: Look, Chagall was in Mexico and he painted—like Chagall!

They had expected to come to the Matisse galleries and be in Mexico.

Only those who do not understand the nature of Chagall's art could have expected such a thing.

Yes, Chagall was in Mexico, came and saw and picked Chagallian material for pictures.

Bible. *Abraham Approaching Sodom with Three Angels*
Etching. 1931–39
Collection of Lionello Venturi, Rome

Courtesy of the Artist

PLATE XXVII

Yes, in Mexico also Chagall did not copy what he saw.

The Mexican landscape is more colorful than around Witebsk, and Chagall's gouaches sparkle more richly and more brightly. There is a new warmth and a new freshness in the pictures that he painted after his visit to Mexico. He brought back some new color values and new patterns. But substantially the canvases remained Chagallian. Compare his pictures from Mexico with the pictures painted by native Mexican painters and you will see at once that Chagall belongs to a different racial temperament and to a different rhythm of life.

And that is as it should be. A new surrounding can bring a new influence, can add a new nuance, a new tone, a change in pattern—but cannot change the artist's psychic make-up.

It is only those artists who live by what they pick up—the surface quality of place and time—that bring from foreign countries their geographic tableaux, as it were.

Chagall had visited Palestine, Syria, Egypt, Spain, Holland—if he were an eclectic he would have come back with bits of styles from every country. But Chagall's artistic roots are deeply planted in a soil that nature and heritage made his own. His artistic personality is too powerfully founded to undergo a sea or land change with every trip he takes.

This is true of all great artists who visit foreign countries to enlarge their experience and vision—whatever they absorb they assimilate.

We have seen what an influence France had on Chagall's painting. But even France did not change the nature of Chagall's artistic psyche.

From the very beginning we have seen that external events do not control Chagall's creative processes. Chagall does not use his material as it comes in through his eye—he lets it be processed in the laboratory of his imagination, under the surveillance of his knowing mind, with the participation of his emotions—until the material is metamorphosed into creatures of his noble breed.

Chagall has said:

"Everything in art must spring from the movement of our whole life-stream, of our whole being—including the unconscious."

We may note here that in his pictures painted in New York you will not find New York—much less than Mexico in his Mexican pictures—which may be interesting but not surprising. New York was unassimilable for Chagall's imagination.

If one does find any influence of the metropolis in his canvases, it must be in the quickened tempo of the rhythm in his compositions, and, perhaps, in the overcrowding of his pictorial space: he does not make free space a part of his compositions, as much as he used to formerly. And there is one other new element that can be picked out—an autumnal yellow color in the leaves of his trees, a shade of color that he had never used before. Perhaps also a cold silver tone in the skies of some of his landscapes.

While in the U. S. the artist worked for a few years in the Catskill mountains, High Falls, near Kingston, where he made his home until he went back to France, in 1948.

Talking about his stay in the United States, Chagall said:

"Above all I am impressed by the greatness of this country and the feeling of freedom that it gives me. But one has to be free oneself to appreciate that freedom. Perhaps during these past few years I have come to know a little the air, the clouds, the trees of this country; perhaps I have learned to understand the great "silent" traits of Americans; perhaps I have been able to let all this pass into my art. I have breathed this stimulating air—though I may not have assimilated this or that local trait, the "reproduction" of which in itself has never constituted art."

Bella's Death

IN SEPTEMBER, 1944, Bella died suddenly of a virus infection.

In the following November the director of the Matisse Galleries made up an exhibition of Chagall's love-pictures, dedicated to the unforgettable Bella who was the inspiration of these pictures.

At the end of February, 1946, the Matisse Galleries exhibited the canvases that Chagall painted after his wife's death.

In these pictures the artist painted in the tenderest and saddest colors his sorrow over the loss of his Princess and his painful yearning for her. Each canvas is full of the memory of her—and that is why they are suffused with the evanescent breath of sad beauty that seems to come from an enchanted world far from the everyday life.

Chagall's soul cannot part with her, he does not want to forget her, but she is now in the valley of the shadow of death—and he tries to bring her back at least in his canvases. He does not leave her and clings to her and goes back with her in the land of memory. And the remembered world in which she still lives is a super-world of pure tender beauty and poetry. She is now for him forever his bride dressed in white, in a white bridal veil, with flowers in her hand. She is always at his side as he goes wandering through the years of the past, in the wonderland of once upon a time—

"Once upon a time"—do not our most beautiful and saddest stories begin like that?

Once upon a time is the dawn of our childhood and the closing hour of the old man before he shuts his eyes for the last time—all his life is now for him once upon a time. When death seals his eyes, the end comes to the beautiful sad tale of once upon a time.

Once upon a time, long ago, there lived a beautiful princess—

What lived long ago lives again in the story of the poet and artist.

Out of the life of his princess Chagall created fairy tales. In these tales his beautiful young princess will live forever, will forever be young and forever beautiful, and forever will her lover stand close to her and tell her of his young love. And forever will spring shower upon them its white blossoms that will not fade and will not lose their fragrance. And over them will always spread the clear blue sky, and under their feet a fresh green earth. And the bird in the tree that sings to them of love will never grow weary and its song will never stop *—as long as there will be people who can be touched by beauty and love.

In these canvases Chagall reached his highest as a lyric poet. He proved again that his art will carry him as high as his poetic imagination will lead.

In his "Green Dream" he created the most rarefied and tenderest poetic mood that one can find in the whole world of modern art. Only a heart touched by love and love's loss and love's sorrow could evoke such purity and innocence. And only Chagall's art could image this dream on canvas in idyllic airy and liquid freshness of color—a green spun of light and tenderness.

Standing in front of his "Naked Cloud," I had a feeling that the artist, holding on to his wife, entered with her the mystery and horror of death, and did not abandon her. He was not frightened in his imagination to remain lying with her on her death bed.

In all other pictures he remembers her as living; he sees her in the different periods of their life, often associated with a certain piece of work painted in their golden period when she was there to inspire him and, later, to rejoice with him when it brought him fame. In this picture, "Naked Cloud," she is dead. The yellow color of the two figures lying together on the bed, gave me an uncanny, dismal and mystic feeling. Near the bed, on the ground, sits a woman in naked blue, yearning and sad. The companion bed is now occupied by a green cow with her violin—a green of gloom and sorrow. In a corner, a figure is falling from the sky spreading violet petals. In the foreground, small town cottages with a fence between—Witebsk. In the last wan light of the setting sun, a white moon rises, a moon without light, without a shimmer, dead,

---

* See Keats' "Ode on a Grecian Urn."

in a background of gray dusk. There is an atmosphere of the border land of the "beyond," where there is no day and no night.

One of the finest canvases of this period is his "One Thought."

I know that Chagall does not like the attribute of master applied to him, or masterpiece applied to his work—and, in truth, it is foreign to Chagall's temperament and to his sense of art.

The term "master" has the connotation of the academic, cold and mechanical. Or, it brings to mind the air of a workshop where rulers and scales are used and everything is cut according to a set of regulations. The "master," it would seem, lets every warm and quickened impulse first grow cold in order to put it on the scales and weigh it carefully. The "master" looks with suspicious eye on each spontaneous, instinctive image, and he must first dissect it for inspection, thus killing the living life of it. A masterpiece may mean cold, compressed thought, frozen inspiration.

And though Chagall has the experience and knowledge of art that makes the master—he knows how—he avoids making "masterpieces." Chagall permits newborn images to come in into his canvases as they may come, uncared for, fresh from birth. He leaves in his work the warm breath of living impulses, sometimes the overflow of his creative energies. In the beginning he may make demarcations and outlines, but in the completed picture you will find the boundary lines overrun and overreached by an afterflow of luxuriant creative abundance.

Chagall is by nature more romantic than classic; more painter than draftsman—that is, he subordinates drawing to color. He will often hurt his drawing for the sake of color and he will distort some drawing intentionally that it may not look too meticulous, too perfect—but he will not arbitrate on his colors.

Sometimes, however, standing in front of a Chagall canvas, the term masterpiece will rise to the tip of my tongue, so perfectly organized are all the plastic elements into a harmonious unity of being. Such a canvas is his "Green Dream," and also "One Thought." I hasten to add that each of these canvases is a living masterpiece, a thing grown, not pressed out of a mould. Feeling, fantasy, form, drawing, color, texture, light, space—everything is perfectly taken care of, and all happily harmonized into a thing of beauty that delights the eye and the mind.

In "One Thought" the sun that is painted in the picture not only lights up the objects in the composition, but seems to enter into their flesh and each thing in turn—also the darker object—emits a warm light as delicate as a perfume. The free spaces in the pictures are not empty, but filled with air that the eye senses, air warmed and lighted by the sun.

For sheer splendor of colors and pictorial beauty I can name a number of canvases of that exhibition, such as "Morning Reveille," "The Wedding Lights," and others.

Looking at the abundance of tender pure beauty, touched by the sadness that the legends of the pictures communicate, you must say with the poet Shelley:

"Our sweetest songs are those that tell of saddest thought."

Bible. *The High Priest Aaron*
Etching. 1931–39
Courtesy of the Artist

PLATE XXVIII

Chagall and the Ballet Theater

IN 1945 Chagall was asked by the Ballet Theater to make the scenery and costumes for "The Fire Bird."

He accepted the commission eagerly. He was glad to go to work on a story of wonderland and tear himself away from the painful reality of a world without Bella.

We have noticed above that in 1942 Chagall went to Mexico to work there on the ballet "Aleko."

We will now give a brief account of Chagall's contribution to the two ballets.

The story of "Aleko" is based on Pushkin's poem "The Gypsies." [Aleko, a restless man, dissatisfied with civilized living, joins a band of wandering gypsies. He falls in love with the beautiful Zemfira and lives with her in her old father's tent. After a while he discovers that Zemfira is having a love affair with a young gypsy. The old father tries to console him, urging him to submit to his fate—no one can compel the heart of a young girl not to change. He himself had had the same experience with Zemfira's mother; she abandoned him and Zemfira and ran away with another man; but he felt that she had the right to do it for love. Aleko does not accept the old man's advice. Finding Zemfira with her lover, he kills them both.

The gypsies now reject Aleko. They break up camp and leave Aleko grieving on the grave of Zemfira and her lover.]

Chagall made four backdrops for the four scenes of the ballet.

The motif of the first is love. A moonlit night, the moon in the sky reflected in a lake. A red cock, the symbol of passionate love, is also in the sky. The head and arm of a lover emerge from a cloud to touch the hair and back of a girl who floats out to him in the sky. Below, in the shadow of a hill, faintly visible, the tents and two covered wagons of the gypsies.

Scene two has as its motif, harvest time: A very large sun with dripping rays, also a large moon. A lake with a man in a boat and a floating branch of a tree on one half of the ground; on the other half, a ripe field with tall stalks and field flowers. A scythe, the blade up, is sticking out above the field.

Scene three, with the motif of a dream: On the side of the hill lies a sprawling village. A large bouquet of flowers in the sky, with a monkey hanging by its tail from it. On the ground a dancing bear with a violin and bow.

Scene four, city life: city buildings in the fore- and background, a long road leading to other city buildings, with a rider on the road. The buildings, road and grounds are all red. In one corner, on a hill, a green cemetery with white grave crosses. In the sky a large gold sun with a rich chandelier and burning candles on the face of the sun. A white horse is running up the sky to the sun, occupying the whole middle and center of the sky.*

The ballet "The Fire Bird" is based on a Russian fairy tale.

[A prince, hunting in a forest, captures the fire bird. She begs him to let her go and offers him one of her gold feathers as a ransom. She tells him to display the feather when he is in danger and she will come to his aid. The prince accepts the feather and lets the fire bird go.

Soon after he finds a group of twelve maidens dancing. He falls in love with one of the maidens, their leader, who is really an enchanted princess. The maiden tells him to leave that part of the forest because it is in the kingdom of an evil magician. But the prince refuses to go.

Suddenly an angry sound is heard. The maidens flee, and the prince is plunged into darkness—but the forest is aflame with blazing lights. The prince tries to escape but is captured by a horde of devils and monsters who carry him to the magician's palace. The maidens, too, are brought there.

The prince now displays the feather of the fire bird, who thereupon comes to his aid, scatters the demons and leads the prince and maidens to a place of safety. Then the fire bird shows the prince an egg, hidden in the hollow of a tree, which contains the soul of the

---

* "Aleko," with music by Tchaikowsky (Piano Trio), choreography by Leonide Massine, scenario by Massine and Chagall, was produced by Ballet Theatre in New York at the Metropolitan Opera House on Oct. 6, 1942.

magician. The prince breaks the egg and the kingdom of magic is destroyed.

The prince now marries the liberated princess, and their wedding is celebrated by a great feast.]

The curtain introducing the ballet has the motif of the fire bird. A magnificent huge figure of a bird-girl with two heads—of a girl and of a bird—with arms and wings, is suspended in mid-air—it occupies almost the entire curtain. The fire bird carries a large bouquet of flowers. On the ground in one corner is a lizard with his head up in the air. In the other corner, on the opposite side, a group of village huts with a church, and a small human figure on top of its tower. There is also the figure of a rider on a road.

The first backdrop is the enchanted forest. The sun shines in it. There are many small figures of birds and animals everywhere on the ground and in the trees. One tree stands out in the foreground with apples on it. A large red bird is prominent in the tree tops.

The next drop is the magician's palace. The palace is built in the body of a huge bird that keeps it in the air. A ladder leads up to the palace, and a girl is climbing up the ladder. On the ground, faintly outlined, a group of buildings. In the center, faintly visible, a palace with stone steps leading to it. A small, bearlike figure, heavy and round, holds a large sword. The back and side grounds are occupied by a very large flower bush, trees and plants.

The third drop has the motif of the wedding feast. It is composed of large and small circles floating in the air. In a very large circle up on top there is a canopy with the bride and groom. The bride's white wedding dress trails all the way down to the ground and gives the impression of a shooting meteor. There are many figures, some carrying candelabras, others playing musical instruments. There is a horse with the head of a drum. One man carries a big cake with candles on it. There are two ladders; two butterflies, one with human hands; a bird (with the face of a girl) brings a bouquet of flowers. In one corner, a group of city buildings; in the other corner, the cupola of a church.*

From the crude notation of the contents and themes of the backdrops, one can see that Chagall's approach to the task of the stage painter is unusual. Instead of painting the scenery as a background for the dancers,

suggesting the place in which the action of the story takes place, a static, spatial layout, Chagall presents in his backdrops a "leit-motif" of each scene. He uses his colors and forms to accompany the dancers in the same manner as the musician. In that sense his paintings of the stage sets are musical. The colors and multi-forms that he uses are dynamic, emotional, rhythmic. The composition has a time element—for the eyes roving over, into, up and down, back and forth—receive the throbbing, moving colors and forms as the ears receive music.

Looking at the curtain and backdrops that Chagall had painted for "Aleko" and "The Fire Bird," one must come to the conclusion that in the forty years of painting Chagall did not really reveal all the opulence, all the magic, all the intensity and purity of the colors he possesses in his brush. In the innumerable canvases that he has painted, he did not have the opportunity to show the full scope of his imagination, nor the magnitude of his constructive power—except twice, in "Aleko" and "The Fire Bird," when he had the space of the stage of the Metropolitan Opera House for his use.

Watching the huge pictures suspended over the stage—and pictures they really are—one can see that even here in the vast space his imagination did not exhaust itself; his energies flow freely and abundantly. His resources seem to be limitless. One would wish a Sistine ceiling, or the walls of a Doges Palace, for the brush of this modern master. It is a pity, indeed, that Chagall's beautiful art was expended on theatre curtains which, most of the time, lie folded up in a storage room to be seen only once in a great while (depending on the whim of the producer) and not on the walls of some public hall. Are there no synagogue or church walls to be decorated?

At first, when your eyes touch the vast canvases of Chagall's stage sets, you are blinded by their splendor of glowing colors—as by the sudden change from a dark room to open, brilliant sunshine. As your eyes become adjusted, you begin to see with amazement the delicacy and purity of the painting. Its striking power, you later realize, comes from the full orchestral ensemble of the colors and their strong contrasts; each object represented, even the big central figures, is lyrical, refined, and charming. Here indeed is painted music or magic—whatever you prefer to call it—vibrant and blazing in space, transparent, airy, rich with

---

* "The Fire Bird," music by Igor Stravinsky, choreography by Adolph Bolm, scenery and costumes by Chagall, was produced by the Ballet Theatre in 1945.

liquid light and emotion, melting into an opulent harmony.

There is no transposition of reality in the pictures hung as backdrops. Each curtain is a pure act of new creation, unfolding before your eyes spontaneously, as a sunrise, fresh, easy-breathing—except for the wonder of it.

There is hardly any need for dancers on the stage. . . . Nor do they have any significance against Chagall's overwhelming enchantment. The spectator can hardly take his eyes and mind off the magnificent stage sets and beautiful costumes to pay attention to the dance patterns, even of a brilliant Markova. Chagall's imagination spreads its magic spell and almost paralyzes the leap of the dancers—at least, such is the effect on the public. It is a vain effort to compete with Chagall's décor.

"Chagall may have visualized a moving drama, gradually unfolding its enchanting reality in living images; yet he starts out with so overwhelming an optical climax that it is hard to equal, let alone surpass, in any subsequent scenic developments. That, precisely, is the danger; for it is almost impossible to conceive of a choreography which would live up to the ideal demands of the artist's vision"—one reviewer said.

And, of course, the old cry of Abraham Efross,* that Chagall "has no theatre blood" is again raised.

This problem cannot be solved by asking Chagall to subdue his genius for the sake of weaker artists.

But the problem is only casual. The feeling of Chagall, if I am not mistaken, is not to waste his powers again on paintings for the storage room.

We are in a way fortunate, therefore, that we have twice seen what he can do with large space.

------

* See page 58.

Chagall 1915

"Thousand and One Nights"

AN INCREASE in Chagall's large number of book illustrations came in 1946 when an American publishing house commissioned the artist to illustrate their New York Pantheon Editions of the "Arabian Nights Entertainments."

The first English translator of the "Arabian Nights," Edward William Lane, was a scholarly orientalist and his aim was not only to entertain his readers but also to instruct them; therefore, in addition to his own innumerable informative notes and comments he looked for an illustrator who would carefully and studiously bring before the reader real types of Arabian men and woman, their national styles of garments and ornaments, their architecture and house furnishing, their customs and ways of life.

It is hard to believe that this was the intent of the publishers when they came with their commission to Chagall. We may safely assume that they were aiming not to instruct but to entertain their readers—and for this purpose they could not find any artist superior to Chagall.

Chagall prepared thirteen gouaches, which were exhibited in the Matisse Galleries in the spring of 1947.

As much as one can venture to say that Chagall's creatures come from any country other than his imagination, I would say that the characters of his "Thousand and One Nights" gouaches are Persian rather than Arabian.

It is not because Chagall discerned Persian original sources behind the Arabian version of the "Nights." We have seen before that he is not concerned with historical values. And so I assume that it was an artistic motif that led him to old Persia instead of Arabia.

The fanatic Islamitic Arabia, observing strictly the Alkoranic prohibition of images, did not create a pictorial or figure art to illustrate the books of its poets and story-tellers. It was under the rule of the Mongol Princes, who cared very little for Mohammedanism, that Persia developed an exquisite art of book illustration.

The Persian miniatures with their rich decorative patterns and brilliant use of color are much admired by modern artists. Henri Matisse was attracted by the Persian illuminators and he studied them with benefit to his art.

But if Chagall did look on this occasion at the Persian illustrations, it was only with one eye and in a passing glance. His gouaches show but a hurried acquaintance with the Persians. The rest is truly and gloriously the wonderland of his own fantasy. And in my opinion, he was right: as far as color is concerned, who could give him a richer palette than what he himself now possessed?

The architectonic of his papers is very far from the mastery of the Persian illuminators. They possess a classicism of their own—while Chagall is romantic. Here Chagall is the improvisator. If in his oils one can discover an underlying plan, a plan used for a period, with modifications, of course, for each individual canvas of the same period—here, behind all Chagall's gouaches there is no general construction plan; each composition seems to have been created impromptu.

I know that art connoisseurs looked at the gouaches and said that Chagall with his oriental fantasy here found suitable material.

Why do they make Chagall an Oriental? Because in all European painting you do not find another one that has in his palette all the fantastic colors that scintillate in Chagall's gouaches.

But may I ask the kind critics to point to one painter in the whole orient, in India, China, Japan, Persia, Arabia, of the old school or new, who painted with such soft, tender, singing, beautiful colors as Chagall? The oriental artists used colors brilliantly—but their colors are unemotional. You can admire a page of their illumination like a casket of gems. Chagall's rich colors are suffused with feeling and do not appeal to the mind, but touch the soul. Matisse is closer to the oriental painters than Chagall.

The material of the "Nights" liberated the artist from the obligation of rational thinking and stimulated unbridled imagining. In his play with the magic stories of the "Nights" no one would ask the artist why he did this or that. Nobody questions the magician as to the reason why. And the freedom to please his own fantasy was all Chagall needed.

For the rest, look at these illustrations: the characters are old Chagallian actors performing in a new enchanted world of Chagallian colors.

Look at the paper showing how "Kamaralkamar carries off the Princess on the ebony horse." Here you have Chagall's lovers clinging together, riding on a horse that soars through the air into the night. An oriental night? No, a Chagallian night. Only Chagall could have created the figures and the night. The horse is made of night and air condensed into a body. And you sense its movement, so graceful and light, above the earth, in mid-air. It transports the lovers who have left the earth and the sun far below. There is no perspective in the composition, and yet you feel deep space filled with air and night, thick, blue, fluid and ethereal. The whole picture is a magic tale of blue nuances of color and texture.

Look at the picture called "The Night of Schaha-razade." I would call it, "Adam and Eve in Paradise."

A pair of nude lovers, painted in white flesh color, lie on a floor of red. Above them blue space. Near them, on the red, stands a large Chagallian bird that reaches up into the blue space. Its feet are blue, the upper parts yellow, and it stands among yellow leaves. On the bird's breast a white sun is rising. From the bird's wings and tail a female figure emerges. The hair of the lying Eve (Schaharazade) is violet.

You have here red, white, blue, yellow and violet. What is there exotic about it? But such colors were seen only by Adam and Eve in Paradise when the earth was fresh, only a few days out of the hands of God, before it was smudged by sin—and now you can only see them in Chagall's gouaches.

The sheer wonder is, how the artist puts down a few patches of yellow on a background of blue, and the yellow patches rise up and float above the ground. The blue is deep, airily transparent and full of light. And see how the yellow of the leaves is transmuted into molten gold before your eyes.

The paper is perfect in its splendor.

New Paintings

TOGETHER with these gouaches, Chagall showed his oils done in 1946 and 1947.

One canvas is particularly memorable for its touching sadness, "Anniversary Flowers."

Against the pure white flowers, the heart of the bouquet, are placed small, fresh blue flowers, delicate and tender and moist, as if moistened by tears—flowers of sorrow—but so soft and tender and beautiful that you do not feel their poignancy as a stab of pain. The yellow figure of the dead bride—the flowers are for her—comes as a shock of sharp contrast—as the cry of pain of a trombone against the singing strings. Draped in sorrow, her lover is still with her, clinging to her.

Another canvas, called simply "Flowers," is magnificent in its beauty and symphonic harmony. It is one of those perfect compositions in which you cannot discover the smallest blemish—a picture that gives you a taste of the perfect peace and ease that is promised to the virtuous in the world to come.

A very interesting composition is "Double Face." The idea is to show the face in two aspects at the same time. Picasso has used this trick innumerable times. Chagall did it a few times before, as in the "Cello Player" (1939), "The Bride With Double Face" (1927), and others.

Here there is a nice structural relationship between the graceful head with its two faces and the breasts of the bust—and again, between the bust and head and the finely modeled animal overhead. The colors are new and different and delightful, with an enamelled cleanliness of brush stroke.

These few examples are enough to give some idea, even if only faintly, of the quality of Chagall's work at this period. More and more he let colors absorb his emotional experiences. He dissolved his creative strength in his color patterns. He did not occupy himself as much with spatial architecture. An exception is his "Wedding Lights"—but about this canvas later.

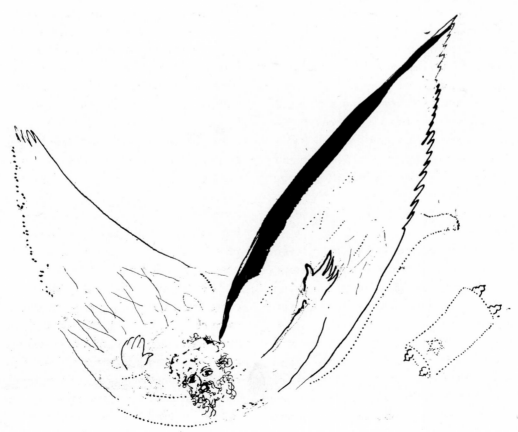

Chagall's Grotesques

GOING ALONG the galleries of Chagall's pictures we have met creatures that belong to a separate order of creation. It is very interesting to look at them in assembly.

Though God had ordained mother earth to bring forth the living creature after his kind, cattle and creeping thing and beast of the earth after his kind, and every winged fowl after his kind, the earth was disobedient. It seems that is her nature. . . . Besides, God is academic and mother earth has modernistic tendencies.

Be that as it may, she did not strictly carry out God's rational plan and brought forth fish that fly, fowls that give suck to their babies, and animals with fins—not at all after their kind. . . .

And her youngest son, perverse man, inherited her propensity in that direction. It is a basic human trait to take pleasure in all kinds of fantastic vagaries. Everywhere, in all parts of the world, in all periods, men have made frightful things, both comic and tragic; all sorts of repulsive and horrid, clever and non-sensical things, to entertain or to scare. Also for symbols and rituals—and for no reason at all.

The poetic imagination of all peoples, when they were young, created myths and legends with stories of many kinds of composite creatures. In Greek mythology we have the Centaur, half man and half horse; Minotaur, half man and half bull; Satyr, half man and half goat, with horns on his head; the Harpy, with the face of a woman and the body of a vulture; Nereids, sea-girls with green hair and fish bodies—and many other creatures.

But the Greeks were a clearminded people and even their most illogical fantasies have the logic of form. Many of the oriental peoples, not to talk of the wild tribes of Asia and Africa, have untamed and uncontrolled fantasies that overrun the boundaries of form.

The Bible contains many grotesque stories and figures: enough to mention Ezekiel's, Daniel's, and Zechariah's visions—but also the Nahosh (Serpent) of the Paradise, the Cherubim, the fallen angels who fell in love with human girls, Jacob's ladder, Joseph's dreams, Pharaoh's cows, Moses' staff, Balaam's ass that spoke Hebrew, Elijah's horses and chariot of fire, Jonah in the belly of the fish, Daniel, Hananiah, Mishael, and Azariah who walked in the fiery furnace—and many more.

Also in the Talmud, in the Aggada and Midrashim there are a great many grotesque stories, fables and symbols.

The modern European countries have a rich heritage of folkloristic poetry with their own fantastic creatures besides those borrowed from the religion or magic of the middle ages.

The great poets of all times are rich in grotesque creations—particularly Homer, Virgil, Dante, Shakespeare, Milton.

Certainly the artists showed a love of the grotesque. Gothic architecture is covered with a great variety of grotesque figures. The great and serious masters did not consider it below their dignity to create grotesque creatures—as witness, Michelangelo, Raphael, Tintoretto, Veronese, Dürer, and others.

To come closer to the present time: Hogarth, Blake, Goya, Delacroix—and the whole host of moderns. Among the moderns: Rousseau, Kandinsky, Klee, Chirico, Duchamp, Picasso. Chagall belongs to this group.

But Chagall stands apart from his colleagues of this group; first, by his Jewishness—he created Jewish grotesque; secondly, by the seriousness of his intent in creating his grotesque figures—the best of them have a soulfulness, spiritual overtones and a feeling bordering on the mystic. They are organic creatures; they possess an organic harmony of being and a completeness, as if nature made them.

This feeling of natural being in his figures may come from Chagall's greater mastery: he leaves no trace of his tools in his creatures. Where others leave over a feeling of technique, of workshop, of cleverness—many times intentionally—Chagall leaves in his creations something of the warm quickening of life's blood that passes from the artist into his creations. He imbues each one of them with meaning, with poetic

Bible. *Abraham Mourns Sarah*
Etching and Drypoint. 1931–39
Courtesy of the Artist

PLATE XXIX

suggestiveness, no matter how slight the thing may be. If this is due to greater mastery, I am satisfied.

In his "fairy tales"—tales that he himself makes up, not borrowed from Jewish or any other folklore, tales that have no meaning other than their art meaning, that are not symbolic and have no other aim except to please with their being—in all his tales which are only adventures in imaginative plastic creation, Chagall has many composite, or "synthetic," species.

You meet in his pictures a man with an ass's head —this character frequently appears, with variations. Chagall introduces a man with a bird's head many times; sometimes the man has wings. He has a girl who is part goat, a man with a flower pot head, in which flowers are growing.

In Mexico, as we have seen, he found a goat that fans itself, a rooster that carries a guitar, and a hen with a human head.

Chagall put a horse in a chair to listen to a speaker. Another horse has two heads—one a woman's. There is a horse with wings; an ass with wings and human hands and feet.

A cow of his sits on a chair and plays a fiddle. A cow takes a walk with an umbrella. A goat carries a drum.

A fish has the head of a Jew in skull-cap, and a long beard. A fish stands up on its tail and plays a fiddle.

A cat with human faces.

He has an animal that has a cow's horns on its head, an almost human face, a tail of a rooster and walks on bird's legs. What would you call this creature? According to Jewish dietary laws this Burbank cow-hen is not kosher; one would not know what ritual blessing to pronounce, when slaughtering it.

Chagall's living creatures are chummy with man, they enter into his affairs and participate in his joys and sorrows.

Also things dumb, silent things, are endowed with a soul by Chagall's art—not of a high category, but they live and have a will of their own. You see a chandelier that goes somewhere to carry out a mission.

In another picture you see a chandelier dancing gracefully; on legs, naturally, and it possesses wings—if my memory does not fool me and begins by itself to imitate Chagall. . . . He has a street lamp that takes a walk; a cello that plays on itself; and many other disporting things.

The inventive, poetic imagination of the artist overflowing with creative ideas, changes and renews the old mold of nature. And all his creatures live their own life—keep their place in the plastic plan of the picture, have their own space and air and their rich color—and what is more, a fresh, sparkling humor. And where there is humor, sometimes gay, sometimes sad, there is fresh life.

But we must not forget, and therefore it is worth repeating, that Chagall himself looks upon these creatures as artistic inventions, form-constructions. And only in this way, through their formal life, by their plastic existence for the picture, do they have their *raison d'etre*. They are pictorial things, conceived by the imagination to be received by the imagination, to be accepted for what they are, in their own right of being—to find joy in them if one has joy in oneself, and if one can find joy in artistic things.

By taking familiar forms, adding to the familiar the charm of the imagination, the artist arouses our interest more keenly than by abstractions and he can more readily convince us of their existential reality, even if only a fictional reality.

Life has such a powerful magnetism that wherever we find a life-pulse beating, we are intensely attracted to it and we respond with warm sympathy. Chagall's things have a life and a soul. That may be partially the result of his giving his creatures human activity familiar to us. And whenever the artist sends one of them on an errand, it is mostly connected with the living ways of his Witebsk folks—with the suggestion, or overtone, of a folklore motif; it seems therefore that these creatures are Jewish because of the association.

Circus Life

CHAGALL painted a large series of pictures with circus motifs; these belong to his grotesques. He comes to the circus arena again and again and brings out his acrobats and clowns—horses and men and girls—with great aplomb, as a successful promoter. He seems to derive great pleasure from them. He approaches them with delicacy and tenderness, and they repay him by performing with gusto. He first attires them all in finery; and bedecked and ornamented he presents them handsomely.

His love for the fantastic and grotesque finds here a spacious stage for play. His performers permit him full freedom of direction and he finds a whole world of fun and tricks for them.

Many artists have made of their clowns pathetic figures that hide tragic experiences behind their comic antics. Some have raised the clown to be a symbol of suffering humanity. The sensitive Chagall, who has felt keenly the suffering of his people, gave all his pathos to his Jewish themes and found his tragic figures in his Jews—but he also gives his full sympathy to the clown, the funny man, the harlequin, the picturesque trickster. Then, too, on these figures he can try his colorful costumes and he can lavish an abundant fantastic magnificence. He finds in the acrobat a free performer who can assume all possible and impossible positions in the pictorial space—and the artist can show his constructive inventiveness. With the performing acrobat the artist created many daring and original decorative and rhythmic patterns. Particularly successful are his circus women, for whom he created beautiful costumes and rich ornaments, using their bodies for flowing and musical lines. His equestrian girls are his best actors; he makes them take safely all dangerous positions on the horse, or under the horse, on its head, or on its tail, and everywhere else—they can even ride on a bird.

"Time is a River without Banks"

THE New York Museum of Modern Art has a famous canvas by Chagall called "Time is a River without Banks," (1930–39). It is a Chagallian grotesque that, as the name indicates, has a symbolic meaning. The explicit title is rather unusual for Chagall. Usually he avoids explanatory names because he wants his canvas to be seen, first of all, as a pictorial composition. But this strange composition would have been unduly puzzling to a speculative spectator —nor could one have read its meaning without the clue of the name. As it is, there is enigma enough in the canvas.

Time, of course, is represented by a clock, an old fashioned clock with a pendulum, enclosed in a glass case with a carved frame. The clock floats in mid-air above the river—to suggest the comparison. But riding on the clock is a fish with spread wings, and a small hand issuing from its head holds a little fiddle. The fish again reminds one of the river. The wings suggest that time flies . . . and the hand and fiddle are added to complete the puzzle . . .

On the banks you see Witebsk cottages. On one side, a pair of hugging lovers. A small rowboat with a figure is on the water.

The clock is often seen in Chagall's pictures, and so are the fish and the fiddle. I have read all kinds of suggestive interpretations of the symbolism of the fish and its association with the clock (time). Fish have been used as a symbol of fecundity (worshipped as a symbol of the god of fertility); as a symbol of the resurrection of the dead; of the coming of the Messiah. But Chagall assures us again and again that he is not concerned with any mystic symbolism. He says:

"There are no stories in my pictures, no fairy tales, no popular legends. For the Cubists a painting was a surface covered with forms in a certain order. For me a picture is a surface covered with representations of things (objects, animals, human beings) in a certain order in which logic and illustration have no importance. The visual effect of the composition is what is paramount. Any other nonstructural consideration is secondary."

The *pictorial* meaning is very clear and very delightful. Its esthetic value may be accepted immediately. The eye takes pleasure in the sensuously painted space that spreads far and deep behind the heavy-bodied fish-clock. It gives you a rich feeling of textured space in contrast to the scaly texture of the fish and the more scratchy texture of the wings. Then again for contrast there is the texture of the smoothly polished wood of the case and frame of the clock. And again in contrast you have the water and the shores. Each has its own texture, form and mass (weight).

Another source of esthetic pleasure is the physical super-reality of the clock and fish. Because of the contrasts their assertiveness of being is powerful. They cut themselves deeply into your awareness. There is a passionate insistence in them—which is enhanced by the strangeness and irrelevancy of their association; and their being up in the air, completely out of their usual place, strikes you as an apparition. The color contrast helps, the movement also. There is a feeling of a swooping motion of the fish. The pendulum sharply falling in the same direction and the inclination of the case of the clock add to the expression of floating, and forward motion, in contrast to the receding shores and cottages. The perspective helps in establishing the direction.

It is very interesting to observe the construction of the wings. They are not bird wings—but definitely wings of a fish: like fins outgrown into wings. There is a structural relationship between wings and tail.

And now you can see *why* the fish has wings—the picture needed them for texture contrast, for floating, for motion, for balance, and for power. Much of the assertive life of the fish-clock depends upon its wings.

The little hand and violin, too, are a fine structural adjustment, though not so apparent. Without it you would feel as if the fish might fly off the slow body of the clock. This little trick relates the fish and the clock as belonging together.

You see how structurally there is no mystery in the picture—except the mystery of the unusual, daring and inventive creativeness of the artist's imagination.

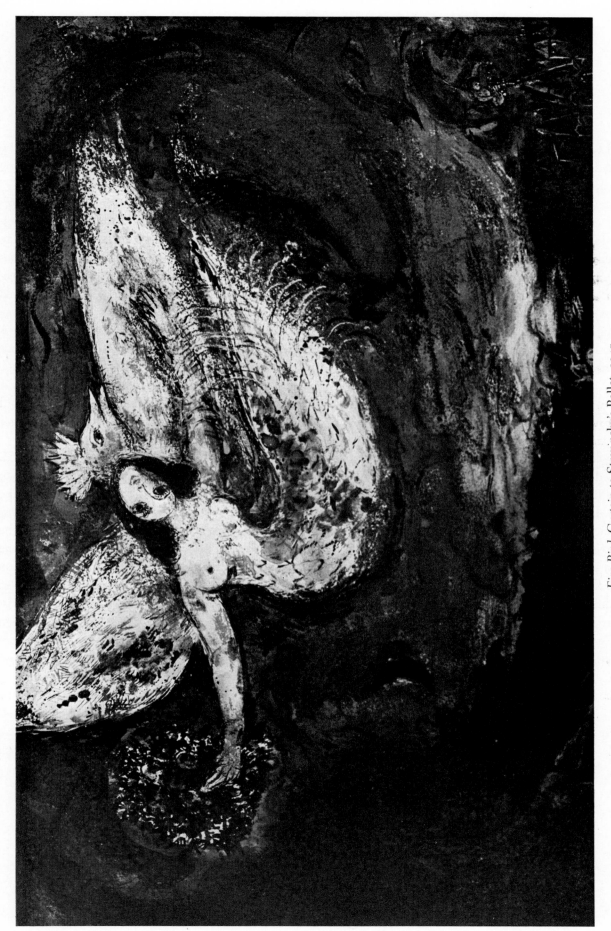

Fire Bird. Curtain to Stravinsky's Ballet. 1945

Courtesy of the Artist

PLATE XXX

"Wedding Lights"

A PARTICULARLY fine piece of Jewish grotesque is Chagall's "Wedding Lights," a vision as out of the apocalypse.

A figure with a head of a he-goat, with one clear human eye in the sun-yellow profile attracts your attention first. He has a pair of blue wings edged with violet, spread out powerfully, though he stands firmly on two human feet. He holds in his hands a flask half-full of wine and a glass filled with the wine. He seems to be waiting for the bride and groom who are approaching. Will he officiate at their wedding ceremony? He has a fine beard like a rabbi and is altogether a reverential personality—some kind of half deity.

A blue man falls from the sky, head down; on his uncovered head a phylactery and at his mouth a long pipe (like an Alpen-horn), blowing a note of doom. A heavy gold chandelier with burning white candles is suspended in the air over the market place where the bride, clad in white and wearing her bridal veil, leads the groom. In the background, behind rich palaces of a strange city, is a flaming sunset. Three musicians, a drummer with his drum, a green bass-viol with crooked shoes (viol and player in one), and a fiddler with his fiddle lead the bridal pair—each of the musicians leading in a different direction. In the very front of the foreground a nude girl and her lover lie reclining; a large bird stands behind their heads.

The gold conflagration of the setting sun touches the profile of the goat-deity and paints it yellow. A roof in the background, standing out diagonally, is covered with light violet and sheds its color onto the edges of the wings of the god.

There is a sweeping curved movement upward on the right, beginning with the bodies of the lying lovers, taken up by the goat-god, carried upward by his wings and ending with the body of the falling man.

As your eyes take in the strangely beautiful color-harmonies and you are busy admiring the epic grandeur of the whole composition, you have no need to know the meaning of it all. But your imagination has been incited, and you follow the figures into the apocalyptic atmosphere, soon to find yourself influenced by the mystic mood. You begin to feel as if you were called upon to witness a mysterious rite and what is happening is heavy with fate. Not only the figures, but also the light of the setting sun, the colors, the strange palaces, the very space, taste of mystic domains—as if the artist had pushed you through the gates beyond the boundaries of dayland into weird regions never visited save by visionaries in dreams.

You cannot linger long in this phantasmal world. Your rational mind asserts its good common sense. Not having any trust in visitations other than from the well-explored earth, you wake up to smile at the art-mysticism that ingratiated itself in your senses by the persuasiveness of its beauty. You know it was all done by the magic brush of a great imaginative master. You turn again to admire the strange life of the picture, so unusual in modern art. How magnificently the artist integrated his invented figures with the plastic design of the picture,—not only their physical appearances but also their supernatural logic and sentiments, and built up a passionate vital canvas!

And because the artist himself remains at the boundary of the rational world and does not himself believe in the occult communication of his brush, we can fully admire this canvas as a masterpiece of Jewish grotesque art.

Mysticism in Art

THE above consideration leads us to take up a question which is sometimes confusing in Chagall. Chagall writes:

"Some people are afraid, for no good reason, of the word 'mystic' to which they attach too much of an orthodox religious meaning. We must remove its old and musty garment and understand it in its pure form, exalted and clean. 'Mystic'—how many times has this word been thrown at me, just as before I had been accused of 'literature.' But can you find anywhere in the world a great picture, one great poem—or even a great social movement—without a mystic element in it? Does not each organism decay and die when you take away from it the mysticism of emotion and thought? I painfully answer myself. It is unjust to attack mysticism when it is the very loss of it that had almost destroyed France. But we must differentiate the various kinds of mysticism. The war must formulate the final aim to secure victory over the falsely conceived mysticism used for evil, a mysticism heartless and one-sided, the mysticism of the enemy."

It is clear, it seems to me, that the artist has created his own concept of mysticism—not the accepted one.

The Mystic believes in a transcendental knowledge and truth which we cannot reach with our fallible senses and erring minds, but may receive as a divine dispensation through spiritual illumination, that is, by direct communication from Heaven.

But if there are many kinds of mysticism and we can have a free choice of selection depending upon our own judgment, then we do not believe in divine guidance and do not wait for directions from God.

Without its "old and musty garment" this blind "mystic" force which Chagall finds in each great picture or poem and in every living organism, is no other force than the dynamic life-energy that shines in the nebular suns and makes the mite and the mote bestir themselves. It is the cosmic force that speaks through instinct in the animal and works intelligently in the poet and artist—as well as in all human endeavor. But sometimes the artist finds that this force works beyond his intelligence. He discovers, or others will, in his canvases something that he did not plan—and it is this "something" that gives his work a superior quality. What is more, he cannot always analyze his artistic impulses. He does not know what impelled him to make certain decisions at a time when his judgment was suspended. And only later does he realize that he was guided right—by what?

Nor does he ever know how to achieve "those thrusts of power beyond the reach of conscious art," as Flaubert termed it.

And no artist will sit with folded arms and wait for those intuitive promptings.

On the other hand, the creative impulses can be dissipated or vitiated, or paralyzed and destroyed by irresoluteness, scepticism and apathy. This is particularly true in a social organism. And therefore Chagall is right in demanding that we use this creative force not for evil, not heartlessly and one-sidedly, but for the good of all.

Chagall has said:

"I have often said to my colleagues, the artists, writers, and philosophers of many lands, that books and pictures are not created only with colors and words, but also with a clean conscience. Only the pure heart and soul can lead us onto the road of pure and exalted creations."

Said Heine:

"Jetzo, da ich ausgewachsen,
  Viel gelesen, viel gereist,
  Schwillt mein Hertz, und ganz von Hertzen
  Glaub' ich an dem Heilgen Geist."

Now when I am grown up,
Have read much, have traveled much,
My heart swells in me and with my
    whole heart
I believe in the Holy Ghost.

Chagall's Place in Modern Art

AGAINST the icy stream of materialism in the French art of our century, two great artists put up strong resistance: the mystic-religious Rouault, and the spiritual-humanistic Chagall.

Rouault's art—a great art—leads back to the middle ages, to the Gothic cathedral with its tenebrous, thick, mystic air, glowing with the rich colors of stained glass, hot and heavy with incense, prayers, gold embroidery, and sin.

Chagall's art leads to fresh, ever overflowing folk poetry, to pantheistic nature, and the human soul. He brings back humanism to modern art, returns man to his own.

Chagall's art wells with the waters of "eternal youth," the pure water that washes free the sky and earth of their blood and mud and sin. He touches the painful human heart with innocent joy and beauty—and while one stands in front of a Chagall canvas, one regains hope for man and his world.

To quote (from memory) William Blake: "Put aside the intellect, put on the imagination; the imagination is the man."

Put on your imagination when you approach Chagall and you will feel all the humanity of Chagall's art.

You need no imagination for Matisse and Picasso.

At first the Paris public refused to accept Chagall's art.

"There is no doubt that my first tendencies were a little strange to the French. And I looked upon the Frenchmen with so much love. It was painful"—he noted.

Not only the general public, also the connoisseurs; the art world was not in the mood to appreciate Chagall's achievement. In the Paris studios the spirit of Picasso—the materialistic frost of his cubism— dominated.

And where the fetish of cubism was not adored there was an altar to Matisse and his no less formalistic catechism. The two artists together were the sovereign law-makers in the art world of those days.

Years later Chagall said:

"Exactly what sort of painter would I have liked to be? I don't say 'could I have been.' I was still very young and did not picture art as a profession or a job. It did not seem to me that pictures were destined solely for decorative or domestic purposes. I said to myself: 'Art is in some way a mission—and don't be afraid of this word.'"

In a previous chapter I have endeavored to project the struggle that Chagall carried on within himself against the powerful materialistic forces of cubism.

Now we have to project the background of Parisian studios and the temper of the art world that Chagall had to meet and challenge.

For the sake of those readers who are not familiar with the history of French art of the last fifty years, we will take a hasty look at its development in order to more fully understand Chagall's position in it.

It began with the Impressionists. They were the first to weaken the interest in the content of a picture.

The Impressionists, as is very well known, were busy studying carefully the changes that take place in the appearance of things when seen in sunlight in the open air.

Monet's interest in sunlight did not come from his love of the sun—the love that the great English landscape painter, Constable, had for the sun. For Constable "the light of nature was the mother of all that is valuable in poetry, in painting, and in everything else that appeals to the soul."

No, Monet did not aim to appeal to the soul. For him, as for his followers, the effect of sunlight had an artistic-scientific interest. He was trying to be more faithful to nature, trying to reproduce exactly what he had before his eyes. He noted carefully the effect of the different intensities of sunlight on the appearance of things, in the different hours of the day, as the sun moves along in its path—and endeavored to find a way of putting colors on canvas to give the eye the sensation of vibrating sunlight reflected from the painted objects, even when viewing the picture in the studio, out of the direct brightness of the sun.

For that purpose one thing in a field was as good as any other. Coming in the field to paint, no one corner of the landscape was preferred; he was indifferent—but carefully studied what he saw. He painted the same haystack three times under the changed light of morning, noon, and afternoon. A grassy field with turkeys in it was as important as the most beautiful piece of landscape. As long as he could make his colors effect the vibration of sunlight, he did not mind what he brought back on his canvas.

The interest in an exhibition now was, not what the artist gave, but how he managed his light-vibration, and how he painted his shadows in the picture.

Up to Monet and the Impressionists artists customarily used bituminous colors (black and dark brown) for shadows. The Impressionists discovered while painting in the open sunlight that the areas in the shadows were not without colors; the colors merely were not as bright and the complementary colors predominated, especially blue. They confirmed their observations by painting winter landscapes, studying the shadows on snow. As a result, Monet stated that black did not exist in nature.

To the discoveries of the Impressionists were added the studies of the optics of colors by Helmholz and others.

Thus, the technical innovations absorbed the interests of the studios and cafes—and the content of the picture fell by the wayside.

A return of interest in subject matter came with the Post-Impressionists, Gauguin and Van Gogh.

Van Gogh revolted against the Impressionists' naturalism. He wrote to his brother from Arles: "I should not be surprised if the Impressionists soon find fault with my way of working. . . . Because, instead of trying to reproduce exactly what I have before my eyes, I use color more arbitrarily so as to express myself forcibly."

Also Gauguin began to use color "remote from nature." And soon the studios were busy again discussing "conventional," "real" and "abstract" (arbitrary) colors.

But Van Gogh's social art had a strong influence on the younger painters and their canvases showed human interest.

Then came a group of painters, with Matisse as

leader, who were known as the "Fauves" (the Wild Beasts). They took over Van Gogh's and Gauguin's idea of free or arbitrary use of color, especially Gauguin's use of patterned zones of pure color—and went into the extreme of intensity and sonority of color orchestration. "The Fauve Matisse wanted to roar" . . .

And again the content of the picture was neglected. But it went even further than that.

Matisse continued to refine his fauve (early) colored patterns—until there was no subject left in his canvas, only a scheme of arrangement . . .

Nature, life, experience, passion, give resistance. But Matisse wanted above all a balanced ensemble. He worked out a scheme of re-proportioning of objects to fit into his decorative patterns. He changed proportions and outlines to attain an over-all balance. He would alter parts of the human body to go with the rest of the decorative, freely patterned design. As he kept changing the colors to harmonize and balance them, so he changed the lines and the natural appearance of his figures to harmonize them with the other patterns—kept on changing and refining them until no vestige of natural life was left in them.

"It is better to modify proportions than to invalidate compositional balance"—he advocated.

As one of his admirers put it: "What in fact he did do was to carry the subject to the extreme limit of transformation."

Matisse put down a law:

"In a picture there must be nothing that can be described in words or which already exists in our memory. . . . When I see a picture I forget what it represents, all that is important is line, form, and colors . . ."

And, again:

"A picture must hang quietly on a wall. The onlooker should not be perturbed or confused, he should not feel the necessity of contradicting himself, of coming out of himself. A picture should give deep satisfaction, relaxation, and pure pleasure to a troubled consciousness."

In other words, the picture must not remember and must not recall the world as it exists outside the walls of the museum. The picture must flatter and pat the owner, must sing him to sleep with the lullaby that all is well in the world. As a paid sweetheart, the picture must yield "pure" pleasure.

By no means must the picture remind the onlooker of the real world and its heartaches. It must speak only of a fantastic, fictional world, a world without reality, without thought, without passion, without conflict. All senses must be put to sleep except the eye. To give pure pleasure to the eye the picture must show pretty things, soft, colorful textiles, rich tapestries, shawls, vases, musical instruments, flower pots, porcelain, jewels, and naked girls. The nudes must not be too voluptuous, not to arouse desire, but only to charm the eye so the beholder may not be disturbed out of his tranquillity. It is best that all objects suggest an exotic world.

At first glance it may seem that such a philosophy of art is also Chagall's. And certainly there are ideas in it that would please every artist. Yes, Chagall, too, leaves the natural world behind, changes reality into a legend. Chagall, too, has no voluptuous nudes. He also aims to give pure pleasure. He loves to paint flowers and pretty textiles. Many of his pictures are idyllic, pure, quiet and peaceful and do not upset the onlooker. He, too, will sing you to sweet dreams.

But Chagall is many sided and rich in experience. The peaceful, pure, and idyllic are part of his emotional experience. But these are moments among others. And in these "pure" pictures Chagall gives much more than Matisse in a human way. Matisse is cold, contemplative and, to a degree, indifferent. Matisse speaks of emotion—but he means the emotion that a colored patterned composition can arouse. His "pure" pleasure is for the eye only. The interest he awakens is mental. Chagall is warm, impulsive, and communicative. He touches your imagination. Chagall's peace is more than the absence of disturbance. His calm is more than repose. His idyllic purity is a singing joy, or sadness. His peace is a serene delight or sorrow.

Not to burden the onlooker with memories of the real world, Matisse leaves only a shadow of reality in his pictures. He removes the living heart of his human figures and the nourishing substance of his things. They become empty of meaning—as the ear of wheat after threshing. Not only his human figures but objects, too, lose their dignity on entering his pictures. He takes away their independent being and they become forms empty of significance, except for the pictorial design. Compare a still-life of Matisse with one painted by Cézanne! It is characteristic that Chagall has painted very few still-life pictures, except flowers.

He must have the glow of life to begin with. His "still-born" objects, his fiddles, clocks, lamps, candles, have in his imagination the living meaning of their human association.

It is characteristic of Matisse that he makes his human beings less vital than his things, and the face less important than other parts of the body. His human figures are less animated, have less vital color than other objects in the picture, and it is seldom the human figures that set the pattern or give the tone to the whole design—partly because his objects come originally with rich textures and colors, like the oriental tapestries, porcelains, jewels, and sumptuous textiles which he introduces into his canvases. The face becomes an empty mask, bloodless and expressionless, and is usually distorted to conform to the patterns dominantly used in the picture. There is really no human being—but line, form and colors.

As a result, you are not interested in the life of Matisse's subjects, nor in their destinies. You can only admire the workmanship of the artist. From one point of view it is a gain—you concentrate on the esthetic value of the picture. On the other hand, your response is light and you are really unconcerned—since the picture was made not to touch you deeply.

The opposite is true of Chagall. Though he, too, does not permit unchanged reality to enter into his canvas, the people and animals that he transforms into subjects for his pictures, once they enter his picture world, bring with them such intensity of life, such passion of being, that you feel concerned about them and you want to know what is happening to them. You have a sympathy for them as for creatures of your own kind. You are not always clear about their doings, but as long as they are before your eyes, you devote your full attention to their life in the picture.

As an illustration, take Chagall's "Burning Village."

Houses are on fire. No human being is to be seen anywhere. A strange bird is sitting in the middle of the deserted street, holding on her lap a human doll saved from the fire. As you look at the picture you become imbued with its dismal air, fear and woe.

Chagall created here a new reality, strange and mystic. But you share with the artist his concern over the fate of the burning village and the bird and its saved doll. . . . You are touched as if you really believed in the strange tale.

While Matisse is busy creating new decorative patterns, Chagall is interested in creating, as in the above picture, patterns of consciousness that speak to you of the fears of the times, of war and destruction.

(Now again, with the preparation of the super-atomic and H-bombs, this picture seems a prophecy of the future—will all our cities go up in flames with the disappearance of all human life, a strange bird and its doll remaining the only inhabitants of the desolation?

William Butler Yeates would say: "The prophetic soul of the wide world dreaming on things to come.")

Whatever its reading may be—this picture also has the value of fantastic poetry for all time, a pure imaginative poetry with a haunting sad beauty, as Poe's "Ulalume," Coleridge's "Kubla Khan," Keat's "Lamia," or some of Baudelaire's sonnets in "Flowers of Evil."

I do not in the least mean to undervalue Matisse—need I say it? In his own inimitable way he had reached a perfection which justifies the sacrifice of the subject. Contrasting Chagall's work against his is done only with the purpose of showing Chagall's place, and what Chagall has restored to French art.

To quote an admirer of Matisse: "Matisse's work has acquired greater order, sumptuousness and plastic perfection, but it has not surpassed the incisive style of his youthful work. One sees this clearly from his colors. In his youth Matisse was at great pains to discover all the secrets of color. For this purpose he made the most complicated experiments and obtained sensational results. But there remained the problem of atmosphere. It is only in the last few years and after long and assiduous efforts that he managed to situate the object in atmosphere and to outline it in space. Today he is the absolute master of color; he has discovered the most subtle relations of tones, and their most intimate fusion." *

It is not hard to see why Matisse found more followers in his time than the more imaginative Chagall. It is easier to follow—I do not say, equal—Matisse and produce pretty decorative patterns, than to follow Chagall who created new patterns of psychic experience in terms of great plastic workmanship.

"Impressionism and cubism," Chagall said, "are comparatively easy to understand because they present but one single aspect of an object for our consideration—simple contrasts of light and shadow. But a single aspect of an object is not enough to make up the complete subject matter of a picture. Every object has diverse aspects. I am not against cubism; I have admired the great Cubists and I have profited from their work. But I have discussed the limitations of its viewpoint even with my friend Apollinaire *, the man who has really given cubism its place. For me, cubism seemed to limit the possibilities of pictorial expression. I needed greater freedom."

What I have said about Matisse and his influence can be said, even more, about Picasso.

When Chagall once asked Apollinaire to introduce him to Picasso, Apollinaire said with a laugh:

"Do you want to commit suicide? All his friends end up that way."

There were many young artists in those days swallowed up by cubism.

And Chagall, too, as we have seen, was for a time a follower of cubism—on his own terms—and, as he admits, has benefited by it.

But for the orthodox Cubists ** Chagall was a nonconformist. He made too many breaches in their discipline and did not accept cubism as an end in itself.

"Art is in some way a mission—and don't be afraid of this old word," he had said to himself, he tells us.

The Cubists objected to Chagall's introducing in his cubistic pictures a spiritual and emotional content—with that, they claimed, he turned painting into "literature."

The accusation of being "literary" was no small matter. The artist with this stigma on him could hope for no hearing.

The crusade against "literary" art was fashionable even before Chagall came to Paris.

It had begun as a healthy reaction against those artists who were attracting the public with sentimental and melodramatic stories on their canvas. Not possessing any real, expressive powers, many of these artists covered their artistic anemia by pretending high aims, hiding their poverty behind well phrased talk of "poetic vision."

The call to throw out literary content and elevate formalism as the only aim of art was a death blow to these pretenders and their practices.

But how could the history of art be forgotten?

* Zervos, quoted by G. Di San Lazzaro in *Painting in France,* published by Philosophical Library.

* See page 25.
** See page 26.

Right behind this new art was Delacroix, who contributed much to its development—Delacroix who was "passionately in love with passion," as Baudelaire put it. "Delacroix's imagination!"—Baudelaire exclaims, "it never feared to scale the difficult heights of religion. Heaven belongs to it as does hell, as do war, Olympus, and sensuality. He is indeed the type of painter-poet!"

And there was Goya, so much admired! Art, indeed, did not begin with Matisse and Picasso. If Delacroix, Goya, Tintoretto, Titian, El Greco, Rembrandt, to mention a few of the highest, were "literary" painters, then there was nothing scandalous about being "literary."

But even the immediate forerunners, Van Gogh and Gauguin, who helped to develop the revolution in French art, were not at all against having "literature" in their pictures. In fact, Gauguin stated that painting "involves a story" like literature, only in painting "the reader can embrace the whole development at once."

Chagall has said: "I admit that when I heard this word ("literature") pronounced by young painters and poets I grew a little pale. I grew pale—not from shame, not from fear on account of myself—but rather for others, for those who said it."

The question is not how much "literary" content there is in a work of art, but how "significant" is the plastic form that contains it. The question is, did the artist neglect his professional workmanship, did he sacrifice any of the plastic needs for the sake of the subject? Did he content himself with the importance of his ideas and a mean plastic form for them?

But as Auguste Rodin has pleaded convincingly:

"Si mon modèle est mauvais, si je commets des fautes d'anatomie, si j'interprète mal les mouvements, si j'ignore la science d'animer le marbre, ces critiques ont cent fois raison. Mais si mes figures sont correctes et vivantes qu'ont-ils donc à y reprendre? Et de quel droit voudraient-ils m'interdire d'y attacher certains intentions? De quoi se plaignent-ils si, en plus de mon travail professionnel, je leur offre des idées et si j'enrichis d'une signification de formes capables de séduire les yeux?"

(If my model is bad, if I commit errors of anatomy, if I interpret the movements badly, if I ignore the science of animating the marble, these critics are a hundred times right. But if my figures are correct and living, then what do they blame them for? And what right have they to forbid me to attach to them certain intentions? What are they complaining of, if in addition to my professional work I offer them ideas and if I enrich with a significance forms that are capable of seducing the eyes?)

Many of the followers of Matisse and Picasso think that this problem is new, an outcome of our modern life. They hold its very "modernism" as a proud proof of the correctness of their position. It may therefore be of interest to them to find this problem, though under a slightly different aspect, noted and commented on by Goethe. He says:

"There are two kinds of dilettanti in poetry: he who neglects the indispensable mechanical part and thinks he has done enough if he shows spirituality and feeling; and he who seeks to arrive at poetry merely by mechanism, in which he can acquire an artist's readiness and is without the soul of the matter."

Of course, in poetry, too, the same demands are raised by the "avant-garde" poets threatening with the same bug-a-boo of "literature":

"Like the wind of morning, crisp and pure,
Which scatters the scent of mint and thyme,
Thus free and careless should be your rime—
And all the rest is literature!"

However, all modern artists do agree that the form of a work of art is of such supreme importance that it demands the primary allegiance of the artist. It must be first in his consciousness, the first aim in the planning of the work. The artist must subject all of his endeavors to the discipline of the plastic idea.

This first principle of modern art Chagall recognizes and follows faithfully. He has a greater variety of new and daring original pictorial designs in his "literary" works than many of the "pure" artists.

You will invariably find, however, that for a great artist the subject is a challenge to creativeness; the importance of the content calls for his effort, for a trial of strength, stirs up his powers and stimulates his imagination to inventiveness. The plastic design of the work grows with the scope and magnitude of the sub-

The Siren. Gouache. 1946–47
Illustration to "Thousand and One Nights"
New York Pantheon Edition
Courtesy of the Artist
PLATE XXXI

ject—the form must be big enough to contain all the possibilities inherent in the subject; it must be strong and subtle, resilient and pliant to express the power and the delicacy of the ideas that press for deliverance in a material investiture of form. Thus the stimulation to creativeness will benefit the formal development of the work of art.

Sometimes the content gains by the need of the plastic organization. Chagall says that he will often introduce a small figure for no other reason than to fill empty space. But in these cases it mostly happens that the auxiliary little figure will enrich the subject with deeper sense. For instance, Chagall has told us:

"In the case of the headless woman with the milk pail in one of my pictures painted in 1910-11,* it occurred to me to separate her head from her body because I found that I needed an empty space in that particular place. In my painting, "I and the Village," ** I painted a small cow and a milk-maid in the head of a large cow because I needed that kind of shape in that place for my composition."

Very well. But who can deny that the conceptual imagery of the subject in both pictures was enriched by the constructive needs? Yes. And what prompted the artist to introduce a cow and milk-maid in a picture of a village? . . .

Chagall has said:

"Before the war of 1914, I was accused of falling into "literature." Today people call me a painter of fairy tales and fantasies. Actually, my first aim is to construct my paintings architecturally—exactly as the Impressionists and Cubists have done in their own fashion and by using the same formal means. The Impressionists filled their canvases with patches of light and shadow; the Cubists filled them with cubes, triangles, and cones. I try to fill my canvases in some way with objects and figures treated as forms . . . sonorous forms like sounds . . . passionate forms designated to add a new dimension which neither the geometry of the Cubists nor the patches of the Impressionists can achieve.

"I am against the term 'fantasy' and 'symbolism.' Our whole inner world is reality—perhaps more real than the apparent world."

* See page 30.
** See page 29.

The form of a work of art is a self-sufficient end—but also a means of communication. The more significant the form, the greater the power of its expressiveness, and, therefore, an excellent means of revealing the "state of the soul" of the artist, or of transmitting the "mission" of the artist—even if the "mission" is only, as Matisse wanted it, "an appeasing influence."

("What I dream of is an art of balance, of purity and serenity devoid of troubling and depressing subject matter, an art which might be for every mental worker, be he businessman or writer, like an appeasing influence, like a mental soother, something like a good arm-chair in which to rest from physical fatigue"—said Matisse.)

There were many outside influences that helped prepare the minds of the younger leaders in art and letters to accept the works of Matisse and Picasso and to formulate ideological concepts in support of them. These "new" ideas were propagated in poems, in magazine articles, and in the cafes.

One such influence came all the way from Japan.

For about 200 years, beginning with the second half of the 17th century, a popular art developed in Japan known as the school of "Ukiyoye," which has been translated as "Pictures of the Floating World," or "Pictures of the Passing Scene." These were pictures of beautiful women and their fashionable dresses or hair-dos, portraits of famous actors, or scenes from popular plays with leading actors in them, illustrations of poems, with a stanza or two, and also well known landscapes, or birds, or flowers. The pictures were printed on paper with wooden blocks and cost only a few pennies.

After the International Exhibition held in London in 1862 and the Exhibition of 1867 held in Paris, these Japanese prints became known in Europe and much admired.

There was an oriental shop in Paris, "La Porte Chinoise," where artists bought Japanese costumes, china, prints and fans. It became a fashion among the artists. Japanese prints and fans could be seen in almost every studio. You can see them now in many paintings made during that period. The Paris literary and artistic cafes were busy discussing oriental art, particularly the Japanese prints. The Impressionists were interested, also Manet, Renoir, Van Gogh, Gauguin, Toulouse-Lautrec, Degas, Whistler, and Matisse.

For the European artists the subjects of these prints

had no interest and no meaning—but the art language appealed to them strongly. Their graphic charm, decorative quality, subtle line, organization of patterned space—the whole approach of the Japanese painters to the picture was fresh and new to the Parisian artists and they studied them.

Matisse had an interest also in the other oriental arts known to the Europeans. He made a careful study of the Persian and Arabian miniatures, tiles, and tapestries—and learned from their idioms. He learned how to put down color contrasts, how to represent men and women in flat patches of colors without shadows, to make fine patterns of them.

"The Persian miniatures do more than illustrate a text. They represent spiritual values unknown to Western illustration, being born out of necessity after many a conquest and brought about by a desire to enforce and preserve the Persian cultural and spiritual tradition.

"The painter must employ every resource at his command. His colors must be of singular purity. His design must have melody, fluency, and refinement of inflection"—to quote an authority.*

One cannot say, therefore, that the cultural and spiritual demands on the Persian artist were in the way of his achieving artistic excellence. Nor did this excellence come to him without conscious effort. On the contrary. The knowledge that he was entrusted with a sacred mission did inspire him to "employ every resource at his command"—and he achieved in his own way as fine artistic results as the European artists who work only for "pure" art.

Matisse did not disdain to learn from the artists who had other aims beside line, color, and form. But the spiritual and cultural qualities of the oriental artists left no impression on him—he was blind to it; perhaps that is the reason why Chinese art did not interest him much.

Another influence in the Parisian art world came from Africa. And through Picasso it became a force more telling than the Japanese prints.

Vlaminck, one of the Fauves, claims the honor of the discovery of African Negro sculpture in the junk shops of Paris. Through him Matisse became interested and Matisse introduced the Negro sculpture to Picasso.

Nobody seems to have noticed the African sculpture before—the time for its influence was not ripe. Now with the new gospel that all that a work of art need give you is pure esthetic pleasure which it can give only by its formal qualities, now the African Idols could find worshipers in Paris.

In their native home these sculptures had a ceremonial and magic significance. The Negro artist did not carve his piece of sculpture to be admired as a work of art, but as a means of communication between him and his tribal brothers, and between them and the spirit world. He aimed at a powerful formal expression to convey his powerful emotion and meaning—though undoubtedly his artistic instinct directed his efforts to an artistic end.

To the godless Parisians the gods of the wild African tribes had nothing to communicate. The Parisian could only judge them as works of art. They saw that they themselves were affected by an art that has no meaning, no communication, but a strong constructive plastic. This confirmed them in their theory that the artist must keep to his plastic mastery and nothing else matters.

Matisse could make no use of the Negro sculpture, but Picasso did.

Picasso had already made the acquaintance of the ancient Iberian sculpture (the pre-Roman sculpture of Spain). Some new pieces of sculpture were then discovered and they were displayed in the Louvre. Picasso made studies of these, and when he saw the Negro sculpture his interest was aroused.

From elements that he had borrowed from Cézanne, together with what he had learned from the Iberian and African sculptures, he now began to develop his cubistic art *—with the help of Braque and others.

The art world of Paris cannot exist long without new ideologies, without revolutionary slogans which the young artists use as weapons to attain leadership. That is what keeps artistic Paris fresh and young.

After the Impressionists, the Neo-Impressionists, and the Post-Impressionists, came the Fauves and Matisse. Then came Picasso with his cubism. (Chagall reached Paris in 1910, when cubism and Picasso were dominant.)

To have a more complete picture, we must also consider, even if only hastily, the socio-political causes that helped to dehumanize art.

---

* Sir W. Arnold, "Painting in Islam."

---

* See page 25.

The decline and fall of man in the eyes of his fellow men began early in our century. The cult of individualism, the cult of the value and, therefore, the prerogative of the heroic individual, reached its culmination with the full development of capitalism. Hero worship, that passed from the knight to the general, from the general to the merchant-prince and captain of industry, came to a speedy end. The historic mission of the capitalist to organize industrial production had been accomplished. The capitalist was no longer socially necessary and he could not keep up his role of benefactor to humanity. His philanthropy could no longer hide his parasitic position in society.

The intellectual class that had served him and was subservient to his interest could no longer continue to propagate the legend of his superman birth-right, neither to itself nor to the masses, not even to the progressive capitalist himself. Nor could it defend ideologically his claims to the divine right of ownership of the vast heaps of wealth he controlled.

In the midst of his possessions, in his magnificent palaces, private museums and libraries, surrounded by the splendor he had collected in many countries, of many centuries, he looked small and insufficient. In the rich frame and brilliant setting, his portrait as a man looked pale and faded.

His almightiness had been successfully challenged by the organizations of his workers, and his political power was on the decline.

The Century of Progress which began with the Industrial Revolution opened with high hopes of unlimited achievement and happiness for humanity— and ended in war and annihilation. Man stands defeated and appalled by the machine.

Man lost.

And individualism lost its ideologists.

Darwin's principle of the survival of the fittest as a factor in the evolution of species lost its scientific validity; it had been disproved in modern biology. Scientists have also noted that mutual aid among animals, especially those that live in herds, is a greater factor in the struggle for survival than the strength of the individual.

Nietzsche with his dream of a superman that possesses unlimited free will and stands beyond good and evil, found his last admirers among the Nazis.

Modern psychology has denied altogether the myth of the integrated human personality. According to Freud man has no free choice of action. He is heir to biologic instincts and impulses that came down to him from his ancestral primeval past, that lie coiled in the abysmal pit of his psyche, hungry and repressed, always in readiness, waiting for a crisis, for a moment of his weakening, to overpower him and take control of his actions.

Man is burdened with a fate he cannot avoid. Before he crosses the threshold of his conscious life, before he knows good from evil, his way into the future is determined for him by forces of which he has no knowledge and over which he has no control.

On what can he pride himself, the little man?

Freud's pessimistic teachings have had, and still have, a tremendous influence on the arts and letters of the century.

Perhaps even before Freud's influence spread, it was Bergson's lectures on "Creative Evolution" which he gave in the *College de France,* that made a strong impression on the intellectual world of Paris. He became fashionable.

According to Bergson, evolution has no end, no goal, though it is purposive and truly creative like the work of an artist. There exists an urge to realization, though there is no way of knowing the nature of the result of the urge.

He compares cosmic evolution to an explosion of a shell into fragments that are shells again, that explode into shells—continuously. Life is one great force, one vast vital impulse, élan vital, given once and for all time.

All organized beings, from the humblest to the highest, from the first origins of life to the time in which we are and in all places as in all times, do but evidence a single impulsion, the inverse of the movement of matter, and in itself indivisible.

On earth the evolution of life manifested itself in the following way: first the life current divided itself into plants and animals. Among the animals, in a later stage, a new division of the life stream took place, resulting in instinct and intellect.

Instinct in its highest form is intuition.

"By intuition I mean instinct that has become disinterested, self-conscious, capable of reflecting upon its object and of enlarging it indefinitely."

The life stream becoming consciousness can only be reached by intuition—not by the intellect. Of the current of consciousness the intellect is only a specialized function and it can therefore grasp only a separate division, a concretization of a part of the current, but not the current in its fullness, in its living flux.

To put it vulgarly: the intellect is like a fisherman on the shore of the current, who catches a fish, one concrete form of the life-stream—and while the fisherman, the intellect, is busy with the dead fish, dead since it became a concrete separate thing, the living, full current of consciousness flows by. With the aid of intuition we can become submerged in the current, suspended, as it were, in midstream, letting the fullness and flow of the living current inundate our being with an awareness of it.

But the intellect dominates our mind and tyrannizes over the subconsciousness. Intuition has been pushed by the intellect to the fringe of it. We must put the intellect into a faint, into "a spiritualized hypnotic trance," then our intuition can become active and take us into the subconscious current of life in its flow.

Bergson wishes to make the intellect "turn inward on itself and awaken the potentialities of intuition which still slumbers within it."

Intelligence or intellect, "as it leaves the hands of nature, has for its chief object the inorganic solid."

"The intellect always behaves as if it were fascinated by the contemplation of inert matter."

"The intellect is characterized by a natural inability to understand life."

Instinct and intuition are opposed to intellect.

Intellect is contemplative and not active as our life ought to be, following freely the urge within us of the élan vital.

Philosophers have always found praise for the contemplative moment of life. The highest good is the intellectual love of God, according to Spinoza.

But Bergson condemns the intellect and has no place in his philosophy for contemplation.

Communication between the artist and the public can be reached by intellectual means only. But no truth can be communicated by the intellect and therefore the art and literature that aim at communication are bad and harmful. Only the reports of instinct and intuition are important.

By his disparaging intellectual activity and all that man can attain by reason and intelligence, by his praise of the instincts and intuition, by urging man to give in to his impulses, to the urge of the élan vital, Bergson opened the gates to irrationality, mystification and confusion for the artist. If the artist must avoid communication, then he can create his personal language, his personal symbols and make a virtue of obscurity. The act of creation itself becomes then the sole aim of the artist.

"We are free," says Bergson, "when our acts spring from our whole personality, when we express it, when they have the indefinable resemblance to it that we sometimes find between the artist and his work."

Bergson thus not only liberates the artistic act, but frees man from responsibility for all his acts—as long as they are acts of his instincts and are in his image. The artist therefore is doubly free as man and as artist, free to follow his urges without responsibility except to himself.

It was this part of Bergson's philosophical system that appealed to the poet and artist.

If Bergson and Freud were not enough—war came.

The First World War was man's biggest breach of faith with man.

When social ideals have outlived their usefulness and become discredited, and no new ones are born to take their place, a decadence and impoverishment in art, in literature, as well as in other spheres of culture sets in.

Without faith in some social ideal the artist becomes "free." At such times the issue of "pure" art, art for art's sake, is suddenly raised, as if it were a new issue, and it finds advocates everywhere among the young artists.

The artists begin to play with their means of expression; form becomes the preoccupation of the creative mind. You can say nothing as long as you say it beautifully—no, significantly. Art becomes overrefined, overripe. Art loses its vitality, and the formal means, such as line, color, organization become the subject of experiment.

The artist feels he is overfed and yet he lusts for foreign and exotic diets. He is satiated with culture and will set out to look for strange, barbaric and forgotten or still undiscovered patterns of culture. He is tired and wants a "new shudder."

Suddenly the artist becomes interested in the barbaric ceremonial masks of the African Negro, in the sculpture of Chaldea, in the archaic beginnings of Egyptian and Greek art, in the Etruscan and Iberian sculptures; and as Chagall reminds me, he turns with a new interest to the pictures of Piero della Francesca, of Pallajuola, of Paola Uccello and Masaccio, or to the primitive art of cavemen, or Byzantine frescos. At the same time, Matisse goes for the highly stylized decorative art of Persia and Japan.

In such a period, if there are creative artistic personalities they will make renovations of old forms and bring in innovations in the use of the language of expression, and even discover new forms. Their achievements, depending on their genius, will have an enduring and significant value.

But man will degenerate in their art into a decorative or structural pattern. Or he will be lost sight of altogether. Art will assume the pessimistic intellectualism of Picasso, or the superficial hedonistic spirit of Matisse.

Matisse remained faithful to his ideal of a hedonistic art even in the years of the first World War, as well as in Hitler's days. Never to this day has he "sinned" as Picasso did with his "Guernica."

But not all the artists, even the followers of Matisse, could remain "happy" in the general breakdown of the war and in the years after. Not all the artists could remain consistently blind to what was happening in the world—and the result was *Dada*.

Dada appeared first in 1916 in New York and Zurich, Switzerland; then it spread to Berlin, Cologne, Paris, Hanover. In New York the French painters Marcel Duchamp and Francis Picabia, war refugees, together with the American Man Ray, began a revolution of the type of Dada, though without that name.

The name Dada was found in Zurich "with the aid of a paper-knife slipped at random in a dictionary." * The name was a great success, it added mystery to confusion. It was quickly adopted in all the art and literary centers.

The apologists of the Dada movement claim that it was a reaction to the war. The Dada artists and poets were exasperated by the catastrophic madness of the war and in despair over the insane peace, inflation, and the rearmament that followed; in protest they began to act in a manner befitting a crazy world. In a hypocritical, false, stupid and insane society, why make a pretence of honesty, decency, and sanity? The Dadaists declared that their guiding principle was irrationality. They declared war on the so-called "re-

spectable" society which they held responsible for the war, the Versaille Treaty and the chaos that followed.

What were the weapons that the Dadaists used? Mockery, madness and foolery. In their art and poems and stories they violated all sense and all reason—as the statesmen did. They aimed at shocking the world as the world leaders shocked them.

Whimsicality, absurdity, buffoonery, folly, pranks, wantonness and insolence were offered to the public with a seriousness as if it were great art, or poetry. Most of it they consumed themselves. They railed at everybody and at themselves, at art and culture and at reason. They denied the value of art and of culture generally. They attacked not only the political leaders, but also leaders in all fields of culture. They mocked all accepted ethic and esthetic principles. They were the new Nihilists.*

What did the Dadists accomplish? Only in Berlin where the Dadaist group was under a left leadership did Dada have a real revolutionary character and its bitter irony and mordant satire, especially in the work of George Grosz, assumed the function of a social criticism. In other centers the leaders themselves were confused and added more confusion to a chaotic world.

Where are the Dadaists now? The groups fell apart. Dada died in Paris officially in 1925. But the confusion remained. Many of the Dadaists became Surrealists. Before, there was purposeful irrationality and irresponsibility; now, irrationality with mystification and self-delusion.

If the positive value of the Dadaists, of their leadership and direction in art and in social criticism was of minimal importance, they were the victims of the times and their sickness was symptomatic.

Matisse and Picasso turned the picture into an artistic-intellectual problem. On the other hand, many of the followers of the Dadaists declared that the "true" way of painting a picture is to paint "automatically," that is, to let the subconscious lead your brush—to allow intuition, the creative impulses, free play, without any directives from the intellect.

---

* George Hugnet. See "Fantastic Art Dada Surrealism," pub. by The Museum of Modern Art.

* As an example of how far their madness reached:
In 1917 Duchamp entered in the New York Independents' exhibition a porcelain urinal with the title "Fountain" and signed R. Mutt. By this act he wished to show his disgust for art and his preference for a useful article. When R. Mutt's entry was rejected, Duchamp resigned in protest from the executive committee of which he was a member. See "Fantastic Art Dada Surrealism," published by The Museum of Modern Art.

Chagall said:

"When I came back to Paris in 1922, I was pleasantly surprised to find a new generation of artists, the Surrealist group, which in some sense redeemed the pre-war term 'literature.' And one was now almost inclined to encourage that which had been harmful in 1910. Sometimes among certain artists this took on a symbolic character, and sometimes it was truly literary.

"It is to be regretted greatly that the art of this period should have shone much less with the natural and technical mastery which the masters of the heroic epoch before 1914 had possessed so abundantly. Since, in 1922, I had not yet become fully acquainted with their art, I had the impression of finding in them what I, myself (between 1908–1914), had felt obscurely and yet correctly. But why, I thought, is it necessary to proclaim the so-called 'automatism'?

"However fantastic or illogical the construction of my painting may appear, I should be horrified to think of them as having a mixture of 'automatism.' If in my picture of 1908 I have painted death in the streets and the violin player on the roof,* or in another picture of 1911, entitled 'I and the Village,' I have painted a little cow with a milkmaid in the head of the large cow,** I did not do all this by 'automatism.'

"Even if automatism has helped some to paint good pictures or to write good poems, still this does not permit us to set up automatism as a method. Nor can all those who paint trees with blue shadows be called 'Impressionists.' Everything in art must spring from the movement of our whole lifestream, of our whole being—including the unconscious.

"I am afraid that as a conscious method automatism generates automatism. And if I was right in saying that the realistic period of technical rebirth was declining, then the automatism of surrealism is laid bare."

Chagall has been claimed as one of the forerunners of surrealism. They bring his pictures such as "Paris Through My Window"† and "Dedicated to My Fiancée"‡ as witnesses. While Chagall influenced some surrealist artists like Max Ernst,* he is not one of them.

"What was gratifying about the young movement of French painting after the First World War was its eagerness for the new. But this drop of new blood was poured into an old organism with little vitality . . .

"Surrealism was the most recent awakening of the desire to liberate art from traditional modes of expression. If it had been more profound in its internal and external expression, it might have crystallized into an artistic movement comparable to the period immediately preceding it."
And again:

"All the phrases about so-called 'pure art' and about bad 'literary' art have quite easily led to the very shaky position of these last years. Lack of 'humanism' in art—don't be afraid of the word— was a sinister presentiment of a sinister present. The examples of the great schools and the great masters of the past teach us that a true and genuine quality in painting is not in harmony with the anti-human tendencies displayed in certain works of the so-called 'avant-garde schools.'"

Now, a third of a century later, it is not hard to see that Chagall was justified in maintaining his own way in art; that he was justified in revolting against the materialistic spirit of the studios of Paris—now the world has learned to appreciate his art and is honoring him as a great master who made a valuable contribution to the art of our century.

It was the sheer stubbornness of genius for the young Witebsk artist to stand up alone against the whole empire of the Cubists.

That Paris would not or could not accept him on his own terms is no wonder—the wonder is that he found the strength to believe in his own (Witebsk) ideals; the strength to endure against the corrosive influence of the art milieu in which he lived and to overcome the neglect or indifference of the Paris public. He did not submit and did not commit suicide (as an artist) even after he met Picasso.**

It always takes time for the original artist to find recognition—even if he is not a foreigner. It happened to native French artists too, witness Cézanne, Manet,

* See page 16.
** See page 29.
† See page 32.

‡ See page 28.
* See page 61.
** See page 109.

Monet, Renoir, and Gauguin. The new artist has to develop his admirers.

But Chagall had a very unusual success. Seldom does an artist win fame in his own lifetime as Chagall did. With every new exhibition he gained new admirers and with each succeeding year the renown of his art spread until it became known in all the art centers of Europe and America.

Innumerable articles and books in all modern languages now began to appear in response to the growing interest in Chagall's art.

Chagall was greatly honored in 1946 when the Museum of Modern Art of New York, together with the Art Institute of Chicago, arranged a retrospective exhibition of his works, gathered from many private and museum collections of Europe and America. After the exhibition in the Modern Museum, the whole collection was shown in the Art Institute of Chicago.

The exhibitions in both cities were a great success. Hundreds of thousands of people came to see Chagall's work. In Chicago, seventy-five thousand visitors came to see it the first week after the opening.

On the occasion of the exhibition, the Museum of Modern Art with the collaboration of the Art Institute of Chicago published a book on Chagall written by James Johnson Sweeney, then the director of painting and sculpture of the Museum. A contribution to this book on Chagall the graphic artist came from Carl O. Schniewind of the Chicago Art Institute.

Mr. Sweeney concludes his appreciation of the artist with a few very interesting remarks. Among other things, he writes:

"He is an artist with a full color sense. He has a deep regard for technique. He is a subtle craftsman who, rather than dull his hand in virtuosity, affects clumsiness . . . In an age that has fled from sentiment he has drawn constantly on it for stimulation. And our debt to Chagall is to an artist who has brought poetry back into painting through subject matter, without any sacrifice of his painter's interest in the picture for itself, and entirely aside from any communication that can be put into words."

Mr. Schniewind remarks among other things:

"Almost completely unknown to the print world, Chagall nevertheless must be regarded as one of the great etchers of our day. From the be-ginning, he has shown a love and an understanding of black and white which is unique among his contemporaries. He has never fallen into the fatal routine performance of the professional printmaker. He has always preserved the freedom of the painter and, above all else, in every one of his prints his great imagination always leads to new and interesting results."

Apropos of Mr. Schniewind's statement that Chagall must be regarded as one of the great etchers of our time, it is a pleasure to note here that the renewed bi-annual International Art Exhibition held in Venice, Italy, in 1948 awarded its first prize for graphic art to Chagall.

In October 1947, the Musée National D'Art Moderne, in Paris, arranged by itself a new retrospective exhibition of Chagall's works (1908–1947).

This was a national honor never before accorded a living artist. Up to that time only the works of the dead masters whose fame was securely established received that honor. The fact that Chagall, not a native Frenchman, and a Jew, was the first of the living artists to receive this distinction, though France is not lacking in native artists of world fame, such as Matisse, Bonnard, or Rouault, proves how highly Chagall is now regarded in Paris.

The invitation to the exhibition was sent out in the name of the French Minister of Art. The introduction to the catalogue was written by Mons. Jean Cassou, Curator in Chief of the Musée D'Art Moderne.

With the enthusiasm with which only a Frenchman can speak of great art, Mons. Cassou says, among other things:

"Marc Chagall comes back to us to take his place as a French painter . . . Through him our painting has become enriched with all the fantasies, with all the effusions, with all the dreams, with all the tragedy, as much as a biblical soul could bring with it from an enchanted infancy of immemorial traditions. The memories of who knows what legendary exotic imagery, an authentic genius of a popular story-teller, a humanity made up of gentleness, of sad tenderness, of dismayed sensibility, the inspiration of a religious spirit, in the highest sense of the term, all have united to produce in Chagall's originality the finest gift with which we could have seen our-

Study for Mural, Moscow Jewish Theater. Oil. 1918–1919

Courtesy of the Artist

PLATE XXXII

Illustration to "Dead Souls"
Etching. 1937. Edition Tériade, Paris. 1949

Courtesy of the Artist

PLATE XXXIII

Moses. Passover Dish. Ceramic. 1950

Courtesy of the Artist

PLATE XXXIV

selves favored. His colors possess a sonority that we have not heard before, and sing an irridescent song of moving lyricism. If the title of poet has a meaning, it has it plainly when applied to this inventor who is always surprising and who, in his ingenuousness and in his sciences, in his emotions and caprices, puts such sound and evident authority . . . At the moment when he is getting ready to continue here among us to produce his masterpieces for the honor of French art, the Musée D'Art Moderne saw fit to dedicate to Marc Chagall its first temporary exhibition and in this way greet the return to Paris of this great creator and great poet."

From Paris the whole exhibition went to Holland and was shown in the Amsterdam Museum.

The Arts Council of Great Britain then brought the exhibition to England and showed it at the Tate Gallery in London. (The Tate Gallery is similar in character to the Museum of Modern Art of New York.)

On the occasion of the exhibition in the Tate Gallery, the very popular English weekly, *The Listener*, published by the British Broadcasting Corporation, appeared with a full-page reproduction of Chagall's "The Rabbi of Witebsk" ("A Jew Prays") on its front page.

With a speech by Prime Minister Attlee and an article by the Bishop of Hanover, the magazine featured a critical review of the exhibition written by Michael Ayrton.

The introduction to the catalogue was written by R. H. Wilensky, one of the best known English art historians and critics.

Among other things, Michael Ayrton wrote:

"The mastery of his medium, his fluent and certain technique derives from France, the logical, exquisite, sober France of Ingres, of Seurat and of Braque. The pride, the religious conviction, the vitality and the profound vein of sadness which runs through even the gayest of his work is Jewish. . . .

"At the Tate Gallery you may see at least half-a-dozen of these masterpieces, at least half-a-dozen pictures which rank with the best that contemporary painting has produced: the two very large, 'Double Portraits,' one gay and one sombre; the Tate's own 'Poet Dreaming'; the wonderful 'Rabbi of Witebsk'— one of the finest of all twentieth century portraits—an austere, a monumental picture in contrast to so many of Chagall's voluptuous and intoxicated explosions; the poetic cubist picture 'I and the Village,' which is Chagall at his most personal but most disciplined; and to show that his vision has not weakened in thirty years, the superb picture dated 1947 and called 'The Cock,' the vision of a majestic white bird standing upon the painter's palette with all the pride of Chanticleer, and in whose tail feathers may be seen the sentimental colloquy of two lovers . . .

"Between the first and the last of the paintings exhibited runs a gamut of the emotions of forty years—forty years of passionate life. The ecstatic, the lyrical, the noble, and the absurd, separate the tragic extremes. But the body of all this work is filled with the joy of life."

The above quotations are evidences of the recognition and honor bestowed upon Chagall by the highest authorities in the most important art centers of the world.

Now the Musée D'Art Moderne announces a new distinguished honor for the artist—that pleases him most—its opening La Salle Chagall—a hall reserved for a permanent collection of Chagall's masterpieces. It is an honor which only few of the very greatest living artists have received. The artist himself has contributed some of his early canvases that he has valued highly. It is a pleasure to think that there will be a permanent home for Chagall's works in the art capital of the world, and an interested visitor will be able to view representative masterpieces of the different periods of the artist's creative life meeting in one place.

"Hope springs eternally in the breast of man. . . ." Humanity cannot endure on pessimism and negation. And already the younger artists in France and in the rest of the world are groping for a way out of the cul-de-sac into which the formalists and purists have brought them. There is evident everywhere in the artistic and intellectual world a searching for a way to return to peace, to hopeful life and a new man.

The world honors Chagall for the great value of his art—but it may also honor him for the mission ("and don't be afraid of the word") his art has for the young generations. It points out to them that great art can be new, original, inventive, and yet be communicative and human; that "true and genuine quality in painting is not in harmony with anti-human tendencies"—

To put it in his own words again:

"The good old times have passed when art nourished itself exclusively on the elements of the external world, the world of form, lines, and color. We are interested in everything, not only in the external world, but also in the inner world of dream and imagination—"

For this mission the Salle Chagall will serve admirably.

But Chagall has another mission for the artist as well as for the cultured man generally.

"The war is over and again there is talk of wars. But perhaps a new kind of struggle must be undertaken by cultured and spiritual humanity, to create artists, prophets—men with weapons of justice who as new soldiers of culture would spread over the world and call peoples and nations to an equitable peace. . . .

"We must carry on a war against automatic and atomic evil in life and in culture, against heartlessness in art and in life, though it covers itself with a so-called 'beauty' of form and pure 'technique'; and if you think that it is a dreamer talking, perhaps it is so much the better.

"Only out of dreams a new reality can grow—but dreams that have their foundation in an all-human love and justice."

The taller the tree, the deeper and wider its roots spread in the soil—and the greater the artist, the deeper he is rooted in the heart and soul of his people, reaching down to the subsoil which is common ground of all humanity.

It is a truism that only the artist who is great enough to become a national artist, who nourishes his art from the deep heart and soul sources of his own people, can bring a real and valuable contribution to all humanity. This is true of the great creators of all time and it is true of Chagall.

The honors that are given to Chagall are also honors for the Jewish people.

The artist and his family live now in Vence, Alpes Maritimes, France.

Not only the radiant skies of the south of France are conducive to artistic creation, but also its good earth. Chagall found the earth near his home so good for ceramics that he began working with this for his new medium and created a number of plates and vases with biblical themes. These have been exhibited at the Maegth Gallery, Paris, together with the latest of his paintings.

To the large number of books that he illustrated is now added a volume of Boccaccio's tales with 26 wash-drawings and cover title page (appeared as "Verve" No. 24) to be published by Tériade, Paris.

Chagall has now reached the maturity of his creative life in full possession of the unabated powers of his genius. He is full of enthusiasm for new work —and to work at his easel is still the necessity of his life. Beside preparing for an exhibition in Zurich, he is now working on a project of large murals with biblical subjects.

The latest honor that the artist received gives him great pleasure—an invitation by the Government of Israel to come for a visit.

The invitation reads:

"State of Israel,
    Office of Education and Culture,
        Jerusalem, Aug. 10, 1950.
In honor of the Artist
    Marc Chagall.
Great Artist and Dearly beloved friend,
    From the bottom of my heart I was happy to hear from the writer Abraham Suzkever that you would at last be able to overcome the difficulty of interrupting your great work to come and visit us in Eretz.
    The Office of Education and Culture of the State of Israel has the great privilege of inviting you as an honored guest.
    During your visit it will be our pleasure to show you the artistic and precious treasures which belong to our State.
    We shall be grateful if you would let us know when you will come to visit us so that we may make all the necessary preparations for your visit.
My blessing and great esteem,
                As always, yours,
                        Z. Shazar
        Minister of Education and Culture."

To Minister Shazar's blessing and expression of great esteem I humbly add my Amen!

                                The Author.

Index

All index entries which are italicized refer to Chagall's work.

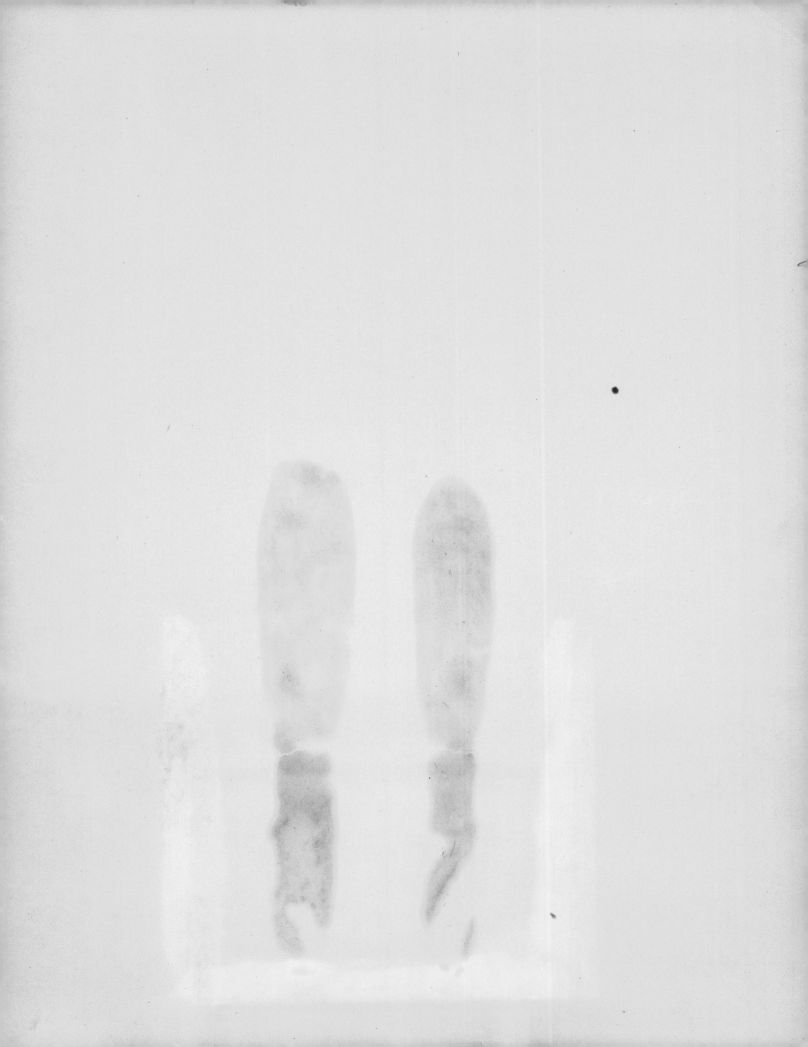

3/4/52